FROM ADAM SMITH TO MICHAEL PORTER

Evolution of Competitiveness Theory

ASIA-PACIFIC BUSINESS SERIES

Series Editors: Richard Brislin *(University of Hawaii)*
Lane Kelley *(University of Hawaii)*

Published

Vol. 1 Guanxi and Business
Yadong Luo (University of Hawaii)

ASIA-PACIFIC BUSINESS SERIES – VOL. 2

FROM ADAM SMITH TO MICHAEL PORTER

Evolution of Competitiveness Theory

Dong-Sung Cho

Seoul National University, Korea

Hwy-Chang Moon

Seoul National University, Korea

World Scientific
Singapore • New Jersey • London • Hong Kong

Published by

World Scientific Publishing Co. Pte. Ltd.

P O Box 128, Farrer Road, Singapore 912805

USA office: Suite 1B, 1060 Main Street, River Edge, NJ 07661

UK office: 57 Shelton Street, Covent Garden, London WC2H 9HE

British Library Cataloguing-in-Publication Data
A catalogue record for this book is available from the British Library.

First published 2000

HF
1414
.C456
.2001

ISBN   981-02-4662-5 (pbk)

Printed by FuIsland Offset Printing (S) Pte Ltd, Singapore

To Our Colleagues Past, Current and Future

FOREWORD

Some people view academic theories as impractical and useless, and make strategic decisions based on their personal ideas. In fact these personal ideas are their personal theories. These decisions may lead to disastrous consequences if they are based on personal theories that are not fully discussed. In contrast, good academic theories have been discussed and tested by scholars. Strategies should be formulated based on the good academic theories, rather than on unproven personal theories. A good theory is a shortcut to understanding the complex real world.

This book deals with important theories of international competitiveness and their strategic implications. The theories range from classical theories such as Adam Smith's absolute advantage to new theories such as Michael Porter's diamond model. This book also incorporates the latest theoretical advances such as the generalized double diamond, the nine-factor model, and new stage models of economic development.

A theory is often complex and controversial. In addition, a theory can be misused and overused. A theory, like a medicine, is most effective when it is appropriately used. Applying a theory without considering its weaknesses is like taking a medicine without knowing its side-effects. To develop a critical perspective, readers first need to fully understand each theory. They should then study its strengths and weaknesses; and previous research and the need for further study; and its strategic implications.

This book is suitable for Business Strategy and International Business courses on both the graduate and upper-division undergraduate levels. This book is also suitable for policy makers and corporate managers. We hope that educators, students, and practitioners will find useful implications from this book's systematic integration of important competitiveness models.

ACKNOWLEDGEMENTS

We were lucky to have a dedicated assistant, Young-Kyun Hur. Without his extraordinary effort this book could not have been completed within a reasonable time. He is a man of talent and responsibility. Warm thanks go to Diana Hinds, for editing the manuscripts. Additional thanks go to Yubing Zhai and Karen Quek of World Scientific Publishing Co., for their valuable help. Our most profound acknowledgement, however, is to Professor Michael E. Porter who introduced a new paradigm of competitiveness and Professor Alan M. Rugman who sparked the debate on competitiveness.

We would also like to thank the following publishers for allowing us to reproduce their articles.

Reprinted by permission of Foreign Affairs, (March/April: 28-44 and July/August: 186-203). Copyright (1994) by the Council on Foreign Relations, Inc.

Reprinted by permission of Harvard Business Review. From (The Competitive Advantage of Nations) by (Michael E. Porter, March-April: 73-93, 1990.)

Reprinted from (International Business Review, 7, H. Chang Moon, Alan M. Rugman and Alain Verbeke, A Generalized Double Diamond Approach to the Global Competitiveness of Korea and Singapore, pages 135-150, copyright (1998)), with permission from Elsevier Science.

Reprinted by permission of (Journal of Far Eastern Business). From (A Dynamic Approach to International Competitiveness: The Case of Korea by Dong-Sung Cho, 1(1): 17-36, 1994.)

CONTENTS

Contents

LIST OF TABLES & FIGURES

xiv *List of Tables and Figures*

INTRODUCTION

The effect of *The Wealth of Nations* was revolutionary. Adam Smith's thoughts on trade gave businessmen a significant place in history. Their pursuit of profit was justified. Their social respectability as an important class was identified. Most importantly, a new concept of a nation's wealth was introduced.

Some economists argue that very little of what Smith said on the subject of trade was new, but the scope of Smith's work, the completeness of his analysis and the timeliness of its appearance all conspired to make his book a landmark in economic thought. Since Smith published his book in 1776, many economists have made important contributions to this theory. However, many of the new trade theories are based on two important concepts— specialization and free exchange—which were introduced by Smith more than two hundred years ago. This is why we respect Adam Smith as the grandfather of economics.

Although Smith and his followers provided some important bases for economic thoughts, today's global economy is too complicated to be understood with this rather simple version of trade theory. There was a breakthrough in 1990. Michael Porter introduced a new competitiveness theory, the diamond model. According to Porter, nations are most likely to succeed in industries or industry segments where the national "diamond" is the most favourable. The diamond has four interrelated components—(1) factor conditions, (2) demand conditions, (3) related and supporting industries, and (4) firm strategy, structure, and rivalry. In addition, there are two exogenous factors—chance and government.

The principle of the diamond is excellent, but its geographical constituency has to be established on different criteria. In particular, Porter's single diamond is not very relevant in small economies because their domestic variables are limited. They have to actively utilize international variables to enhance their competitiveness. In fact, Porter recognized the importance of international or global variables for a nation's competitiveness, but his diamond model did not explicitly include these variables. The debate on the diamond model in Chapter 4 has thus centered on the treatement of international variables.

Notwithstanding, the extended models by other scholars are based on the principle of the diamond model that was originally introduced by Porter. Likewise, the debate in Chapter 2 is based on the principle of Adam Smith and his followers. The debates are sometimes very harsh and acute, but we can understand the theories better through these debates. In addition to the diamond model, Porter also introduced a stage model of economic development. This is an important model but has not been much discussed. In Chapter 7 and 8, we discuss the stage model. In Chapter 9, we discuss how to measure the concept of competitiveness. The overall structure of this book is illustrated in the next page. To sum up, Adam Smith is the pioneer of trade theory and Michael Porter is the pioneer of competitiveness theory. Yet, no theory is perfect in a changing environment. We need to go further.

Evolution from Trade Theory to Competitiveness Theory

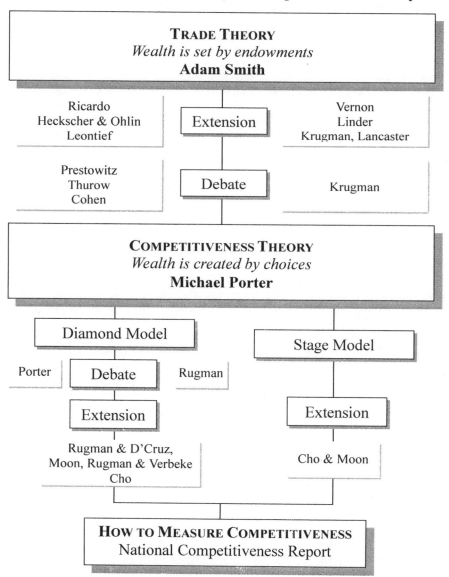

TRADE THEORY
Wealth is set by endowments
Adam Smith

Ricardo
Heckscher & Ohlin
Leontief

Extension

Vernon
Linder
Krugman, Lancaster

Prestowitz
Thurow
Cohen

Debate

Krugman

COMPETITIVENESS THEORY
Wealth is created by choices
Michael Porter

Diamond Model

Porter

Debate

Rugman

Stage Model

Extension

Rugman & D'Cruz,
Moon, Rugman & Verbeke
Cho

Extension

Cho & Moon

HOW TO MEASURE COMPETITIVENESS
National Competitiveness Report

1. TRADITIONAL MODEL: THEORY

Mercantilism
Absolute Advantage   Smith, 1937(1776)
Comparative Advantage   Ricardo, 1971(1817)
Factor Endowments   Heckscher, 1949(1919); Ohlin, 1933
Leontief Paradox   Leontief, 1953
Product Cycle   Vernon, 1966
Country Similarity   Linder, 1961
Economies of Scale   Krugman, 1979; Lancaster, 1979

Summary and Key Points

Mercantilism viewed trade as a zero-sum game in which a trade surplus of one country is offset by a trade deficit of another country. In contrast, Adam Smith viewed trade as a positive-sum game in which all trading partners can benefit if countries specialize in the production of goods in which they have absolute advantages. Ricardo extended absolute advantage theory to comparative advantage theory. According to Ricardo, even if a country does not have an absolute advantage in any good, this country and other countries would still benefit from international trade. However, Ricardo did not satisfactorily explain why comparative advantages are different between countries. Heckscher and Ohlin explained that comparative advantage arises from differences in factor endowments. This theory appears to be virtually self-evident. However, Leontief found a paradoxical result. Some economists have developed alternative theories because the Heckscher-Ohlin model did not work well in the real world. These theories include product cycle, country similarity, and trade based on economies of scale. All of the theories discussed in this chapter are useful in understanding many of today's industrial and trade policies. They are also helpful in understanding and evaluating the debate over competitiveness in Chapter 2.

Sources:
Smith, Adam. 1937 (1776). *An inquiry into the nature and causes of the wealth of nations.* In Charles W. Eliot, editor, The Harvard Classics. New York: P. F. Collier & Son Corporation.
Ricardo, David. 1971 (1817). *The principles of political economy and taxation.* Baltimore: Penguin.
Heckscher, Eli F. 1949 (1919). The effect of foreign trade on the distribution of income. In Howard. S. Ellis & Lloyd A. Metzler, editors, *Readings in the theory of international trade.* Homewood: Irwin.
Leontief, Wassily. 1953. Domestic production and foreign trade: The American capital position re-examined. *Proceedings of the American Philosophical Society,* 97: 331-349. Reprinted in Richard Caves and Harry Johnson, editors, *Readings in International Economics* (Homewood, Illinois: Richard D. Irwin, Inc., 1968).
Vernon, Raymond. 1966. International investments and international trade in the product cycle. *Quarterly Journal of Economics,* May: 190-207.
Linder, Staffan B. 1961. *An essay on trade and transformation.* New York: John Wiley.
Krugman, Paul R. 1979. Increasing returns, monopolistic competition and international trade. *Journal of International Economics,* 9: 469-479.
Lancaster, Kelvin J. 1979. *Variety, equity and efficiency.* New York: Columbia University Press.

MERCANTILISM

In 1492 Columbus reached the New World; in 1501 Amerigo Vespucci discovered the mainland of the continent; and in 1519 Magellan reached the Philippines around the southern tip of South America and opened the Western route to India. These discoveries were possible because of scientific development in the areas such as astronomy and shipbuilding. Merchants and traders wanted to expand their business to the East because trading Eastern and Western products was profitable. International business became important in the age of discovery and exploration during the 15th century.

An economic theory at this time was called mercantilism. It continued to be the dominant economic thought until the 18th century. The mercantilists thought of wealth as gold and silver, or treasure, a term common at that time. The policy of accumulating precious metals was called bullionism. In the earliest period, bullionist philosophy translated into encouraging imports and forbidding exports of bullion. This policy soon shifted toward regulating international trade to achieve a favorable balance of trade. Mercantilism emphasized the necessity of a country to acquire an abundance of precious metals. To do this, the country had to export the maximum of its own manufactures and to import the minimum from other countries. The excess of exports over imports would be paid for in gold and silver.

The policy then shifted toward encouraging domestic production. The rationale was that the country, producing more goods for export, could achieve a favorable balance of trade and thus a bullion inflow. This policy was well explained by Thomas Mun (1571-1641), a director of the East India Company and a principal mercantile theorist. His main contention was that to increase the wealth of the nation, England must sell to other countries more than she bought from them. He advised his people to cultivate unused lands; reduce the consumption of foreign wares; be frugal in the use of natural resources, saving them as much as possible for export; develop industries at home to supply necessities. These are the tenets of the thrifty businessman. However, these are not only the responsibility of individual merchants. The government should also have an obligation. It could thus be advised for the government to prohibit imports and subsidize exports.

At this time a tax policy was important. The country could achieve mercantilist goals by lowering taxes for exports and imposing high tariffs on imports. However, taxes were often superimposed on the areas which were not directly related to exports. For example, in England, there were even taxes on windows, births, burials, marriages, and bachelors. In addition, high tariffs on imported items caused the smuggling industry to thrive. Another important policy was to grant monopoly for certain important sectors such as glass manufacturing, paper manufacturing, and copper mining. However, this policy was also abused frequently and became less helpful to the industrial structure.

ABSOLUTE ADVANTAGE

The major problem with mercantilism was that it viewed trade as a zero-sum game in which a trade surplus of one country is offset by a trade deficit of another country. In contrast, Adam Smith viewed trade as a positive-sum game in which all trading partners can benefit. A large part of *The Wealth of Nations* (Smith, 1776) was devoted to an attack upon mercantilism. Smith believed in the operation of natural law, or invisible hand, and thus favored individualism and free trade. Smith said that each man is more understanding than any other as to his own needs and desires. If each man were allowed to seek his own welfare, he would in the long run contribute most to the common good. Natural law, rather than government restraint, would serve to prevent abuses of this freedom. Specifically, the advantage of this natural law in Smith's eyes came from the division of labor. Smith explained this with the example of a pin factory:

"To take an example,....the pin-maker; a workman not educated to this business, not acquainted with the use of the machinery employed in it, could make one pin in a day, and certainly could not make twenty. But in the way in which this business is divided into a number of branches,...One man draws out the wire, another straights it, a third cuts it, a fourth points it, a fifth grinds it at the top for receiving the head; to make the head requires two or three distinct operations; to put it on, is a peculiar business, to whiten the pins is another; it is even a trade by itself to put them into the paper; and the important business of making a pin is, in this manner, divided into about eighteen distinct operations, which, in some manufactories, are all performed by distinct hands, though in others the same man will sometimes perform two or three of them. I have seen a small manufactory of this kind

where ten men were employed....Those ten persons could make 48,000 pins in a day. Each person, therefore, making a tenth part, might be considered as making 4,800 pins in a day. But if they had all wrought separately and independently, they certainly could not each of them have made twenty, perhaps not one pin in a day... (Smith, 1776, p. 10)"

Smith extended this idea of "division of labor" to that of "international division of labor." Now consider how much more production there would be if countries specialized in production just as the pin-makers did in his example. Specialization, cooperation, and exchange were responsible for the world's economic progress, and therein lay the road to future achievements. International trade was thus a positive game to Smith. In practice, however, Smith saw various barriers set by governments that restricted the free flow of international trade. His famous passage is as follows:

"It is the maxim of every prudent master of a family, never to attempt to make at home what it will cost him more to make than to buy. The taylor does not attempt to make his own shoes, but buys them of the shoemaker. The shoemaker does not attempt to make his own clothes, but employs a taylor. The farmer attempts to make neither the one nor the other, but employs those different artificers...."

"What is prudence in the conduct of every private family, can scarce be folly in that of a great kingdom. If a foreign country can supply us with a commodity cheaper than we ourselves can make it, better buy it of them with some part of the produce of our own industry, employed in a way in which we have some advantage...."

"The natural advantages which one country has over another in producing particular commodities are sometimes so great, that it is acknowledged by all the world to be in vain to struggle with them. By means of glasses, hotbeds, and hotwalls, very good grapes can be raised in Scotland, and very good wine too can be made of them at about thirty times the expence for which at least equally good can be brought from foreign countries. Would it be a reasonable law to prohibit the importation of all foreign wines, merely to encourage the making of claret and burgundy in Scotland? (pp. 336-338)"

In criticizing mercantilism, Smith showed how all forms of government interference, such as granting monopolies, subsidizing exports, restricting imports, and regulating wages, hampered the natural growth of economic activity. In contrast, Smith argued the advantages of specialization by regions and nations. Beginning with such reasoning, Smith showed how each nation would be far better off economically by concentrating on what it could do best rather than following the mercantilist doctrine of national self-sufficiency.[1] Following Smith's thoughts, the protection of trade as a government policy actually reduced in England.

Competition was important in the society that Smith proposed. Competition assured that each person and nation would do what they was best fitted to do, and it assured each one the full reward of their services and the maximum contribution to the common good. Therefore, the role of the government, or *sovereign*, should be minimum. Smith argued as follows:

"All systems either of preference or of restraint, therefore, being thus completely taken away, the obvious and simple system of natural liberty establishes itself of its own accord. Every man, as long as he does not violate the laws of justice, is left perfectly free to pursue his own interest his own way, and to bring both his industry and capital into competition with those of any other man,....According to the system of natural liberty, the sovereign has only three duties to attend to: three duties of great importance, indeed, but plain and intelligible to common understandings; first, the duty of protecting the society from the violence and invasion of other independent societies; secondly, the duty of protecting, as far as possible, every member of the society from the injustice or oppression of every other member of it, or the duty of establishing an exact administration of justice; and, thirdly, the duty of erecting and maintaining certain public works and certain public institutions, which it can never be for the interest of any individual, or small number of individuals, to erect and maintain; because the profit could never repay the expence to any individual or small number of individuals, though it may frequently do much more than repay it to a great society. (pp. 445-446)"

---

[1] Very little of what Smith said on the subject of trade was new, most of it had been said before; but the scope of Smith's work, the completeness of his analysis and the timeliness of its appearance all conspired to make his book a landmark in economic thought.

The most important economic policy of government was thus to eliminate monopolies and preserve competition. However, Smith's position on the government regulation was not absolute. As shown in the third duty of the government, Smith admitted that necessary projects that were too large for private enterprise should be undertaken by public authority. He also believed The Navigation Acts, requiring the use of English vessels to transport goods to and from England, were necessary to safeguard the marine service as a matter of national defense. Smith said, "The act of navigation is perhaps the wisest of all the commercial regulations of England (p. 344)."

It has often been said that it was more than a coincidence that both the Declaration of Independence and *The Wealth of Nations* were given to the world in 1776. One was a declaration of political freedom. The other was a declaration of commercial independence. The effect of *The Wealth of Nations* was revolutionary. Smith's thoughts on trade gave businessmen a significant place in history. Their pursuit of profit was justified. Their social respectability as an important class was identified. In the same year of 1776, individuals attained political freedom in the United States and economic freedom in England.

COMPARATIVE ADVANTAGE

Since Adam Smith published his book in 1776, many economists have made important contributions to this theory. Among them, David Ricardo's contribution to international trade theory was so important that this classical theory is sometimes referred to as Ricardian theory.[2] There was a problem with the theory of absolute advantage. What if one country had an absolute advantage in both goods? According to Smith, such a superior country might have no benefits from international trade. In contrast, according to Ricardo, the superior country should specialize where it has the greatest absolute advantage and the inferior country should specialize where it has the least absolute disadvantage. This rule is known as the theory of comparative advantage. One important implication of this theory is that even if a country did not have an absolute advantage in any good, this country and other countries would still benefit from international trade.

---

[2] Although Ricardo is known as the author of the theory of comparative advantage, some economists say there is substantial evidence that Robert Torrens developed the notion of comparative advantage years earlier, in 1808.

To explain this, Ricardo used an illustration (see "On Foreign Trade" in Ricardo, 1817). In trade between England and Portugal, if Portugal could produce cloth with the labor of 90 men and wine with the labor of 80 men, and England could produce the same quantity of cloth with 100 men and the wine with 120, it would be advantageous for these nations to exchange English cloth for Portuguese wine. By concentrating upon what each nation could do with the least effort, each had a greater comparative advantage. Thus each nation had more wine and more cloth than it could have had by producing each commodity independently without the benefit of exchange.

In this example Portugal can benefit from trading with the less efficient England because Portugal's cost advantage is relatively greater in wine than in cloth. Portugal's production cost of wine is only two-thirds the cost in England, but its cost of cloth is nine-tenths the cost in England. Portugal has thus greater efficiency in wine than in cloth, while England has less inefficiency in cloth than in wine.

Table 1-1. Ricardo's Comparative Advantage

Ricardo's Comparative Advantage		
	Production Cost	
Country	Cloth	Wine
Portugal	90	80
England	100	120

Ricardo used another illustration which resulted in the same point. Two men could both make shoes and hats, and one was superior to the other in both employments; but in making hats, he could only exceed his competitor by one-fifth or 20 percent, and in making shoes he can exceed him by one-third or 33 percent. Would it not be for the interest of both, that the superior man should employ himself exclusively in making shoes, and the inferior man in making hats? Ricardo contended that imports could be profitable to a nation even though that nation could produce the imported article at a lower cost. Therefore, it was not true, as Adam Smith believed, that under free trade each commodity would be produced by that country which produced it at the lowest real cost.

It is the principle of comparative advantage that underlies the advantages of the division of labor, whether between individuals, regions, or nations.

The Ricardian model of international trade is thus a very useful tool for explaining the reasons why trade may happen and how trade increases the welfare of the trading partners. However, this model is incomplete. In particular, there are two major problems. First, the simple Ricardian model predicts an extreme degree of specialization, but in practice countries produce not one but many products including import-competing products. Second, it explains trade based on differences in productivity levels between countries, but it does not explain why these differences exist.

The first problem can be solved when we assume diminishing returns to scale (i.e., a convex production possibility frontier), implying that as resources are shifted from one sector to another sector, the opportunity cost of each additional unit of another sector increases. Such increasing costs may arise because factors of production vary in quality and in suitability for producing different commodities. Under these circumstances, the theory can predict that a country will specialize up to the point where gains from specialization become equal to increasing costs of specialization. The theory can then explain the reason why a country does not specialize its production completely. The second problem is solved by the theory of factor endowments.

FACTOR ENDOWMENTS

Ricardo explained that comparative advantage arises from differences in labor productivity, but did not satisfactorily explain why labor productivity is different between countries. In the early twentieth century an important new theory of international trade, the Heckscher-Ohlin (HO) model, was developed by two Swedish economists.[3] Heckscher and Ohlin argued that comparative advantage arises from differences in factor endowments. According to the HO model, there are two basic characteristics of countries and products. Countries differ from each other according to the factors of production they possess. Goods differ from each other according to the factors that are required in their production. The HO model says that a

---

[3] Eli Heckscher's original work, published in 1919 in Swedish, received little attention until it was translated into English in 1949. Bertil Ohlin, Heckscher's student, elaborated on Heckscher's ideas in his doctoral dissertation in 1924, which was also written in Swedish, and did not receive attention until it was published in English in 1933.

country will have comparative advantage in, and therefore will export, that good whose production is relatively intensive in the factor with which that country is relatively well endowed. The logic is that the more abundant a factor is, the lower its cost. Therefore, differences in the factor endowments of various countries explain differences in factor costs, which result in different comparative advantages.

There are two factors of production, capital and labor, in the HO model, while labor is the only factor of production in the Ricardian model. The HO model assumes that technology is identical but production methods are different between countries. Different production methods indicate different combinations of capital and labor. That is, different countries may choose different production methods depending upon factor prices in those countries. Therefore, patterns of production and trade are explained by different factor endowments or factor prices.

The HO model has been expanded by three important theorems: the factor price equalization theorem, the Stolper-Samuelson theorem, and the Rybczynski theorem.

The Factor Price Equalization Theorem

This theorem states that free trade will equalize factors of production between countries.[4] Suppose there is a free trade between the United States and Mexico. With free trade, output of the comparative advantage good increases, thereby demand for the abundant factor and consequently its price increase. At the same time, output of the comparative disadvantage good decreases, thereby demand for the scarce factor and consequently its price decrease. Therefore, rental rates increase and wages decrease in the capital-abundant country (the United States), while the opposite happens in the labor-abundant country (Mexico). Prior to free trade, rental rates were relatively low and wages were relatively high in the United States. With free trade, these prices move in the direction of equalization.

However, we need strong conditions for factor price equalization to occur. These conditions include no transportation costs, no trade barriers, and identical technology. One interesting implication of factor price

---

[4] This theorem was first suggested by Heckscher and Ohlin, and later proved by Samuelson (1948). Interestingly, shortly after Samuelson's article appeared, he learned that Abba Lerner, while a student in England in 1933, had written a term paper that also proved the theorem.

equalization is that foreign investment may not be necessary if there is free trade. We can understand foreign investment as an international transfer of production factors such as technology, capital, and labor. This is a viable strategy only when the prices of these factors are not equal between countries. With factor price equalization, there is no need to invest abroad. In the real world, however, there are many obstacles or market imperfections (for example, see Hymer, 1960/1976) that stand in the way of complete equalization of factor prices.

The factor price equalization theorem is still useful and we can derive some important implications from it. For example, how trade liberalization affects income gaps between countries. The theorem predicts that income gaps will reduce by lowering trade barriers. Two important conclusions can be derived. First, with formation of a trading bloc, the country of low income will benefit more than the country of high income. Second, a less developed country should actively pursue an open door policy to increase its income level.

The Stolper-Samuelson Theorem

This theorem links international trade to the domestic distribution of income. As we have seen in the case of factor price equalization, free trade will increase the price, or income, of the relatively abundant factor and reduce that of the relatively scarce factor. Therefore, according to this theorem, free trade benefits the abundant factor and harms the scarce factor. Why should the scarce factor lose? Precisely because the income of the scarce factor has been too high. With free trade, the scarce factor, say, U.S. labor, has to compete with its foreign competitor, say, Mexican labor. Although labor is immobile between countries, its price can change through international trade because labor is embodied in the goods.

Everyone is a winner in the classical one-factor model. In the two-factor HO model, one factor is a loser. We can now understand why the abundant factor (e.g., U.S. capitalists) is for and the scarce factor (e.g., U.S. workers) is against trade liberalization (e.g., North American Free Trade Agreement). The scarce factor may want to lobby to restrict free trade, but may have to accept a reduction of income in the end. However, it is important to note that although the scarce factor loses, the country as a whole gains from trade liberalization. A policy of income redistribution such as taxation may then be important. Otherwise, a group of people will lose permanently.

The Rybczynski Theorem

This theorem says that at constant prices, an increase in one factor endowment will increase by a greater proportion the output of the good intensive in that factor and reduce the output of the other. Suppose a country's capital stock increases by 10 percent and its labor force is unchanged. As the capital stock increases, the output of the capital-intensive good expands to utilize the extra supply of capital. In contrast, the output of the labor-intensive good decreases because labor is getting out of this sector. As the capital stock increases, the production possibility frontier bulges out in the direction of the capital-intensive good so that the country's production should be larger than before. Since the output of the labor-intensive good decreases absolutely, the output of the capital-intensive good should increase more than 10 percent.

This theorem is useful in explaining the pattern of economic development of Japan and Korea. These countries have had high savings and investment, and produced more capital-intensive goods. Labor-intensive sectors have actually shrunk in these countries because labor force has been released to the booming capital-intensive sectors. Therefore, an important implication of this theorem is that a country can change its relative factor endowments by changing its investment patterns, while factor endowments are fixed in the world of the classical theories of Smith and Ricardo.

The HO model is referred to as the neoclassical theory of international trade because it builds upon and complements the classical theory of comparative advantage. The HO model contains several appealing elements. It is simple, logical, makes common sense, and appears to be virtually self-evident. However, an empirical test produced a paradoxical result.

LEONTIEF PARADOX

The famous empirical study of the HO model was conducted by Leontief (1953), who was awarded the Nobel prize in 1973. Leontief expected that the United States, the most capital-abundant country in the world, should export capital-intensive goods and import labor-intensive goods, but found that U.S. import-competing goods required 30 percent more capital per worker than U.S. export goods. According to his calculations, the capital-labor ratio was about $14,000 per worker-year in export goods and about $18,100 per worker-year in import-competing goods. This finding was the opposite of what the HO model predicted. It has become known as the Leontief Paradox.

How can we reconcile the Leontief's findings with the HO model? Many economists, including Leontief, have attempted to explain this.

Labor Skills

The first attempt was made by Leontief himself. He argued that U.S. workers are much more productive than foreign workers. Specifically, he suggested that one man-year of U.S. labor is equivalent to three man-years of foreign labor. Thus, the number of U.S. workers must be multiplied by three. However, his estimate about the superiority of U.S. labor was overstated. Other studies (e.g., Kreinen, 1965) showed that the superiority was not 300 percent, as Leontief claimed, but about 20 to 25 percent, which was not sufficient to convert the paradox.

Natural Resources

Leontief tested only capital and labor, but omitted other important factors such as resources. Vanek (1963) argued that the United States is relatively scarce in natural resources but abundant in both capital and labor. The production of certain natural resources requires large quantities of capital. Importing natural resources then means importing capital which is embodied in natural resources. Since the HO model includes basically capital and labor, many economists recalculated the factor content of U.S. trade after excluding the natural resource sectors. Studies generally show that the capital intensity of U.S. import-competing sectors drops substantially, but not enough to reverse the paradox.

Factor Intensity Reversals

Because foreign data on trade were not available, Leontief calculated the factor content of U.S. import-competing goods rather than analyzing actual imports. For example, Leontief calculated the factor content of the U.S. textile industry that competed with imports, instead rather than calculating the factor content of the foreign textile industry. However, textiles may be labor-intensive in Mexico, for example, but relatively capital-intensive in the United States. For another example, agriculture is labor-intensive in many foreign countries, but capital-intensive in the United States. Yet, many economists believe that factor intensity reversals are not significant in the real world.

Several other explanations have been attempted, but failed to satisfactorily reconcile the Leontief paradox. The paradox continues. Some economists have developed alternative theories of international trade because the HO model does not work well in the real world. Recognizing the increasing diversity of international trade, the new theories are useful in explaining some special cases of international trade. These theories include product cycle, country similarity, and trade based on economies of scale.

PRODUCT CYCLE

Raymond Vernon (1966) argued that many manufactured goods go through a product cycle of introduction, growth, maturity, and decline. Thus, comparative advantages of these goods shift over time from one country to another. The product cycle hypothesis begins with the assumption that the stimulus to innovation is typically provided by some threat or promise in the market. In other words, firms tend to be stimulated by the needs and opportunities of the market closest at hand, the home market. The home market plays a dual role in this hypothesis. Not only is it the source of stimulus for the innovation firm; it is also the preferred location for production.

In the introduction stage, the United States has been a pioneer in inventing and producing new products such as televisions and computers. Two reasons account for this dominant position. First, the wealth and size of the U.S. market gave U.S. firms a strong incentive to develop new consumer products. Second, the high cost of U.S. labor gave U.S. firms an incentive to develop cost-saving innovations.[5] If innovating firms scan their home markets with special intensity, the chances are greatly increased that their first production facilities will also be located in the home market. The propensity to cluster in the home market is fortified by the fact that there are some well-recognized economies to be captured by an innovating team that is brought together in a common location.

In this introduction stage, the demand for new products tends to be based on non-price factors. Firms can charge relatively high prices for new

---

[5] European technology is material-saving and Japanese technology is space-saving.

products, which obviates the need to look for low-cost production sites in other countries. As the market in the United States and other developed countries matures, the product becomes more standardized, and price becomes the main competitive weapon. Thus the locus of production shifts to other developed countries, and then to less developed countries.

The product cycle model is useful in reconciling the Leontief paradox. Suppose the United States has comparative advantage in new manufactured products. The production method of these new products may be quite labor-intensive because investment in fixed capital is not likely to occur at this stage. Producers still need to know how to manufacture products most efficiently and how the market reacts to these new products. Thus, U.S. exports tend to be labor-intensive. When the product becomes standardized, producers are familiar with the efficient engineering and market feedback. A large amount of fixed capital can now be invested. The production method may thus be quite capital-intensive. The Leontief paradox can be reconciled because the U.S. exports in the introducing stage where the production is labor-intensive and imports in the maturing stage where the production is capital-intensive.

In his later work, Vernon (1979) suggested that the power of the product cycle hypothesis has been changing. Two reasons account for that change: one, an increase in the geographical reach of many of the enterprises that are involved in the introduction of new products, a consequence of their establishment of many overseas subsidiaries; and two, a change in the national markets of the advanced industrialized countries, which has reduced some of the differences that had previously existed between such markets.

In industries such as electronics and chemicals, innovating firms that are limited to their own home markets are no longer very common. Instead, firms with highly developed multinational networks introduce the new products simultaneously in the Triad—the United States, Europe, and Japan—and in some less developed countries. With a multinational network, U.S. firms also feel at ease in foreign production. The interval of time between the introduction of any new product in the United States and its first production in a foreign location has thus been rapidly shrinking.

The U.S. income was higher than that of other developed countries. Recently, however, the income gap has narrowed. This shrinkage weakened a critical assumption of the product cycle hypotheses, namely, that the entrepreneurs of large enterprises confronted different conditions in their respective home markets. As European and Japanese incomes approached those of the United States, these differences were reduced.

The product cycle hypothesis had strong predictive power in the first two or three decades after World War II, especially in explaining the composition of U.S. trade and in projecting the likely patterns of foreign direct investment by U.S. firms. However, Vernon said that certain conditions of that period are now gone. For one thing, the leading multinational firms have developed global networks of subsidiaries; on the other, the U.S. market is no longer unique among national markets. Thus, the predictive power of the hypothesis is weakened. However, the hypothesis is still useful for a multinational firm that has not yet acquired a capacity for global scanning, but tries to move from home-based innovation to the possibility of exports and ultimately of overseas investment. The hypothesis may also provide useful guidelines for many less developed countries that try to absorb a developed country's innovations as introduced earlier.

COUNTRY SIMILARITY

Staffan Linder's (1961) country similarity theory is different from other trade theories because it deals with the demand side rather than the supply side. This theory explains international trade among countries that have similar characteristics. The theory has two assumptions. First, a country exports those manufactured products for which there is a significant home market. According to Linder, manufacturers introduce new products in order to serve the domestic market because they are familiar with the domestic market. Production for the domestic market must be large enough for firms to achieve economies of scale and thus to reduce costs. Second, the country exports the product to other countries with similar tastes and income levels. Linder believed that countries with similar income levels would have similar tastes. Each country will produce primarily for its home market, but part of the output will be exported to other similar countries.

The first assumption, the home-oriented myopic view of the managers, is similar to the product cycle hypothesis in explaining the early stage of product life. In today's global economy, however, this view is less appealing because firms often target the global market rather than domestic markets. For example, artificial Christmas trees are exported by non-Christian countries such as China, where the market for this product is small, to Christian countries such as the United States. For another example, Japan exported typewriters to the United States when the market for this product was not yet developed in Japan. Other counter-examples include OEM manufacturing and international subcontracting, which are popular in many less developed countries. These are not for the domestic market, but for exports.

There is also a problem with the second assumption. Suppose there are two countries with similar tastes and income levels. Why can one country originate a particular product? The United States exports Cadillac cars to Japan while importing Lexus cars from them. The origins of these products may not be explained in Linder's thesis. To explain this, we need to know different factor endowments and different characteristics of technology of the two countries, which can be explained by the HO model. Despite these problems, the Linder model is useful in explaining some trade patterns. Much of the international trade in manufactured goods takes place among the countries with high income: the United States, Europe, and Japan. Much of this trade is in fact the exchange of similar products.

There are two important differences between the HO model and the Linder model. First, in the HO model, there will be more trade between countries that have more dissimilarities in factor endowments because more dissimilarities will give larger differences in relative factor prices. In contrast, in the Linder model there will be more trade between countries that have more similarity in incomes and tastes. Second, in the HO model, a country's exports and imports are different products with different factor proportions. In contrast, in the Linder model a country's exports and imports are similar products. These differences are due to the different perspectives of the two theories: the HO model on a production side and the Linder model on a demand side.

The theoretical contribution of the Linder model is its identification of two important variables, domestic demand and economies of scale, in explaining different types of international trade. These two variables are revitalized in two more recent theories. The first variable, domestic demand, is one of the four determinants of Porter's (1990) diamond model, which will be discussed in Chapter 3. The second variable, economies of scale, is a major explanatory variable in the theory of intraindustry trade, which will be discussed in the next section.

ECONOMIES OF SCALE

The basic HO model assumes constant returns to scale. Thus, if inputs were doubled, output would be doubled. In many industries, however, there exist economies of scale (or increasing returns). Thus, if inputs were doubled, output would be more than doubled. The existence of economies of scale can explain some trade patterns which are not explained by the HO model. If there are economies of scale, countries (or firms) would benefit if they specialize in the production of a limited range of goods. The problem of specifying a market structure consistent with economies of scale internal to firms delayed for many years the formal modeling of trade based on increasing returns to scale. The breakthrough came in the late 1970s, when Krugman (1979) and Lancaster (1979) independently developed models of trade in differentiated products.[6]

Suppose there are two countries (the United States and Japan) and two types of cars (large cars and small cars). Also suppose there is a demand for both cars in each of the two countries. If there are economies of scale, it would be advantageous for each country to specialize in the production of only one type of car rather than both types. If there is free trade between the two countries, consumers in each country can buy both cars. Economies of scale and international trade make it possible for each country to produce goods more efficiently without sacrificing of variety of goods.

There are basically two types of trade: interindustry trade and intraindustry trade. Interindustry trade reflects comparative advantage. Countries that are relatively similar and so have few comparative differences may not engage in interindustry trade. For an extreme example, suppose that two countries have identical factor endowments. The HO model would then predict no trade. If there are economies of scale, however, there would be benefits of trade from specialization by each country. Therefore, we can conclude that trade between countries with dissimilar factor endowments is largely interindustry, but trade between countries with similar factor endowments is largely intraindustry.

The intraindustry trade model, based on economies of scale, is useful in explaining the trade of manufactured goods among developed countries. For example, cars made by General Motors are exported to other countries at the

---

[6] Krugman emphasized individuals' desire for variety in consumption. In contrast, Lancaster introduced consumer heterogeneity. For more information, see Grossman (1992).

same time that the United States imports foreign-made cars. This is similar to the prediction of the country similarity theorem. However, the intraindustry trade model focuses on the production side, while the country similarity theory emphasizes the demand side.

There are two problems with this model. First, the empirical measures of intraindustry trade are overstated because aggregation is too broad. Much of the apparent intraindustry trade would disappear if goods were further disaggregated. Second, the model does not explain which country produces which goods, so the pattern of intraindustry trade is unpredictable. However, the trade pattern may not be just arbitrary, as we have seen in the case of the country similarity theory. In fact, it is not difficult to explain why, for example, the United States exports large cars and Japan exports small cars. This pattern may be based on different factor endowments between the two countries.

CONCLUSION

We have discussed traditional trade theories. None of these theories has died. They remain useful in understanding many of today's industrial and trade policies. For example, the theory of comparative advantage is a basic guideline for many countries when they consider industrial and trade policies. Even mercantilism, a popular theory before Adam Smith, is important for some countries. However, no single theory is satisfactory in explaining today's international trade because today's world is much more complicated than before. The primary goal of model building is to recognize the most important variable or variables to simplify the phenomena and to easily understand the world. For example, the theory of comparative advantage treats only one variable, i.e., factor endowments, but not other important variables such as demand conditions. It was effective at the time this theory was introduced because the world was not so complicated. Today's global economy is different. Several important variables have to be considered simultaneously in the trade or competitiveness formula. One recent, important development that addresses this issue is Michael Porter's (1990) "diamond model," which will be introduced in Chapter 3. In the next chapter we will discuss the relationship between international trade and competitiveness.

REFERENCES

Grossman, Gene M., editor. 1992. *Imperfect competition and international trade.* Cambridge: MIT Press.

Heckscher, Eli F. 1949 (1919). The effect of foreign trade on the distribution of income. In Howard. S. Ellis & Lloyd A. Metzler, editors, *Readings in the theory of international trade.* Homewood: Irwin.

Hymer, Stephen H. 1976 (1960). *The international operations of national firms: A study of direct foreign investment.* Cambridge: MIT Press.

Krugman, Paul R. 1979. Increasing returns, monopolistic competition and international trade. *Journal of International Economics,* 9: 469-479.

Kreinin, Mordechai. 1965. Comparative labor effectiveness and the Leontief scarce factor paradox. *American Economic Review,* 64 (April): 143-155.

Lancaster, Kelvin J. 1979. *Variety, equity and efficiency.* New York: Columbia University Press.

Leontief, Wassily. 1953. Domestic production and foreign trade: The American capital position re-examined. *Proceedings of the American Philosophical Society,* 97: 331-349. Reprinted in Richard Caves and Harry Johnson, editors, *Readings in International Economics* (Homewood, Illinois: Richard D. Irwin, Inc., 1968).

Linder, Staffan B. 1961. *An essay on trade and transformation.* New York: John Wiley.

Porter, Michael E. 1990. *The competitive advantage of nations.* New York: Free Press.

Ricardo, David. 1971 (1817). *The principles of political economy and taxation.* Baltimore: Penguin.

Samuelson, Paul. 1948. International trade and the equalization of factor prices. *Economic Journal* 58: 165-184.

Smith, Adam. 1937(1776). An inquiry into the nature and causes of the wealth of nations. In Charles W. Eliot, editor, The Harvard Classics. New York: P. F. Collier & Son Corporation.

Stolper, Wolfgang and Paul Samuelson. 1941. Protection and real wages, Review of Economic Studies 9: 58-73.

Vanek, Jaroslav. 1963. The natural resource content of United States foreign trade, 1870-1955, Cambridge: MIT Press.

Vernon, Raymond. 1966. International investments and international trade in the product cycle. Quarterly Journal of Economics, May: 190-207.

Vernon, Raymond. 1979. The product cycle hypothesis in a new international environment. OBES, 41 (4): 255-267. Reprinted in Heidi Wortzel and Lawrence Wortzel, editors, Strategic Management of Multinational Corporations: The Essentials (New York: John Wiley & Sons, 1985).

2. TRADITIONAL MODEL: DEBATE

What Is Competitiveness?

Competitiveness: A Dangerous Obsession	Krugman, 1994
Response 1: Playing to Win	Prestowitz, 1994
Response 2: Microchips, Not Potato Chips	Thurow, 1994
Response 3: Speaking Freely	Cohen, 1994
Counter-Response: Proving My Point	Krugman, 1994

Summary and Key Points

The rhetoric of competitiveness—the view that, in the words of President Clinton, each nation is "like a big corporation competing in the global marketplace"—has become pervasive. According to Krugman, competitiveness poses three dangers. First, it could result in the waste of money to enhance U.S. competitiveness. Second, it could lead protectionism and trade wars. Finally, it could result in bad public policy. Here are his key points and responses by others. Krugman argues that trade is not a zero-sum game, while competition between firms is a zero-sum game. Prestowitz responds that Krugman is correct in the case of trade between the United States and Costa Rica, but not between the United States and Europe. Krugman argues that a country's economic fortunes are determined not by its success on world markets, but by its domestic productivity. Thurow responds that if the domestic economy is to succeed in productivity, it must first compete successfully in the global economy. Krugman warns that an obsession with competitiveness is dangerous and advises cathecting onto productivity. Cohen responds that an exclusive focus on productivity has some dangers. Krugman counter-responds that if the concept of competitiveness cannot be well defined, it should not be used to guide policy.

The debate is highly intellectual and practical, but sometimes confusing. The knowledge of trade models discussed in Chapter 1 is useful in evaluating this debate. For example, Krugman argues that many policy makers and economists are mercantilists because they view trade as a zero-sum game. However, Krugman can also be criticized for not clearly distinguishing between competitive advantage and comparative advantage as a basis of a nation's competitiveness. There are two important issues in this debate. First, it is difficult to define competitiveness. Second, trade balance may not be a good measure for competitiveness. We need a new, comprehensive model that can effectively deal with these two issues. For this purpose, Michael Porter has provided the diamond model, which will be discussed in Chapter 3.

Source:
March/April 1994 and July/August 1994 issues of *Foreign Affairs*

COMPETITIVENESS: A DANGEROUS OBSESSION

PAUL KRUGMAN

The Hypothesis is Wrong

In June 1993, Jacques Delors made a special presentation to the leaders of the nations of the European Community, meeting in Copenhagen, on the growing problem of European unemployment. Economists who study the European situation were curious to see what Delors, president of the EC Commission, would say. Most of them share more or less the same diagnosis of the European problem: the taxes and regulations imposed by Europe's elaborate welfare states have made employers reluctant to create new jobs, while the relatively generous level of unemployment benefits has made workers unwilling to accept the kinds of low-wage jobs that help keep unemployment comparatively low in the United States. The monetary difficulties associated with preserving the European Monetary System in the face of the costs of German reunification have reinforced this structural problem.

It is a persuasive diagnosis, but a politically explosive one, and everyone wanted to see how Delors would handle it. Would he dare tell European leaders that their efforts to pursue economic justice have produced unemployment as an unintended by-product? Would he admit that the EMS could be sustained only at the cost of a recession and face the implications of that admission for European monetary union?

Guess what? Delors didn't confront the problems of either the welfare state or the EMS. He explained that the root cause of European unemployment was a lack of competitiveness with the United States and Japan and that the solution was a program of investment in infrastructure and high technology.

It was a disappointing evasion, but not a surprising one. After all, the rhetoric of competitiveness—the view that, in the words of President Clinton, each nation is "like a big corporation competing in the global marketplace"—has become pervasive among opinion leaders throughout the world. People who believe themselves to be sophisticated about the subject take it for granted that the economic problem facing any modern nation is essentially one of competing on world markets—that the United States and Japan are competitors in the same sense that Coca Cola competes with Pepsi—and are unaware that anyone might seriously question that proposition. Every few months a new best seller warns the American public of the dire consequences of losing the "race" for the 21st century.[7] A whole industry of councils on competitiveness, "geo-economists" and managed trade theorists has sprung up in Washington. Many of these people, having diagnosed America's economic problems in much the same terms as Delors did Europe's, are now in the highest reaches of the Clinton administration formulating economic and trade policy for the United States. So Delors was using a language that was not only convenient but comfortable for him and a wide audience on both sides of the Atlantic.

Unfortunately, his diagnosis was deeply misleading as a guide to what ails Europe, and similar diagnoses in the United States are equally misleading. The idea that a country's economic fortunes are largely determined by its success on world markets is a hypothesis, not a necessary truth; and as a practical, empirical matter, that hypothesis is flatly wrong. That is, it is simply not the case that the world's leading nations are to any

---

[7] See, for just a few examples, Laura D'Andrea Tyson, *Who's Bashing Whom: Trade Conflict in High-Technology Industries*, Washington: Institute for International Economics, 1992; Lester C. Thurow, *Head to Head: The Coming Economic Battle among Japan, Europe, and America*, New York: Morrow, 1992; Ira C. Magaziner and Robert B. Reich, *Minding America's Business. The Decline and Rise of the American Economy*, New York: Vintage Books, 1983; Ira C. Magaziner and Mark Patinkin, *The Silent War: Inside the Global Business Battles Shaping Americas Future*, New York: Vintage Books, 1990; Edward N. Luttwak, *The Endangered American Dream: How to Stop the United States from Becoming a Third World Country and How to Win the Geo-economic Struggle for Industrial Supremacy*, New York: Simon and Schuster, 1993; Kevin P. Phillips, *Staying on Top: The Business Case for a National Industrial Strategy*, New York: Random House, 1984; Clyde V. Prestowitz, Jr., *Trading Places: How We Allowed Japan to Take the Lead*, New York: Basic Books, 1988; William S. Dietrich, *In the Shadow of the Rising Sun: The Political Roots of American Economic Decline*, University Park: Pennsylvania State University Press, 1991; Jeffrey E. Garten, *A Cold Peace: America, Japan, Germany, and the Struggle for Supremacy*, New York: Times Books, 1992; and Wayne Sandholtz et al., *The Highest Stakes: The Economic Foundations of the next Security System*, Berkeley Roundtable on the International Economy (BRIE), Oxford University Press, 1992.

important degree in economic competition with each other, or that any of their major economic problems can be attributed to failures to compete on world markets. The growing obsession in most advanced nations with international competitiveness should be seen, not as a well-founded concern, but as a view held in the face of overwhelming contrary evidence. And yet it is clearly a view that people very much want to hold—a desire to believe that is reflected in a remarkable tendency of those who preach the doctrine of competitiveness to support their case with careless, flawed arithmetic.

This article makes three points. First, it argues that concerns about competitiveness are, as an empirical matter, almost completely unfounded. Second, it tries to explain why defining the economic problem as one of international competition is nonetheless so attractive to so many people. Finally, it argues that the obsession with competitiveness is not only wrong but dangerous, skewing domestic policies and threatening the international economic system. This last issue is, of course, the most consequential from the standpoint of public policy. Thinking in terms of competitiveness leads, directly and indirectly, to bad economic policies on a wide range of issues, domestic and foreign, whether it be in health care or trade.

Mindless Competition

Most people who use the term "competitiveness" do so without a second thought. It seems obvious to them that the analogy between a country and a corporation is reasonable and that to ask whether the United States is competitive in the world market is no different in principle from asking whether General Motors is competitive in the North American minivan market.

In fact, however, trying to define the competitiveness of a nation much more problematic than defining that of a corporation. The bottom line for a corporation is literally its bottom line: if a corporation cannot afford to pay its workers, suppliers, and bondholders, it will go out of business. So when we say that a corporation is uncompetitive, we mean that its market position is unsustainable—that unless it improves its performance, it will cease to exist. Countries, on the other hand, do not go out of business. They may be happy or unhappy with their economic performance, but they have no well-defined bottom line. As a result, the concept of national competitiveness is elusive.

One might suppose, naively, that the bottom line of a national economy is simply its trade balance, that competitiveness can be measured by the ability of a country to sell more abroad than it buys. But in both theory and practice a trade surplus may be a sign of national weakness, a deficit a sign of strength. For example, Mexico was forced to run huge trade surpluses in the 1980s in order to pay the interest on its foreign debt since international investors refused to lend it any more money; it began to run large trade deficits after 1990 as foreign investors recovered confidence and began to pour in new funds. Would anyone want to describe Mexico as a highly competitive nation during the debt crisis era or describe what has happened since 1990 as a loss in competitiveness?

Most writers who worry about the issue at all have therefore tried to define competitiveness as the combination of favorable trade performance and something else. In particular, the most popular definition of competitiveness nowadays runs along the lines of the one given in Council of Economic Advisors Chairman Laura D'Andrea Tyson's *Who's Bashing Whom?*: competitiveness is "our ability to produce goods and services that meet the test of international competition while our citizens enjoy a standard of sustainable." This sounds reasonable. If you think about it, however, and test your thoughts against the facts, you will find out that there is much less to this definition than meets the eye.

Consider, for a moment, what the definition would mean for an economy that conducted very little international trade, like the United States in the 1950s. For such an economy, the ability to balance its trade is mostly a matter of getting the exchange rate right. But because trade is such a small factor in the economy, the level of the exchange rate is a minor influence on the standard of living. So in an economy with very little international trade, the growth in living standards—and thus "competitiveness" according to Tyson's definition—would be determined almost entirely by domestic factors, primarily the rate of productivity growth. That's domestic productivity growth, period—not productivity growth relative to other countries. In other words, for an economy with very little international trade, "competitiveness" would turn out to be a funny way of saying "productivity" and would have nothing to do with international competition.

But surely this changes when trade becomes more important, as indeed it has for all major economies? It certainly could change. Suppose that a country finds that although its productivity is steadily rising, it can succeed in exporting only if it repeatedly devalues its currency, selling its exports ever more cheaply on world markets. Then its standard of living, which depends on its purchasing power over imports as well as domestically produced goods, might actually decline. In the jargon of economists, domestic growth might be outweighed by deteriorating terms of trade.[8] So "competitiveness" could turn out really to be about international competition after all.

There is no reason, however, to leave this as a pure speculation; it can easily be checked against the data. Have deteriorating terms of trade in fact been a major drag on the U.S. standard of living? Or has the rate of growth of U.S. real income continued essentially to equal the rate of domestic productivity growth, even though trade is a larger share of income than it used to be?

To answer this question, one need only look at the national income accounts data the Commerce Department publishes regularly in the Survey of Current Business. The standard measure of economic growth in the United States is, of course, real GNP—a measure that divides the value of goods and services produced in the United States by appropriate price indexes to come up with an estimate of real national output. The Commerce Department also, however, publishes something called "command GNP." This is similar to real GNP except that it divides U.S. exports not by the export price index, but by the price index for U.S. imports. That is, exports are valued by what Americans can buy with the money exports bring. Command GNP therefore measures the volume of goods and services the U.S. economy can "command"—the nation's purchasing power—rather than the volume it produces.[9] And as we have just seen, "competitiveness" means

---

[8] An example may be helpful here. Suppose that a country spends 20 percent of its income on imports, and that the prices of its imports are set not in domestic but in foreign currency. Then if the country is forced to devalue its currency—reduce its value in foreign currency—by 10 percent, this will raise the price of 20 percent of the country's spending basket by 10 percent, thus raising the overall price index by 2 percent. Even if domestic *output* has not changed, the country's real *income* will therefore have fallen by 2 percent. If the country must repeatedly devalue in the face of competitive pressure, growth in real income will persistently lag behind growth in real output. It's important to notice, however, that the size of this lag depends not only on the amount of devaluation but on the share of imports in spending. A 10 percent devaluation of the dollar against the yen does not reduce U. S. real income by 10 percent—in fact, it reduces U.S. real income by only about 0.2 percent because only about 2 percent of U.S. income is spent on goods produced in Japan.

[9] In the example in the previous footnote, the devaluation would have no effect on real GNP, but command GNP would have fallen by two percent. The finding that in practice command GNP has grown almost as fast as real GNP therefore amounts to saying that events like the hypothetical case in footnote one are unimportant in practice.

something different from "productivity" if and only if purchasing power grows significantly more slowly than output.

Well, here are the numbers. Over the period 1959-73, a period of vigorous growth in U.S. living standards and few concerns about international competition, real GNP per worker-hour grew 1.85 percent annually, while command GNP per hour grew a bit faster, 1.87 percent. From 1973 to 1990, a period of stagnating living standards, command GNP growth per hour slowed to 0.65 percent. Almost all (91 percent) of that slowdown, however, was explained by a decline in domestic productivity growth: real GNP per hour grew only 0.73 percent.

Similar calculations for the European Community and Japan yield similar results. In each case, the growth rate of living standards essentially equals the growth rate of domestic productivity—not productivity relative to competitors, but simply domestic productivity. Even though world trade is larger than ever before, national living standards are overwhelmingly determined by domestic factors rather than by some competition for world markets.

How can this be in our interdependent world? Part of the answer is that the world is not as interdependent as you might think: countries are nothing at all like corporations. Even today, U.S. exports are only 10 percent of the value-added in the economy (which is equal to GNP). That is, the United States is still almost 90 percent an economy that produces goods and services for its own use. By contrast, even the largest corporation sells hardly any of its output to its own workers; the "exports" of General Motors—its sales to people who do not work there—are virtually all of its sales, which are more than 2.5 times the corporation's value-added.

Moreover, countries do not compete with each other the way corporations do. Coke and Pepsi are almost purely rivals: only a negligible fraction of Coca Cola's sales go to Pepsi workers, only a negligible fraction of the goods Coca Cola workers buy are Pepsi products. So if Pepsi is successful, it tends to be at Coke's expense. But the major industrial countries, while they sell products that compete with each other, are also each other's main export markets and each other's main suppliers of useful imports. If the European economy does well, it need not be at U.S. expense; indeed, if anything a successful European economy is likely to help the U.S. economy by providing it with larger markets and selling it goods of superior quality at lower prices.

International trade, then, is not a zero-sum game. When productivity rises in Japan, the main result is a rise in Japanese real wages; American or European wages are in principle at least as likely to rise as to fall, and in practice seem to be virtually unaffected.

It would be possible to belabor the point, but the moral is clear: while competitive problems could arise in principle, as a practical, empirical matter the major nations of the world are not to any significant degree in economic competition with each other. Of course, there is always a rivalry for status and power—countries that grow faster will see their political rank rise. So it is always interesting to compare countries. But asserting that Japanese growth diminishes U.S. status is very different from saying that it reduces the U.S. standard of living and it is the latter that the rhetoric of competitiveness asserts.

One can, of course, take the position that words mean what we want them to mean, that all are free, if they wish, to use the term "competitiveness" as a poetic way of saying productivity, without actually implying that international competition has anything to do with it. But few writers on competitiveness would accept this view. They believe that the facts tell a very different story, that we live, as Lester Thurow put it in his best-selling book, *Head to Head*, in a world of "win-lose" competition between the leading economies. How is this belief possible?

Careless Arithmetic

One of the remarkable, startling features of the vast literature on competitiveness is the repeated tendency of highly intelligent authors to engage in what may perhaps most tactfully be described as "careless arithmetic." Assertions are made that sound like quantifiable pronouncements about measurable magnitudes, but the writers do not actually present any data on these magnitudes and thus fail to notice that the actual numbers contradict their assertions. Or data are presented that are supposed to support an assertion, but the writer fails to notice that his own numbers imply that what he is saying cannot be true. Over and over again one finds books and articles on competitiveness that seem to the unwary reader to be full of convincing evidence but that strike anyone familiar with the data as strangely, almost eerily inept in their handling of the numbers. Some examples can best illustrate this point. Here are three cases of careless arithmetic, each of some interest in its own right.

Trade Deficits and the Loss of Good Jobs. In a recent article published in Japan, Lester Thurow explained to his audience the importance of reducing the Japanese trade surplus with the United States. U.S. real wages, he pointed out, had fallen six percent during the Reagan and Bush years, and the reason was that trade deficits in manufactured goods had forced workers out of high-paying manufacturing jobs into much lower-paying service jobs.

This is not an original view; it is very widely held. But Thurow was more concrete than most people, giving actual numbers for the job and wage loss. A million manufacturing jobs have been lost because of the deficit, he asserted, and manufacturing jobs pay 30 percent more than service jobs.

Both numbers are dubious. The million job number is too high, and the 30 percent wage differential between manufacturing and services is primarily due to a difference in the length of the workweek, not a difference in the hourly wage rate. But let's grant Thurow his numbers. Do they tell the story he suggests?

The key point is that total U.S. employment is well over 100 million workers. Suppose that a million workers were forced from manufacturing into services and as a result lost the 30 percent manufacturing wage premium. Since these workers are less than 1 percent of the U.S. labor force, this would reduce the average U.S. wage rate by less than 1/100 of 30 percent— that is, by less than 0.3 percent.

This is too small to explain the 6 percent real wage decline *by a factor of 20*. Or to look at it another way, the annual wage loss from deficit induced deindustrialization, which Thurow clearly implies is at the heart of U.S. economic difficulties, is on the basis of his own numbers roughly equal to what the U.S. spends on health care every week.

Something puzzling is going on here. How could someone as intelligent as Thurow, in writing an article that purports to offer hard quantitative evidence of the importance of international competition to the U.S. economy, fail to realize that the evidence he offers clearly shows that the channel of harm that he identifies was not the culprit?

High Value-added Sectors. Ira Magaziner and Robert Reich, both now influential figures in the Clinton Administration, first reached a broad audience with their 1982 book, *Minding America's Business*. The book advocated a U.S. industrial policy, and in the introduction the authors offered a seemingly concrete quantitative basis for such a policy: "Our standard of living can only rise if (I) capital and labor increasingly flow to industries with high value-added per worker and (II) we maintain a position in those industries that is superior to that of our competitors."

Economists were skeptical of this idea on principle. If targeting the right industries was simply a matter of moving into sectors with high value-added, why weren't private markets already doing the job?[10] But one might dismiss this as simply the usual boundless faith of economists in the market; didn't Magaziner and Reich back their case with a great deal of real world evidence?

Well, *Minding America's Business* contains a lot of facts. One thing it never does, however, is actually justify the criteria set out in the introduction. The choice of industries to cover clearly implied a belief among the authors that high value-added is more or less synonymous with high technology, but nowhere in the book do any numbers compare actual value-added per worker in different industries.

Such numbers are not hard to find. Indeed, every public library in America has a copy of the *Statistical Abstract of the United States*, which each year contains a table presenting value-added and employment by industry in U.S. manufacturing. All one needs to do, then, is spend a few minutes in the library with a calculator to come up with a table that ranks U.S. industries by value-added per worker.

The table shows selected entries from pages 740-744 of the 1991 *Statistical Abstract*. It turns out that the U.S. industries with really high value-added per worker are in sectors with very high ratios of capital to labor, like cigarettes and petroleum refining. (This was predictable: because capital-intensive industries must earn a normal return on large investments, they must charge prices that are a larger markup over labor costs than labor-intensive industries, which means that they have high value-added per worker). Among large industries, value-added per worker tends to be high in traditional heavy manufacturing sectors like steel and autos. High-technology sectors like aerospace and electronics turn out to be only roughly average.

---

[10] "Value-added" has a precise, standard meaning in national income accounting: the value added of a firm is the dollar value of its sales, minus the dollar value of the inputs it purchases from other firms, and as such it is easily measured. Some people who use the term, however, may be unaware of this definition and simply use "high value-added" as a synonym for "desirable."

Table 2-1. Value Added Per Worker

Value Added Per Worker, 1988 *(in thousands of dollars)*	
Cigarettes	488
Petroleum Refining	283
Autos	99
Steel	97
Aircraft	68
Electronics	64
All Manufacturing	66

This result does not surprise conventional economists. High value-added per worker occurs in sectors that are highly capital-intensive, that is, sectors in which an additional dollar of capital buys little extra value-added. In other words, there is no free lunch.

But let's leave on one side what the table says about the way the economy works, and simply note the strangeness of the lapse by Magaziner and Reich. Surely they were not calling for an industrial policy that would funnel capital and labor into the steel and auto industries in preference to high-tech. How, then, could they write a whole book dedicated to the proposition that we should target high value-added industries without ever checking to see which industries they meant?

Labor Costs. In his own presentation at the Copenhagen summit, British Prime Minister John Major showed a chart indicating that European unit labor costs have risen more rapidly than those in the United States and Japan. Thus he argued that European workers have been pricing themselves out of world markets.

But a few weeks later Sam Brittan of the *Financial Times* pointed out a strange thing about Major's calculations: the labor costs were not adjusted for exchange rates. In international competition, of course, what matters for a U.S. firm are the costs of its overseas rivals measured in dollars, not marks or yen. So international comparisons of labor costs, like the tables the Bank of England routinely publishes, always convert them into a common currency. The numbers presented by Major, however, did not make this standard adjustment. And it was a good thing for his presentation that they didn't. As Brittan pointed out, European labor costs have not risen in relative terms when the exchange rate adjustment is made.

If anything, this lapse is even odder than those of Thurow or Magaziner and Reich. How could John Major, with the sophisticated statistical resources of the U.K. Treasury behind him, present an analysis that failed to make the most standard of adjustments?

These examples of strangely careless arithmetic, chosen from among dozens of similar cases, by people who surely had both the cleverness and the resources to get it right, cry out for an explanation. The best working hypothesis is that in each case the author or speaker wanted to believe in the competitive hypothesis so much that he felt no urge to question it; if data were used at all, it was only to lend credibility to a predetermined belief, not to test it. But why are people apparently so anxious to define economic problems as issues of international competition?

The Thrill of Competition

The competitive metaphor—the image of countries competing with each other in world markets in the same way that corporations do—derives much of its attractiveness from its seeming comprehensibility. Tell a group of businessmen that a country is like a corporation writ large, and you give them the comfort of feeling that they already understand the basics. Try to tell them about economic concepts like comparative advantage, and you are asking them to learn something new. It should not be surprising if many prefer a doctrine that offers the gain of apparent sophistication without the pain of hard thinking. The rhetoric of competitiveness has become so widespread, however, for three deeper reasons.

First, competitive images are exciting, and thrills sell tickets. The subtitle of Lester Thurow's huge best-seller, *Head to Head*, is "The Coming Economic Battle among Japan, Europe, and America"; the jacket proclaims that "the decisive war of the century has begun . . . and America may already have decided to lose." Suppose that the subtitle had described the real situation: "The coming struggle in which each big economy will succeed or fail based on its own efforts, pretty much independently of how well the others do." Would Thurow have sold a tenth as many books?

Second, the idea that U.S. economic difficulties hinge crucially on our failures in international competition somewhat paradoxically makes those difficulties seem easier to solve. The productivity of the average American worker is determined by a complex array of factors, most of them unreachable by any likely government policy. So if you accept the reality that our "competitive" problem is really a domestic productivity problem pure and simple, you are unlikely to be optimistic about any dramatic turnaround. But if you can convince yourself that the problem is really one of failures in international competition—that imports are pushing workers out of high-wage jobs, or subsidized foreign competition is driving the United States out of the high value-added sectors—then the answers to economic malaise may seem to you to involve simple things like subsidizing high technology and being tough on Japan.

Finally, many of the world's leaders have found the competitive metaphor extremely useful as a political device. The rhetoric of competitiveness turns out to provide a good way either to justify hard choices or to avoid them. The example of Delors in Copenhagen shows the usefulness of competitive metaphors as an evasion. Delors had to say something at the EC summit; yet to say anything that addressed the real roots of European unemployment would have involved huge political risks. By turning the discussion to essentially irrelevant but plausible sounding questions of competitiveness, he bought himself some time to come up with a better answer (which to some extent he provided in December's white paper on the European economy—a paper that still, however, retained "competitiveness" in its title).

By contrast, the well-received presentation of Bill Clinton's initial economic program in February 1993 showed the usefulness of competitive rhetoric as a motivation for tough policies. Clinton proposed a set of painful spending cuts and tax increases to reduce the Federal deficit. Why? The real reasons for cutting the deficit are disappointingly undramatic: the deficit siphons off funds that might otherwise have been productively invested, and thereby exerts a steady if small drag on U. S . economic growth. But Clinton was able instead to offer a stirring patriotic appeal, calling on the nation to act now in order to make the economy competitive in the global market—with the implication that dire economic consequences would follow if the United States does not.

Many people who know that "competitiveness" is a largely meaningless concept have been willing to indulge competitive rhetoric precisely because they believe they can harness it in the service of good policies. An overblown fear of the Soviet Union was used in the 1950s to justify the building of the interstate highway system and the expansion of math and science education. Cannot the unjustified fears about foreign competition similarly be turned to good, used to justify serious efforts to reduce the budget deficit, rebuild infrastructure, and so on?

A few years ago this was a reasonable hope. At this point, however, the obsession with competitiveness has reached the point where it has already begun dangerously to distort economic policies.

The Dangers of Obession

Thinking and speaking in terms of competitiveness poses three real dangers. First, it could result in the wasteful spending of government money supposedly to enhance U.S. competitiveness. Second, it could lead to protectionism and trade wars. Finally, and most important, it could result in bad public policy on a spectrum of important issues.

During the 1950s, fear of the Soviet Union induced the U.S. government to spend money on useful things like highways and science education. It also, however, led to considerable spending on more doubtful items like bomb shelters. The most obvious if least worrisome danger of the growing obsession with competitiveness is that it might lead to a similar misallocation of resources. To take an example, recent guidelines for government research funding have stressed the importance of supporting research that can improve U.S. international competitiveness. This exerts at least some bias toward inventions that can help manufacturing firms, which generally compete on international markets, rather than service producers, which generally do not. Yet most of our employment and value-added is now in services, and lagging productivity in services rather than manufactures has been the single most important factor in the stagnation of U.S. living standards.

A much more serious risk is that the obsession with competitiveness will lead to trade conflict, perhaps even to a world trade war. Most of those who have preached the doctrine of competitiveness have not been old-fashioned protectionists. They want their countries to win the global trade game, not drop out. But what if, despite its best efforts, a country does not seem to be winning, or lacks confidence that it can? Then the competitive diagnosis inevitably suggests that to close the borders is better than to risk having foreigners take away high-wage jobs and high-value sectors. At the very least, the focus on the supposedly competitive nature of international economic relations greases the rails for those who want confrontational if not frankly protectionist policies.

We can already see this process at work, in both the United States and Europe. In the United States, it was remarkable how quickly the sophisticated interventionist arguments advanced by Laura Tyson in her published work gave way to the simple-minded claim by U.S. Trade Representative Mickey Kantor that Japan's bilateral trade surplus was costing the United States millions of jobs. And the trade rhetoric of President Clinton, who stresses the supposed creation of high-wage jobs rather than the gains from specialization, left his administration in a weak position when it tried to argue with the claims of NAFTA foes that competition from cheap Mexican labor will destroy the U.S. manufacturing base.

Perhaps the most serious risk from the obsession with competitiveness, however, is its subtle indirect effect on the quality of economic discussion and policy-making. If top government officials are strongly committed to a particular economic doctrine, their commitment inevitably sets the tone for policy-making on all issues, even those which may seem to have nothing to do with that doctrine. And if an economic doctrine is flatly, completely and demonstrably wrong, the insistence that discussion adhere to that doctrine inevitably blurs the focus and diminishes the quality of policy discussion across a broad range of issues, including some that are very far from trade policy per se.

Consider, for example, the issue of health care reform, undoubtedly the most important economic initiative of the Clinton administration, almost surely an order of magnitude more important to U.S. living standards than anything that might be done about trade policy (unless the United States provokes a full-blown trade war). Since health care is an issue with few direct international linkages, one might have expected it to be largely insulated from any distortions of policy resulting from misguided concerns about competitiveness.

But the administration placed the development of the health care plan in the hands of Ira Magaziner, the same Magaziner who so conspicuously failed to do his homework in arguing for government promotion of high value-added industries. Magaziner's prior writings and consulting on economic policy focused almost entirely on the issue of international competition, his views on which may be summarized by the title of his 1990 book, *The Silent War*. His appointment reflected many factors, of course, not least his long personal friendship with the first couple. Still, it was not irrelevant that in an administration committed to the ideology of competitiveness Magaziner, who has consistently recommended that national industrial policies be based on the corporate strategy concepts he learned during his years at the Boston Consulting Group, was regarded as an economic policy expert.

We might also note the unusual process by which the health care reform was developed. In spite of the huge size of the task force, recognized experts in the health care field were almost completely absent, notably though not exclusively economists specializing in health care, including economists with impeccable liberal credentials like Henry Aaron of the Brookings

Institution. Again, this may have reflected a number of factors, but it is probably not irrelevant that anyone who, like Magaziner, is strongly committed to the ideology of competitiveness is bound to have found professional economists notably unsympathetic in the past—and to be unwilling to deal with them on any other issue.

To make a harsh but not entirely unjustified analogy, a government wedded to the ideology of competitiveness is as unlikely to make good economic policy as a government committed to creationism is to make good science policy, even in areas that have no direct relationship to the theory of evolution.

Advisers with No Clothes

If the obsession with competitiveness is as misguided and damaging as this article claims, why aren't more voices saying so? The answer is, a mixture of hope and fear.

On the side of hope, many sensible people have imagined that they can appropriate the rhetoric of competitiveness on behalf of desirable economic policies. Suppose that you believe that the United States needs to raise its savings rate and improve its educational system in order to raise its productivity. Even if you know that the benefits of higher productivity have nothing to do with international competition, why not describe this as a policy to enhance competitiveness if you think that it can widen your audience? It's tempting to pander to popular prejudices on behalf of a good cause, and I have myself succumbed to that temptation.

As for fear, it takes either a very courageous or very reckless economist to say publicly that a doctrine that many, perhaps most, of the world's opinion leaders have embraced is flatly wrong. The insult is all the greater when many of those men and women think that by using the rhetoric of competitiveness they are demonstrating their sophistication about economics. This article may influence people, but it will not make many friends.

Unfortunately, those economists who have hoped to appropriate the rhetoric of competitiveness for good economic policies have instead had their own credibility appropriated on behalf of bad ideas. And somebody has to point out when the emperor's intellectual wardrobe isn't all he thinks it is.

So let's start telling the truth: competitiveness is a meaningless word when applied to national economies. And the obsession with competitiveness is both wrong and dangerous.

RESPONSE 1: PLAYING TO WIN

CLYDE V. PRESTOWITZ, JR.

Paul Krugman first achieved a measure of public recognition with a study of competition in the aircraft industry, which proved mathematically the potential efficacy of strategic—that is to say managed—trade. That this analysis was considered important might seem odd in view of the fact that the German-American scholar Friedrich List had done more or less the same work nearly 150 years ago and in view of the experience of the Japanese, who had been practicing strategic trade for more than 40 years at the time of Krugman's study. But given the narrow scope of the research considered permissible by the conventional wisdom of U.S. economists, as well as their ignorance of history and other disciplines, Krugman's analysis was a notable, iconoclastic achievement.

Indeed, it may have been too daring because ever since its publication Krugman has been running away from the implications of his own findings. His diatribe in *Foreign Affairs* (March/April) against the concept of competitiveness and those who espouse it is only the most recent example.

Krugman not only claims that concern with competitiveness is misplaced. He attacks all those who think otherwise—Including leading members of the Clinton administration such as Robert B. Reich, Ira C. Magaziner, Laura D'Andrea Tyson and the president himself—as protectionists whose work is careless if not dishonest and whose motives run from simple greed to chauvinism and demagoguery.

Krugman contends that concern about competitiveness is silly because as a practical matter the major countries of the world are not in economic competition with each other. He attempts to prove this by making three points. First he argues that trade is not a zero-sum game. Trade between the United States and Japan is not like competition between Coca-Cola and Pepsi because whereas Pepsi's gain is almost always Coke's loss, the United States and its trading partners can both be winners through the dynamics of comparative advantage.

Although true to some extent, this rationale ignores that different kinds of trade take place. Surely Krugman is correct in the case of trade between the United States and Costa Rica, where America imports bananas it does not grow and exports airplanes and machinery that Costa Rica does not make. Both countries come out winners by devoting their resources to what each does best. But what about the kind of trade typified by the recent Saudi Arabian order for $6 billion of new airplanes? Why were the Europeans so upset and Clinton so happy when the Saudis announced that U.S. producers would win all the orders? Both the Europeans and the Americans make airplanes, and this order means that the United States will gain jobs and income that Europe might have had but lost. This was largely a zero-sum trade situation, and ironically it was precisely the case that first brought Krugman to prominence. Maybe he was right the first time.

It's Living Standards, Stupid

In fact, Krugman later concedes the point by allowing that "in principle" competitiveness problems could arise between countries. But he insists that they do not in practice because trade is a relatively small part of GNP in the major countries. Consequently, living standards are determined almost wholly by how well the economy works domestically rather than by international performance. In this vein, he observes that exports constitute only 10 percent of U.S. output, apparently leaving 90 percent of the economy to purely domestic factors. Moreover, he attributes 91 percent of the 1973 to 1990 stagnation in U.S. living standards to declining domestic productivity growth and only 9 percent to deteriorating terms of trade.

But competitiveness proponents have never denied the importance of domestic economic performance. Indeed, virtually all competitiveness prescriptions emphasize domestic savings and investment rates, education, cost of capital and research and development. Trade is typically treated as a secondary issue—more a symptom than a cause of subpar competitiveness. Second, Krugman ignores America's imports—which equal 11 percent of GNP and nearly half of U.S. manufacturing output. Thus, overall trade is equivalent to about 21 percent of GNP, and by some estimates the impact of trade is felt directly by at least half the U.S. economy. Take the U.S. auto industry. It is not a big exporter, and imports account for only about 15 percent of the U.S. market. But the prices and quality of those imports help determine the retail prices U.S. automakers can charge, wages of U. S . auto workers and incomes of those who service the U.S. auto industry.

Krugman does not explain the slowdown in U.S. productivity growth, but he implies that domestic factors are the sole culprits. Yet the slowdown came just when U.S. imports were soaring and entire industries such as consumer electronics were being wiped out by foreign competitors pursuing mercantilist tactics. Surely these dislocations had some impact on U.S. productivity growth.

Krugman's third and final argument is that although countries may be rivals for status and power, such rivalry is something apart from economics and has no impact on living standards. A high relative growth rate may enhance Japan's status, for example, but it does not reduce the living standard of other countries. Although this notion may be true in the short-term, absolute sense, it is not necessarily true in the long-term, potential sense. Since the end of World War II, the United States has grown faster than Great Britain. The United States has done so in part by taking British inventions such as jet planes and radar and commercializing them faster than the British, thereby closing off those industries as potential avenues of British growth. Of course, if Britain could enter other high-growth, high-wage industries, the U.S. position would make no difference. But at any one time the number of those industries is limited; missing the boat on one can mean losing potential gains in living standards. In the extreme, loss of economic competitiveness can weaken national security and cause greater vulnerability to political regimes and international cartels that may severely constrain a country's economic potential. This competition is, after all, what imperialism and its opposition has been all about.

Splitting Hairs

To buttress his arguments, Krugman attacks his critics' arithmetic as careless. Yet Krugman's own arithmetic is careless and selective. His analysis of how manufacturing job loss affects real average wages ignores the relationship between service and manufacturing wages. American barbers are not notably more productive than Bangladeshi barbers. But their wages are much higher because their customers work with much higher productivity than the customers of their Bangladeshi counterparts. Loss of high-wage U.S. manufacturing jobs also depresses not only manufacturing wages, but service industry wages as well. Krugman, however, fails to mention this drag.

Krugman's discussion of value added is even more questionable. He may have a point in that "high value added" has become a kind of shorthand for technology-intensive and high-wage industries when that is not always the case. But Krugman uses very broad industry categories to make his point, although the data he draws on clearly show that a huge industry like electronics consists of many sectors, some with high value added and others with low. Overall, Krugman notes a figure of value added per worker in the electronics industry of only $64,000. But why did he ignore the tables showing the figures of $443,000 for computers and $234,000 for semiconductors?

Krugman concludes by expressing fear of the possible distortion of the U.S. economy through the application of flawed competitiveness policies. He could, of course, be right. But can the United States be confident that an analyst who has such obvious gaps of his own and who has now argued both sides of the competitiveness issue can be relied on as the guide? Perhaps he is wrong, and competitiveness, far from being a dangerous obsession, is an essential concern.

RESPONSE 2: MICROCHIPS, NOT POTATO CHIPS

LESTER C. THUROW

The Gang of Eight (Bill Clinton, John Major, Jacques Delors, Robert Reich, Laura D'Andrea Tyson, Mickey Kantor, Ira Magaziner, Lester Thurow) pleads not guilty to Paul Krugman's charges that it is grossly exaggerating the importance of international competitiveness.

Krugman asserts that, economically, nations have "no well-defined bottom line." Wrong! Nations seek to raise the living standards of each citizen. Higher living standards depend on rising productivity, and in any economy the rate of productivity growth is principally determined by the size of domestic investments in plant and equipment, research and development, skills and public infrastructure, and the quality of private management and public administration.

I have written articles referring to strategic trade policies as the "seven percent solution." Ninety-three percent of economic success or failure is determined at home with only seven percent depending on competitive and cooperative arrangements with the rest of the world. My book, *The Zero-Sum Solution: Building a World-Class American Economy*, contains 23 pages on competitiveness issues, 45 pages on the importance of international cooperation and 333 pages on getting things right at home. The centrality of domestic invention and innovation is precisely why I agreed to lead the Lemelson-MIT program in invention and innovation, one part of which is a $500,000 prize for the American inventor and innovator of the year. The corpus of writings, speeches and actions of the rest of the Gang of Eight contains similar quotations, proportions and actions.

But remembering this sense of proportion, what is the role for competitiveness? Clearly something is wrong with Krugman's arithmetic that shows international trade cannot make much difference to American productivity. If his arithmetic were correct, then it follows that a lot of American protection might be quite a good thing.

Today 6 million Americans are working part-time who would like to work full-time, and almost 9 million are unemployed. In the last 20 years the bottom two-thirds of the male work force has taken a 20 percent reduction in real wages. The American work force could use a few million extra high-wage jobs. Suppose the United States were to impose quotas on manufactured imports so as to bring American imports (now 14 percent of gross domestic product) down to the 10 percent of GDP currently exported— that is, increase the domestically produced GDP by $250 billion. According to the U.S. Department of Commerce, if one divides manufacturing output by manufacturing employment, every $45 billion in extra output represents one million jobs. Production of current imports would absorb more than 5 million of those 15 million underemployed and unemployed people.

Since more Americans would be working in a sector with above-average productivity, national output and earnings would rise. The losses to the American consumer in the form of higher prices would be smaller than the gains to American producers in the form of higher earnings unless American producers were less than half as efficient as those abroad (an unlikely event). But even if that were the case, the economic burden of their inefficiency would be trivial relative to American GDP of $6.5 trillion. The gains to workers would be well worth the loss in output. But certainly none of the Gang of Eight advocates such policies, although they would seem to be called for by Krugman's simple arithmetic. Why?

Welcome to the Real World

The simple arithmetic of what economists call "comparative statics" is technically right but economically wrong. If the domestic economy is to succeed in moving to higher levels of productivity and income, it must first compete successfully in the global economy. Foreign competition simultaneously forces a faster pace of economic change at home and produces opportunities to learn new technologies and new management practices that can be used to improve domestic productivity. Put bluntly, those who don't compete abroad won't be productive at home.

Although he denies saying it, Michael J. Boskin, chairman of President Bush's Council of Economic Advisers, will go down in history as the man who said, "It doesn't make any difference whether a country makes potato chips or computer chips!" The statement is wrong because wages and rates of return to capital are not everywhere equal.

The real world is in a perpetual state of dynamic disequilibrium where differentials in wages and rate of return to capital by industry are both large and persistent (these above-average wages or returns to capital are technically called disequilibrium quasi-rents). Within manufacturing in 1992 there was an almost four-to-one wage gap between those working in the highest- and lowest-paid industries. The industries at the top and bottom have changed little since World War II. Rates of return to capital similarly ranged from plus 27 percent in pharmaceuticals to minus 26 percent in building materials.

Pharmaceuticals top the rate of return charts every year. The market is always eliminating the high rates of return on existing drugs, but disequilibrium quasi-rents are always being created on new drugs. Because every successful pharmaceutical firm requires huge amounts of time and capital to build physical and human infrastructure, those already in the industry find it relatively easy to stay ahead of those who might seek to enter.

Putting People First

Those who lost jobs in autos and machine tools as American firms lost market share at home and abroad typically took a 30 to 50 percent wage reduction, if they were young. If they were over 50 years of age, they were usually permanently exiled to the periphery of the low-wage, part-time labor market. Their losses might not be a large faction of GDP, but those losses are important to the millions of affected workers and their families. The correct redress for their problems, however, is not to keep Japanese autos or machine tools out of the American market but to organize ventures such as the government-industry auto battery consortium that seeks to expand the American auto industry's market share by taking the lead in producing tomorrow's electric cars.

Since aircraft manufacturing generates technologies that later spread to the rest of the economy and above-average wages, the United States cannot simply ignore the government-financed European Airbus Industry challenge in an industry America currently dominates.

The fastest-growing and technologically most exciting industry over the next decade is expected to be the industry that lies at the intersection of telecommunications, computers, television and the media arts. Given this prospect the United States cannot afford to let itself be locked out of the Japanese wireless telecommunications market or permit the Europeans to limit American movies and television programs to 40 percent of their markets. To do so is to make the entire American economy less dynamic and less technologically sophisticated and to generate lower American incomes than would otherwise be the case.

In the traditional theory of comparative advantage, Boskin and Krugman are correct. Natural resource endowments and factor proportions (capital-labor ratios) determine what countries should produce. Governments can and should do little when it comes to international competitiveness. With a world capital market, however, all now essentially borrow in London, New York or Tokyo regardless of where they live. There is no such thing as a capital-rich or capital-poor country. Modern technology has also pushed natural resources out of the competitive equation. Japan, with no coal or iron ore deposits, can have the best steel industry in the world.

This is now a much more dynamic world of brainpower industries and synthesized comparative advantage. Industries such as microelectronics, biotechnology, the new materials industries, telecommunications, civilian aircraft production, machine tools, and computer hardware and software have no natural geographic home. They will be located wherever someone organizes the brainpower to capture them. With man-made comparative advantage, one seeks not to find disequilibrium quasi-rents (the gold mine of yore) but to create the new products and processes that generate above-average wages and rates of return.

In their funding of education, skills and research and development, governments have an important role to play in organizing the brainpower necessary to create economic leadership. Just as military intelligence estimates about U.S.S.R. intentions partly guided yesterday's strategic military research and development, so the actions of U.S. economic competitors will partly guide tomorrow's civilian research and development. If the Japanese have an insurmountable lead in flat-screen video technology, it does not make sense to invest government or private resources or talent in a hopeless attempt to catch up.

The smart private firm benchmarks itself vis-à-vis its best domestic and international competition. Where it is not the world's best, it seeks to adopt the better practices found elsewhere. A smart country will do the same. Is America's investment in plant and equipment, research and development, skills and infrastructure world class? Do American managers, private and public, have something to learn from practices in the rest of the world? The purpose of such benchmarking is not to declare economic warfare° on foreign competitors but to emulate them and elevate U.S. standards of performance.

Obsessions are not always wrong or dangerous. A passion for building a world-class economy that is second to none in generating a high living standard for every citizen is exactly what the United States and every other country should seek to achieve. Achieving that goal in any one country in no way stops any other country from doing likewise.

RESPONSE 3: SPEAKING FREELY

STEPHEN S.COHEN

Paul Krugman contends that those who speak of competitiveness fail to understand three important points. First, nations are not like companies. No single number indicates their bottom line and the analogy does not apply. Second, he says that competitiveness is at best a meaningless concept. If it has any meaning whatever, it is "a poetic way of saying productivity." Productivity is the robust and unique measure of the performance of a national economy. Third, international trade is not a zero-sum game.

These are not stinging revelations but merely oft-repeated truisms. All his assertions are set out mundanely in The Report of the President's Commission on Competitiveness, written for the Reagan administration in 1984. The report provides what even Krugman acknowledges has become the standard definition:

Competitiveness has different meanings for the firm and for the national economy .... A nation's competitiveness is the degree to which it can, under free and fair market conditions, produce goods and services that meet the test of international markets while simultaneously expanding the real

incomes of its citizens. Competitiveness at the national level is based on
superior productivity performance.

So all of Krugman's revelations are on page one of the basic text: no simple
analogy equates a nation and a business, productivity lies at the center of
competitiveness, and trade is not a zero-sum game; it can and should be free
and fair.

What then, if anything, is Krugman flailing at? Nobody with whom
Krugman should deign to take difference has ever said the silly things he
pokes with his jousting spear. Lots of people vulgarize competitiveness, but
that is true of just about every other idea in economics.

Krugman objects to President Clinton's likening of the U.S. economy to
"a big corporation competing in the global marketplace." Presidential
metaphors, which try to encapsulate complicated matters for purposes of
political mobilization, have their own logic and history. Perhaps Clinton's
simile is akin to Franklin D. Roosevelt's famous likening of the Lend-Lease
Act to lending a neighbor a fire hose. Clinton was neither mendacious nor
wrong. To remind Americans that in many ways they are all in this together
is important, and in a sense the national economy can be likened to a huge
corporation—not big in the rude, trivializing example Krugman uses, Pepsi
versus Coke, but big in the Mitsubishi, Mitsui or Sumitomo sense. The six
main *keiretsu*—massive structures of grouped companies—which for many
purposes come very close to being the Japanese economy, produce about
half the Japanese total output of transportation equipment, banking,
insurance, oil, glass, cement and shipping. Over one-half of all intermediate
products are produced and bought within the cozy network of the six main
groups, not to mention the lesser vertical *keiretsu*.

Lots of people, not just politicians, use "competitiveness" as a metaphor
and do so a bit freely. Scientists talk of national competitiveness in biology;
educators, in math. Part of the problem is the need for a single substantive
term for "competitive position." Part is a heightened awareness, all to the
good, that the United States is no longer supreme, benchmarking is a first
step toward serious improvement, and comparative measures—even of
economic welfare—have important and legitimate meanings.

Krugman criticizes those who write about competitiveness for their
tendency to "engage in what may perhaps most tactfully be described as
'careless arithmetic.'" Yet Krugman's own arithmetic is, to say the least,
careless. He provides a table that purports to demonstrate arithmetically that
value-added production correlates not with technology but with capital

intensity. But relating capital intensity to value added by sector contains a concealed correlation because the same table also ranks sectors by degree of monopoly power. And nothing generates more value added than monopoly. Furthermore, Krugman omitted at least one sector: pharmaceuticals. This sector should be number three on his list, with value added almost twice as high as autos. But value added in pharmaceuticals is not explained by lots of capital per worker; instead the pharmaceutical industry has lots of research per worker along with lots of sales effort and monopoly concentration. And for a more sophisticated understanding, one should look beyond production to sales figures in the United States, which include competition from imports. In cigarettes, the number-one industry in value added and number-one in monopoly concentration, competition from imports is trivial. That is a major reason for the high value added in cigarette production. But that raises big questions, such as what determines productivity? What operationally can and cannot be done with simple productivity numbers?

Krugman warns that an obsession with competitiveness is dangerous and advises cathecting onto productivity. A near-exclusive focus on productivity, however, has some particular dangers and problems. Competitiveness puts productivity at the center of its concerns but not as an explanation. Instead competitiveness points out that overall productivity rates, which are very complex syntheses, are the things to explain, and that economics does not know how to do that.

Beggar-Thy-Question

Krugman unwittingly illustrates the problem of relying on a single number for overall production rates when he provides an alternative to a competitiveness approach. To say that 91 percent of the slowdown in the growth of per capita GNP "was explained by a decline in domestic productivity growth" does not explain the decline but rephrases it. To say that GNP grew slowly because the growth in output per hour grew slowly is simply to push aside the real question: What caused the decline? Krugman's numerical exercise does not even adequately fulfill the smaller role he assigns to it—to show that foreign competition played a trivial part in lowering the rate of growth of national welfare. This failure occurs because Krugman counts only the prices and quantities of imports, not their impact on profits, investment, jobs and wages. The typical case outlining the advantages of trade to the U.S. economy always focuses on these elements because they are much bigger than the simple, first-round effects of the prices and quantities of imports, which, with a modicum of craftsmanship, can be manipulated to demonstrate whatever one wishes. Similar problems of logic and data flaw the calculations that yield Krugman's most sweeping single-number assertion—that the U.S. trade deficit in manufactured goods has only a very small impact on wages, a reduction at most of only 0.3 percent. The problem, again, is not just with the single number but with the static approach Krugman adopts. Only a dynamic understanding and methodology can appreciate those impacts because that is how they proceed, iteratively, with real and consequential feedback. Finally, national productivity data have several smaller, technical difficulties that radically reduce the reliability of the numbers. It is impossible to get reliable productivity numbers for the core sectors of the service economy, for example well over a third of GNP. And operationally, market and institutional structures lead economists to assign low productivity growth rates to industries such as semiconductors although engineers know that productivity has grown at fabulous rates.

The clean simplicity and apparent analytic power of the simple, one-number approach, though it fits snugly with the models and methods of traditional American economics, has given rise to efforts to define a different organizing concept—competitiveness—in order to open a broader, more open-minded and modest approach. The competitiveness approach poses a sensible question: How are we doing as an economy? No single number sums it all up, especially given the follow-up: How are we doing compared to the other guys? And why? Competitiveness is a reconsideration of a broad set of indicators, none of which tells the whole story but that together provide a highly legitimate focus.

COUNTER-RESPONSE: PROVING MY POINT

PAUL KRUGMAN

My article in the March/April issue of *Foreign Affairs* has obviously upset many people. Some of my critics claim that I misrepresented their position, that despite their insistent use of the word "competitiveness" they have never believed that the major industrial nations are engaged in a competitive economic struggle. Others claim that I have gotten the economics wrong:

that countries are engaged in a competitive struggle. Indeed, some of them make both claims in the same response.

Moving Target

Lester C. Thurow vigorously denies ever asserting that international competition is a central issue for the U.S. economy. In particular, he cites page counts from his 1985 book, *The Zero-Sum Solution*, to demonstrate that domestic factors are his principal concern. But Thurow's most recent book is *Head to Head*, which follows its provocative title with the subtitle, *The Coming Battle Among Japan, Europe and America*. The book jacket asserts that the "decisive war of the century has begun." The text asserts over and over that the major economic powers are now engaged in "win-lose" competition for world markets, a competition that has taken the place of the military competition between East and West. Thurow now says that international strategic competition is no more than seven percent of the problem; did the typical reader of *Head to Head* get this message?

Similarly, Stephen S. Cohen denies that he, or indeed anyone else with whom I should "deign to take difference," has ever said the things I claim competitiveness advocates believe. But in 1987 Cohen, together with John Zysman, published *Manufacturing Matters*, a book that seemed to say two (untrue) things: the long-term downward trend in the share of manufacturing in U. S. employment is largely due to foreign competition, and this declining share is a major economic problem.

After their initial denial, both Cohen and Thurow proceed to argue that international competition is of crucial importance after all. In this they are joined by Clyde V. Prestowitz, Jr., who at least makes no bones about believing that trade and trade policy are the central issue for the U.S. economy. Does Cohen believe that Prestowitz—or James Fallows, who expressed similar views in his new book, *Looking at the Sun*—is one of those people with whom I should not deign to argue?

Sloppy Math: Part II

Of all the elements in my article, the section on careless arithmetic—the strange pattern of errors in reporting or using data in articles and books on competitiveness—has enraged the most people. Both Thurow and Prestowitz have taken care to fill their responses with a blizzard of numbers and calculations. However, some of the numbers are puzzling.

For example, Thurow says that imports are 14 percent of U.S. GDP, while exports are only l0 percent, and that reducing imports to equal exports would add $250 billion to the sales of U.S. manufacturers. But according to Economic Indicators, the monthly statistical publication of the Joint Economic Committee, U.S. imports in 1993 were only 11.4 percent of GDP, while exports were 10.4 percent. Even the current account deficit, a broader measure that includes some additional debit items, was only $109 billion. If the United States were to cut imports by $250 billion, far from merely balancing its trade as Thurow asserts, the United States would run a current account surplus of $140 billion—that is, more than the 2 percent maximum of GDP U.S. negotiators have demanded Japan set as a target!

Or consider Prestowitz, who derides my claim that high-technology industries, commonly described as "high value" sectors, actually have much lower value added per worker than traditional "high volume," heavy industrial sectors. I have aggregated too much by looking at broad sectors like electronics, he says; I should look at the highest-tech lines of business, like semiconductors, where value added per worker is $234,000. Prestowitz should report the results of his research to the Department of Commerce, whose staff has obviously incorrectly calculated (in the *Annual Survey of Manufactures*) that in 1989 value added per worker in Standard Industrial Classification 3674 (semiconductors and related devices) was $96,487— closer to the $76,709 per worker in SIC 2096 (potato chips and related snacks) than to the $187,569 in SIC 3711 (motor vehicles and car bodies).[11]

Everyone makes mistakes, although it is surprising when men who are supposed to be experts on international competition do not have even a rough idea of the size of the U.S. trade deficit or know how to look up a standard industrial statistic. The interesting point, however, is that the mistakes made by Thurow, Prestowitz and other competitiveness advocates are not random errors; they are always biased in the same direction. That is, the advocates always err in a direction that makes international competition seem more important than it really is.

Beyond these petty, if revealing, errors of fact are a series of conceptual misunderstandings. For example, Prestowitz argues that productivity in

---

[11] I don't know why Thurow thinks the U.S. trade deficit is four times as big as it actually is. I have, however, tracked down Prestowitz's number. It is not value added per employee; it is shipments (which are always larger than value added) divided by the number of production workers (who are only a fraction of total employment, especially in high-technology industries).

sectors that compete on world markets is much more important than productivity in non-traded service sectors because the former determine wage rates throughout the economy. For example, because U.S. manufacturing workers are much more productive than their Third World counterparts, U.S. barbers, who do not have a comparable productivity advantage, also get high wages. But Prestowitz fails to notice that the converse is also true: service productivity affects the real wages of manufacturing workers. Because the high relative productivity of U.S. manufacturing is not matched in the haircut sector, haircuts by those well-paid barbers are much more expensive than haircuts in the Third World; as a result real wages of U. S . manufacturing workers (that is, wages in terms of what they can buy, including haircuts) are not as high as they would be if U.S. barbers were more productive. With careful thought, one realizes that real wages depend on the overall productivity of the economy, with no special presumption that productivity in manufacturing—or in internationally traded sectors in general—deserves any more attention or active promotion than productivity elsewhere.

Cohen makes essentially the same mistake when he complains that I underestimated the effects of competitive pressure because I focused only on import and export prices and did not consider the further impacts of that pressure on profits and wages. He somehow fails to realize that a change in wages or profits that is not reflected in import or export prices cannot change overall U.S. real income—it can only redistribute profits to one group within the United States at the expense of another. That is why the effect of international price competition on U.S. real income can be measured by the change in the ratio of export to import prices—full stop. And the effects of changes in this ratio on the U.S. economy have, as I showed in my article, been small.

Or consider Thurow's analysis of the benefits that would accrue to the United States if it could roll back imports (leaving aside the inaccuracy of his numbers). He asserts that the United States could create five million new jobs in import-competing sectors, and he assumes that all five million jobs represent a net addition to employment. But this assumption is unrealistic. As this reply was being written, the Federal Reserve was raising interest rates in an effort to rein in a recovery that it feared would proceed too far, that is, lead to excessive employment, producing a renewed surge in inflation. Some people think that the Fed is tightening too soon, but the essential point is that the growth of employment is not determined by the ability of the United States to sell goods on world markets or to compete with imports, but by the Fed's judgement of what will not set off inflation. So suppose that the United States were to impose import quotas, adding millions of jobs in import-competing sectors. The Fed would respond by raising interest rates to prevent an overheated economy, and most if not all of the job gains would be matched by job losses elsewhere.

Things Add Up

In each of these cases, my critics seem to have forgotten the most basic principle of economics: things add up. Higher employment in import-competing industries must come either through a reduction in unemployment, in which case one must ask whether the implied unemployment rate (about three percent in Thurow's example) is feasible, or at the expense of jobs elsewhere in the economy, in which case no overall job gain takes place. If higher manufacturing wages lead to a higher wage rate for barbers without higher tonsorial productivity, the gain must come at someone else's expense. Since it is hard to see how foreigners pay for more expensive American haircuts, that wage gain can only redistribute the benefits of manufacturing productivity from one set of American workers to another, not increase the total gains. In their haste to assign great importance to international competition, my critics, like the inventors of perpetual motion machines, have failed to realize that there are conservation principles that any story about the economy must honor.

But perhaps Cohen, Thurow and Prestowitz stumble on economic basics because they are so eager to get to their main point, which is that advanced economic theory, and in particular the theory of strategic trade policy, supports their obsession with competitiveness.

Prestowitz's central assertion is that the theory of strategic trade policy, which he for some reason thinks I invented in a paper about aircraft competition (the actual inventors were James Brander and Barbara Spencer, who never mentioned aircraft), justifies aggressively interventionist trade policies. He further asserts that economists in general, and I in particular, have run away from that implication for ideological reasons.

Well, that's not quite the real story. It is true that in the early 1980s professional economists became aware that one of the implications of new theories of international trade was a possible role for strategic policies to promote exports in certain industries. Confronted with a new idea that was exciting, potentially important but untested, these economists began a sustained process of research, probing the weak points, confronting the new idea with the data. After all, lots of things could be true in principle. For example in certain theoretical situations a tax cut could definitely stimulate the economy so much that government revenues would actually rise, and it would be very nice if that were the actual situation; but unfortunately it isn't. Similarly, it is definitely possible to imagine a situation in which, because of all of the market imperfections Thurow dwells on, a clever strategic trade policy would sharply raise U.S. real income. And it would be very nice if the United States could devise such a policy. But is that possibility really there? To answer that question requires looking hard at the facts.

And so over the course of the last ten years a massive international research program has explored the prospects for strategic trade policy.[12] Two broad conclusions emerge. First, to identify which industries should receive strategic promotion or the appropriate form and level of promotion is very difficult. Second, the payoffs of even a successful strategic trade policy are likely to be very modest—certainly far less even than Thurow's "seven percent solution," which is closer to the entire share of international trade in the U.S. economy.

Research results are always open to challenge, especially in an inexact field like economics. If Prestowitz wants to point out specific failings in the dozens of painstaking empirical studies of strategic trade that have been carried out over the past decade, by all means let him do so. His remarks about the subject, however, strongly suggest that while he is happy to mention strategic trade theory in support of his policy writing, Prestowitz has not read any of the economic literature.

I do, however, agree with Prestowitz on one point. More people should read the works of Friedrich List. If they do, they may wonder why this turgid, confused writer—whose theory led him to predict that Holland and Denmark would be condemned to permanent economic backwardness unless they sought political union with Germany—has suddenly become a favorite of

---

[12] The original paper on strategic trade policy was James Brander and Barbara Spencer, "Export Subsidies and International Market Share Rivalry," *Journal of International Economics*, February 1985, pp. 83-100. See also Paul Krugman, ed., *Strategic Trade Policy and the New International Economics*, Cambridge: MIT Press, 1986; Robert Feenstra, ed., *Empirical Methods for International Trade*, Chicago: University of Chicago Press, 1988; Robert Baldwin, ed., *Trade Policy Issues and Empirical Analysis*, Chicago: University of Chicago Press, 1988; and Paul Krugman and Alasdair Smith, eds., *Empirical Studies of Strategic Trade Policy*, Chicago: University of Chicago Press, 1994.

Fallows, Prestowitz and others. The new cult of List bears an uncanny resemblance to the right-wing supply-siders' canonization of the classical French economist Jean-Baptiste Say, who claimed that the economy as a whole could never suffer from the falls in aggregate demand that produce recessions.[13] The motive of the supply-siders was, of course, to cover simplistic ideas with a veneer of faux scholarship.

In contrast to Prestowitz and Thurow, who offer coherent if flawed reasons to worry about international competition, Cohen offers a more difficult target. Basically, he asks us to accept "competitiveness" as a kind of ineffable essence that cannot be either defined or measured. Data that seem to suggest the importance of this essence are cited as "indicators," whatever that means, while those that do not are dismissed as unreliable. Both in his article and other writings he has persistently used a rhetoric that seems to portray international trade as a game with winners and losers, but when challenged on any particular point he denies having said it. I guess I don't understand how a concept so elusive can be a useful guide to policy.

My original article in *Foreign Affairs* argued that a doctrine that views world trade as a competitive struggle has become widely accepted, that this view is wrong but that there is nonetheless an intense desire to believe in that doctrine. The article enraged many, especially when it asserted that the desire to believe in competitive struggle repeatedly leads highly intelligent authors into surprising lapses in their handling of concepts and data. I could not, however, have asked for a better demonstration of my point than the responses published in this issue.

---

[13] Fallows officially elevated List to guru status in his article "How the World Works," *The Atlantic Monthly*, December 1993, pp. 60-87. Readers may wish to compare the elevation of Say by Jude Wanniski in his influential supply-side tract, *The Way the World Works*, New York: Basic Books, 1978.

3.   NEW MODEL: THEORY

The Diamond Model
Porter, 1990

Factor Conditions
Demand Conditions
Related and Supporting Industries
Firm Strategy, Structure and Rivalry

Summary and Key Points

To investigate why nations gain competitive advantage in particular industries and the implications for company strategy and national economies, Porter (1990) conducted a four-year study of ten important trading nations. Porter defined a nation's industry as internationally successful if it possessed competitive advantage relative to the best worldwide competitors. As the best indicators he chose the presence of substantial and sustained exports and/or significant outbound foreign investment based on skills and assets created in the home country. Porter concluded that nations succeed in particular industries because their home environment is the most forward-looking, dynamic, and challenging. Specifically, the determinants are factor conditions; demand conditions; related and supporting industries; and firm strategy, structure, and rivalry. In addition, there are two outside variables: government and chance.

Porter criticized the traditional doctrine, whose origins date back to Adam Smith and David Ricardo, that it is at best incomplete and at worst incorrect. According to Porter, national prosperity is created, not inherited. Porter model is thus dynamic. Porter model is also comprehensive because it includes not just factor conditions, as most traditional models do, but also other important variables simultaneously. However, Porter model is not without criticism. In particular, Porter's treatment of multinational activities and government is not convincing. We will discuss this in Chapter 4.

Source:

Porter, Michael E. 1990. The competitive advantage of nations. *Harvard Business Review*, March-April: 73-93.

THE COMPETITIVE ADVANTAGE OF NATIONS

National prosperity is created, not inherited. It does not grow out of a country's natural endowments, its labor pool, its interest rates, or its currency's value, as classical economics insists.

A nation's competitiveness depends on the capacity its industry to innovate and upgrade. Companies gain advantage against the world's best competitors, because of pressure and challenge. They benefit from having strong domestic rivals, aggressive home-based suppliers, and demanding local customers.

In a world of increasingly global competition, nations have become more, not less, important. As the basis of competition has shifted more and more to the creation and assimilation of knowledge, the role of the nation has grown. Competitive advantage is created and sustained through a highly localized process. Differences in national values, culture, economic structures, institutions, and histories all contribute to competitive success. There are striking differences in the patterns of competitiveness in every country; no nation can or will be competitive in every or even most industries. Ultimately, nations succeed in particular industries because their home environment is the most forward-looking, dynamic, and challenging.

These conclusions, the product of a four-year study of the patterns of competitive success in ten leading trading nations, contradict the conventional wisdom that guides the thinking of many companies and national governments—and that is pervasive today in the United States. (For more about the study, see Appendix A "Patterns of National Competitive Success.") According to prevailing thinking, labor costs, interest rates, exchange rates, and economies of scale are the most potent determinants of competitiveness. In companies, the words of the day are merger, alliance, strategic partnerships, collaboration, and supranational globalization. Managers are pressing for more government support for particular industries. Among governments, there is a growing tendency to experiment with various policies intended to promote national competitiveness—from efforts to manage exchange rates to new measures to manage trade to policies to relax antitrust—which usually end up only undermining it. (See Appendix B "What is National Competitiveness?")

These approaches, now much in favor in both companies and governments, are flawed. They fundamentally misperceive the true sources of competitive advantage. Pursuing them, with all their short-term appeal, will virtually guarantee that the United States—or any other advanced nation—never achieves real and sustainable competitive advantage.

We need a new perspective and new tools—an approach to competitiveness that grows directly out of an analysis of internationally successful industries, without regard for traditional ideology or current intellectual fashion. We need to know, very simply, what works and why. Then we need to apply it.

How Companies Succeed in International Markets

Around the world, companies that have achieved international leadership employ strategies that differ from each other in every respect. But while every successful company will employ its own particular strategy, the underlying mode of operation—the character and trajectory of all successful companies—is fundamentally the same.

Companies achieve competitive advantage through acts of innovation. They approach innovation in its broadest sense, including both new technologies and new ways of doing things. They perceive a new basis for competing or find better means for competing in old ways. Innovation can be manifested in a new product design, a new production process, a new marketing approach, or a new way of conducting training. Much innovation is mundane and incremental, depending more on accumulation of small insights and advances than on a single, major technological breakthrough. It often involves ideas that are not even "new"—ideas that have been around, but never vigorously pursued. It always involves investments in skill and knowledge, as well as in physical assets and brand reputations.

Some innovations create competitive advantage by perceiving an entirely new market opportunity or by serving a market segment that others have ignored. When competitors are slow to respond, such innovation yields competitive advantage. For instance, in industries such as autos and home electronics, Japanese companies gained their initial advantage by emphasizing smaller, more compact, lower capacity models that foreign competitors disdained as less profitable, less important, and less attractive.

In international markets, innovations that yield competitive advantage anticipate both domestic and foreign needs. For example, as international concern for product safety has grown, Swedish companies like Volvo, Atlas

Copco, and AGA have succeeded by anticipating the market opportunity in this area. On the other hand, innovations that respond to concerns or circumstances that are peculiar to the home market can actually retard international competitive success. The lure of the huge U.S. defense market, for instance, has diverted the attention of U.S. materials and machine-tool companies from attractive, global commercial markets.

Information plays a large role in the process of innovation and improvement—Information that either is not available to competitors or that they do not seek. Sometimes it comes from simple investment in research and development or market research; more often, it comes from effort and from openness and from looking in the right place unencumbered by blinding assumptions or conventional wisdom.

This is why innovators are often outsiders from a different industry or a different country. Innovation may come from a new company, whose founder has a nontraditional background or was simply not appreciated in an older, established company. Or the capacity for innovation may come into an existing company through senior managers who are new to the particular industry and thus more able to perceive opportunities and more likely to pursue them. Or innovation may occur as a company diversifies, bringing new resources, skills, or perspectives to another industry. Or innovations may come from another nation with different circumstances or different ways of competing.

With few exceptions, innovation is the result of unusual effort. The company that successfully implements a new or better way of competing pursues its approach with dogged determination, often in the face of harsh criticism and tough obstacles. In fact, to succeed, innovation usually requires pressure, necessity, and even adversity: the fear of loss often proves more powerful than the hope of gain.

Once a company achieves competitive advantage through an innovation, it can sustain it only through relentless improvement. Almost any advantage can be imitated. Korean companies have already matched the ability of their Japanese rivals to mass-produce standard color televisions and VCRs; Brazilian companies have assembled technology and designs comparable to Italian competitors in casual leather footwear.

Competitors will eventually and inevitably overtake any company that stops improving and innovating. Sometimes early-mover advantages such as customer relationships, scale economies in existing technologies, or the loyalty of distribution channels are enough to permit a stagnant company to retain its entrenched position for years or even decades. But sooner or later, more dynamic rivals will find a way to innovate around these advantages or create a better or cheaper way of doing things. Italian appliance producers, which competed successfully on the basis of cost in selling midsize and compact appliances through large retail chains, rested too long on this initial advantage. By developing more differentiated products and creating strong brand franchises, German competitors have begun to gain ground.

Ultimately, the only way to sustain a competitive advantage is to *upgrade it*—to move to more sophisticated types. This is precisely what Japanese automakers have done. They initially penetrated foreign markets with small, inexpensive compact cars of adequate quality and competed on the basis of lower labor costs. Even while their labor-cost advantage persisted, however, the Japanese companies were upgrading. They invested aggressively to build large modern plants to reap economies of scale. Then they became innovators in process technology, pioneering just-in-time production and a host of other quality and productivity practices. These process improvements led to better product quality, better repair records, and better customer-satisfaction ratings than foreign competitors had. Most recently, Japanese automakers have advanced to the vanguard of product technology and are introducing new, premium brand names to compete with the world's most prestigious passenger cars.

The example of the Japanese automakers also illustrates two additional prerequisites for sustaining competitive advantage. First, a company must adopt a global approach to strategy. It must sell its product worldwide, under its own brand name, through international marketing channels that it controls. A truly global approach may even require the company to locate production or R&D facilities in other nations to take advantage of lower wage rates, to gain or improve market access, or to take advantage of foreign technology. Second, creating more sustainable advantages often means that a company must make its existing advantage obsolete—even while it is still an advantage. Japanese auto companies recognized this; either they would make their advantage obsolete, or a competitor would do it for them.

As this example suggests, innovation and change are inextricably tied together. But change is an unnatural act, particularly in successful companies; powerful forces are at work to avoid and defeat it. Past approaches become institutionalized in standard operating procedures and management controls. Training emphasizes the one correct way to do anything; the construction of specialized, dedicated facilities solidifies past practice into expensive brick and mortar; the existing strategy takes on an aura of invincibility and becomes rooted in the company culture.

Successful companies tend to develop a bias for predictability and stability; they work on defending what they have. Change is tempered by the fear that there is much to lose. The organization at all levels filters out information that would suggest new approaches, modifications, or departures from the norm. The internal environment operates like an immune system to isolate or expel "hostile" individuals who challenge current directions or established thinking. Innovation ceases; the company becomes stagnant; it is only a matter of time before aggressive competitors overtake it.

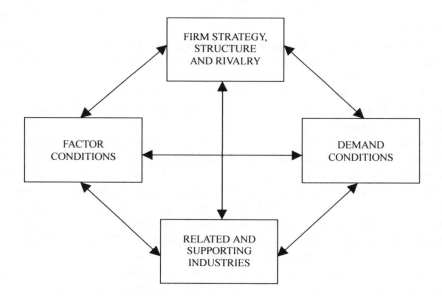

Figure 3-1. Determinants of National Competitiveness

The Diamond of National Advantage

Why are certain companies based in certain nations capable of consistent innovation? Why do they ruthlessly pursue improvements, seeking an ever-more sophisticated source of competitive advantage? Why are they able to overcome the substantial barriers to change and innovation that so often accompany success?

The answer lies in four broad attributes of a nation, attributes that individually and as a system constitute the diamond of national advantage, the playing field that each nation establishes and operates for its industries. These attributes are:

1. *Factor Conditions*. The nation's position in factors of production, such as skilled labor or infrastructure, necessary to compete in a given industry.

2. *Demand Conditions*. The nature of home-market demand for the industry's product or service.

3. *Related and Supporting Industries*. The presence or absence in the nation of supplier industries and other related industries that are internationally competitive.

4. *Firm Strategy, Structure, and Rivalry.* The conditions in the nation governing how companies are created, organized, and managed, as well as the nature of domestic rivalry.

These determinants create the national environment in which companies are born and learn how to compete. (See figure 3-1 "Determinants of National Competitive Advantage.") Each point on the diamond—and the diamond as a system—affects essential ingredients for achieving international competitive success: the availability of resources and skills necessary for competitive advantage in an industry; the information that shapes the opportunities that companies perceive and the directions in which they deploy their resources and skills; the goals of the owners, managers, and individuals in companies; and most important, the pressures on companies to invest and innovate. (See Appendix C "How the Diamond Works: The Italian Ceramic Tile Industry.")

When a national environment permits and supports the most rapid accumulation of specialized assets and skills—sometimes simply because of greater effort and commitment—companies gain a competitive advantage. When a national environment affords better ongoing information and insight into product and process needs, companies gain a competitive advantage. Finally, when the national environment pressures companies to innovate and invest, companies both gain a competitive advantage and upgrade those advantages over time.

Factor Conditions. According to standard economic theory, factors of production—labor, land, natural resources, capital, infrastructure—will determine the flow of trade. A nation will export those goods that make most use of the factors with which it is relatively well endowed. This doctrine, whose origins date back to Adam Smith and David Ricardo and that is embedded in classical economics, is at best incomplete and at worst incorrect.

In the sophisticated industries that form the backbone of any advanced economy, a nation does not inherit but instead creates the most important factors of production—such as skilled human resources or a scientific base. Moreover, the stock of factors that a nation enjoys at a particular time is less important than the rate and efficiency with which it creates, upgrades, and deploys them in particular industries.

The most important factors of production are those that involve sustained and heavy investment and are specialized. Basic factors, such as a pool of labor or a local raw-material source, do not constitute an advantage in knowledge-intensive industries. Companies can access them easily through a global strategy or circumvent them through technology. Contrary to conventional wisdom, simply having a general work force that is high school or even college educated represents no competitive advantage in modern international competition. To support competitive advantage, a factor must be highly specialized to an industry's particular needs—a scientific institute specialized in optics, a pool of venture capital to fund software companies. These factors are more scarce, more difficult for foreign competitors to imitate—and they require sustained investment to create.

Nations succeed in industries where they are particularly good at factor creation. Competitive advantage results from the presence of world-class institutions that first create specialized factors and then continually work to upgrade them. Denmark has two hospitals that concentrate in studying and treating diabetes—and a world-leading export position in insulin. Holland has premier research institutes in the cultivation, packaging, and shipping of flowers, where it is the world's export leader.

What is not so obvious, however, is that selective disadvantages in the more basic factors can prod a company to innovate and upgrade—a disadvantage in a static model of competition can become an advantage in a dynamic one. When there is an ample supply of cheap raw materials or abundant labor, companies can simply rest on these advantages and often deploy them inefficiently. But when companies face a selective disadvantage, like high land costs, labor shortages, or the lack of local raw materials, they must innovate and upgrade to compete.

Implicit in the oft-repeated Japanese statement, "We are an island nation with no natural resources," is the understanding that these deficiencies have only served to spur Japan's competitive innovation. Just-in-time production, for example, economized on prohibitively expensive space. Italian steel producers in the Brescia area faced a similar set of disadvantages: high capital costs, high energy costs, and no local raw materials. Located in Northern Lombardy, these privately owned companies faced staggering logistics costs due to their distance from southern ports and the inefficiencies of the state-owned Italian transportation system. The result: they pioneered technologically advanced minimills that require only modest capital investment, use less energy, employ scrap metal as the feedstock, are efficient at small scale, and permit producers to locate close to sources of scrap and end-use customers. In other words, they converted factor disadvantages into competitive advantage.

Disadvantages can become advantages only under certain conditions. First, they must send companies proper signals about circumstances that will spread to other nations, thereby equipping them to innovate in advance of foreign rivals. Switzerland, the nation that experienced the first labor shortages after World War II, is a case in point. Swiss companies responded to the disadvantage by upgrading labor productivity and seeking higher value, more sustainable market segments. Companies in most other parts of the world, where there were still ample workers, focused their attention on other issues, which resulted in slower upgrading.

The second condition for transforming disadvantages into advantages is favorable circumstances elsewhere in the diamond—a consideration that applies to almost all determinants. To innovate, companies must have access to people with appropriate skills and have home-demand conditions that send the right signals. They must also have active domestic rivals who create pressure to innovate. Another precondition is company goals that lead to sustained commitment to the industry. Without such a commitment and the presence of active rivalry, a company may take an easy way around a disadvantage rather than using it as a spur to innovation.

For example, U.S. consumer-electronics companies, faced with high relative labor costs, chose to leave the product and production process largely unchanged and move labor-intensive activities to Taiwan and other Asian countries. Instead of upgrading their sources of advantage, they settled for labor-cost parity. On the other hand, Japanese rivals, confronted with intense domestic competition and a mature home market, chose to eliminate labor through automation. This led to lower assembly costs, to products with fewer components and to improved quality and reliability. Soon Japanese companies were building assembly plants in the United States—the place U.S. companies had fled.

Demand Conditions. It might seem that the globalization of competition would diminish the importance of home demand. In practice, however, this is simply not the case. In fact, the composition and character of the home market usually has a disproportionate effect on how companies perceive, interpret, and respond to buyer needs. Nations gain competitive advantage in industries where the home demand gives their companies a clearer or earlier picture of emerging buyer needs, and where demanding buyers pressure companies to innovate faster and achieve more sophisticated competitive advantages than their foreign rivals. The size of home demand proves far less significant than the character of home demand.

Home-demand conditions help build competitive advantage when a particular industry segment is larger or more visible in the domestic market than in foreign markets. The larger market segments in a nation receive the most attention from the nation's companies; companies accord smaller or less desirable segments a lower priority. A good example is hydraulic excavators, which represent the most widely used type of construction equipment in the Japanese domestic market—but which comprise a far smaller proportion of the market in other advanced nations. This segment is one of the few where there are vigorous Japanese international competitors and where Caterpillar does not hold a substantial share of the world market.

More important than the mix of segments per se is the nature of domestic buyers. A nation's companies gain competitive advantage if domestic buyers are the world's most sophisticated and demanding buyers for the product or service. Sophisticated, demanding buyers provide a window into advanced customer needs; they pressure companies to meet high standards; they prod them to improve, to innovate, and to upgrade into more advanced segments. As with factor conditions, demand conditions provide advantages by forcing companies to respond to tough challenges.

Especially stringent needs arise because of local values and circumstances. For example, Japanese consumers, who live in small, tightly packed homes, must contend with hot, humid summers and high-cost electrical energy—a daunting combination of circumstances. In response, Japanese companies have pioneered compact, quiet air-conditioning units powered by energy-saving rotary compressors. In industry after industry, the tightly constrained requirements of the Japanese market have forced companies to innovate, yielding products that are *kei-haku-tan-sho*—light, thin, short, small—and that are internationally accepted.

Local buyers can help a nation's companies gain advantage if their needs anticipate or even shape those of other nations—if their needs provide ongoing "early-warning indicators" of global market trends. Sometimes anticipatory needs emerge because a nation's political values foreshadow needs that will grow elsewhere. Sweden's long-standing concern for handicapped people has spawned an increasingly competitive industry focused on special needs. Denmark's environmentalism has led to success for companies in water-pollution control equipment and windmills.

More generally, a nation's companies can anticipate global trends if the nation's values are spreading—that is, if the country is exporting its values and tastes as well as its products. The international success of U.S. companies in fast food and credit cards, for example, reflects not only the American desire for convenience but also the spread of these tastes to the rest of the world. Nations export their values and tastes through media, through training foreigners, through political influence, and through the foreign activities of their citizens and companies.

Related and Supporting Industries. The third broad determinant of national advantage is the presence in the nation of related and supporting industries that are internationally competitive. Internationally competitive home-based suppliers create advantages in downstream industries in several ways. First, they deliver the most cost-effective inputs in an efficient, early, rapid, and sometimes preferential way. Italian gold and silver jewelry companies lead the world in that industry in part because other Italian companies supply two-thirds of the world's jewelry-making and precious-metal recycling machinery.

Far more significant than mere access to components and machinery, however, is the advantage that home-based related and supporting industries provide in innovation and upgrading—an advantage based on close working relationships. Suppliers and end-users located near each other can take advantage of short lines of communication, quick and constant flow of information, and an ongoing exchange of ideas and innovations. Companies have the opportunity to influence their suppliers' technical efforts and can serve as test sites for R&D work, accelerating the pace of innovation.

Figure 3-2 "The Italian Footwear Cluster" offers a graphic example of how a group of close-by, supporting industries creates competitive advantage in a range of interconnected industries that are all internationally competitive. Shoe producers, for instance, interact regularly with leather manufacturers on new styles and manufacturing techniques and learn about new textures and colors of leather when they are still on the drawing boards. Leather manufacturers gain early insights into fashion trends, helping them to plan new products. The interaction is mutually advantageous and self-reinforcing, but it does not happen automatically: it is helped by proximity, but occurs only because companies and suppliers work at it.

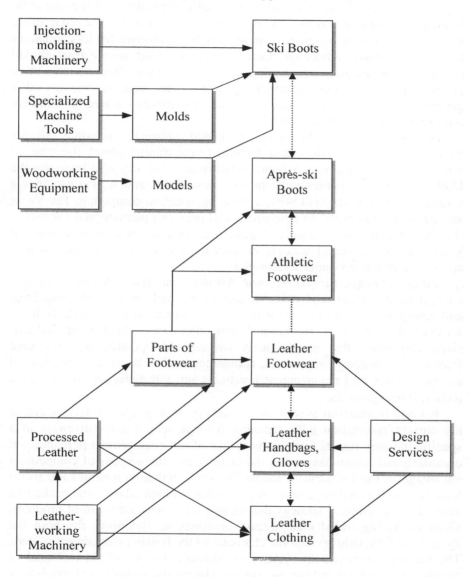

Figure 3-2. The Italian Footwear Cluster

The nation's companies benefit most when the suppliers are, themselves, global competitors. It is ultimately self-defeating for a company or country to create "captive" suppliers who are totally dependent on the domestic industry and prevented from serving foreign competitors. By the same token, a nation need not be competitive in all supplier industries for its companies to gain competitive advantage. Companies can readily source from abroad materials, components, or technologies without a major effect on innovation or performance of the industry's products. The same is true of other generalized technologies—like electronics or software—where the industry represents a narrow application area.

Home-based competitiveness in related industries provides similar benefits: information flow and technical interchange speed the rate of innovation and upgrading. A home-based related industry also increases the likelihood that companies will embrace new skills, and it also provides a source of entrants who will bring a novel approach to competing. The Swiss success in pharmaceuticals emerged out of previous international success in the dye industry, for example; Japanese dominance in electronic musical keyboards grows out of success in acoustic instruments combined with a strong position in consumer electronics.

Firm Strategy, Structure, and Rivalry National circumstances and context create strong tendencies in how companies are created, organized, and managed, as well as what the nature of domestic rivalry will be. In Italy, for example, successful international competitors are often small or medium-sized companies that are privately owned and operated like extended families; in Germany, in contrast, companies tend to be strictly hierarchical in organization and management practices, and top managers usually have technical backgrounds.

No one managerial system is universally appropriate—notwithstanding the current fascination with Japanese management. Competitiveness in a specific industry results from convergence of the management practices and organizational modes favored in the country and the sources of competitive advantage in the industry. In industries where Italian companies are world leaders—such as lighting, furniture, footwear, woolen fabrics, and packaging machines—a company strategy that emphasizes focus, customized products, niche marketing, rapid change, and breathtaking flexibility fits both the dynamics of the industry and the character of the Italian management system. The German management system, in contrast, works well in technical or engineering-oriented industries—optics, chemicals, complicated machinery —where complex products demand precision manufacturing, a careful development process, after-sale service, and thus a highly disciplined management structure. German success is much rarer in consumer goods and services where image marketing and rapid new-feature and model turnover are important to competition.

Countries also differ markedly in the goals that companies and individuals seek to achieve. Company goals reflect the characteristics of national capital markets and the compensation practices for managers. For example, in Germany and Switzerland, where banks comprise a substantial part of the nation's shareholders, most shares are held for long-term appreciation and are rarely traded. Companies do well in mature industries, where ongoing investment in R&D and new facilities is essential but returns may be only moderate. The United States is at the opposite extreme, with a large pool of risk capital but widespread trading of public companies and a strong emphasis by investors on quarterly and annual share-price appreciation. Management compensation is heavily based on annual bonuses tied to individual results. America does well in relatively new industries, like software and biotechnology, or ones where equity funding of new companies feeds active domestic rivalry, like specialty electronics and services. Strong pressures leading to underinvestment, however, plague more mature industries.

Individual motivation to work and expand skills is also important to competitive advantage. Outstanding talent is a scarce resource in any nation. A nation's success largely depends on the types of education its talented people choose, where they choose to work, and their commitment and effort. The goals a nation's institutions and values set for individuals and companies, and the prestige it attaches to certain industries, guide the flow of capital and human resources—which, in turn, directly affects the competitive performance of certain industries. Nations tend to be competitive in activities that people admire or depend on—the activities from which the nation's heroes emerge. In Switzerland, it is banking and pharmaceuticals. In Israel, the highest callings have been agriculture and defense-related fields. Sometimes it is hard to distinguish between cause and effect. Attaining international success can make an industry prestigious, reinforcing its advantage.

The presence of strong local rivals is a final, and powerful, stimulus to the creation and persistence of competitive advantage. This is true of small countries, like Switzerland, where the rivalry among its pharmaceutical companies, Hoffmann-La Roche, Ciba-Geigy, and Sandoz, contributes to a leading worldwide position. It is true in the United States in the computer and software industries. Nowhere is the role of fierce rivalry more apparent than in Japan, where there are 112 companies competing in machine tools, 34 in semiconductors, 25 in audio equipment, 15 in cameras—in fact, there are usually double figures in the industries in which Japan boasts global dominance. (See table 3-1 "Estimated Number of Japanese Rivals in Selected Industries.") Among all the points on the diamond, domestic rivalry is arguably the most important because of the powerfully stimulating effect it has on all the others.

Conventional wisdom argues that domestic competition is wasteful: it leads to duplication of effort and prevents companies from achieving economies of scale. The "right solution" is to embrace one or two national champions, companies with the scale and strength to tackle foreign competitors, and to guarantee them the necessary resources, with the government's blessing. In fact, however, most national champions are uncompetitive, although heavily subsidized and protected by their government. In many of the prominent industries in which there is only one national rival, such as aerospace and telecommunications, government has played a large role in distorting competition.

Static efficiency is much less important than dynamic improvement, which domestic rivalry uniquely spurs. Domestic rivalry, like any rivalry, creates pressure on companies to innovate and improve. Local rivals push each other to lower costs, improve quality and service, and create new products and processes. But unlike rivalries with foreign competitors, which tend to be analytical and distant, local rivalries often go beyond pure economic or business competition and become intensely personal. Domestic rivals engage in active feuds; they compete not only for market share but also for people, for technical excellence, and perhaps most important, for "bragging rights." One domestic rival's success proves to others that advancement is possible and often attracts new rivals to the industry. Companies often attribute the success of foreign rivals to "unfair" advantages. With domestic rivals, there are no excuses.

Geographic concentration magnifies the power of domestic rivalry. This pattern is strikingly common around the world: Italian jewelry companies are located around two towns, Arezzo and Valenza Po; cutlery companies in Solingen, West Germany and Seki, Japan; pharmaceutical companies in Basel, Switzerland; motorcycles and musical instruments in Hamamatsu, Japan. The more localized the rivalry, the more intense. And the more intense, the better.

Another benefit of domestic rivalry is the pressure it creates for constant upgrading of the sources of competitive advantage. The presence of domestic competitors automatically cancels the types of advantage that come from simply being in a particular nation—factor costs, access to or preference in the home market, or costs to foreign competitors who import into the market. Companies are forced to move beyond them, and as a result, gain more sustainable advantages. Moreover, competing domestic rivals will keep each other honest in obtaining government support. Companies are less likely to get hooked on the narcotic of government contracts or creeping industry protectionism. Instead, the industry will seek—and benefit from— more constructive forms of government support, such as assistance in opening foreign markets, as well as investments in focused educational institutions or other specialized factors.

Ironically, it is also vigorous domestic competition that ultimately pressures domestic companies to look at global markets and toughens them to succeed in them. Particularly when there are economies of scale, local competitors force each other to look outward to foreign markets to capture greater efficiency and higher profitability. And having been tested by fierce domestic competition, the stronger companies are well equipped to win abroad. If Digital Equipment can hold its own against IBM, Data General, Prime, and Hewlett-Packard, going up against Siemens or Machines Bull does not seem so daunting a prospect.

The Diamond as a System

Each of these four attributes defines a point on the diamond of national advantage; the effect of one point often depends on the state of others. Sophisticated buyers will not translate into advanced products, for example, unless the quality of human resources permits companies to meet buyer needs. Selective disadvantages in factors of production will not motivate innovation unless rivalry is vigorous and company goals support sustained investment. At the broadest level, weaknesses in any one determinant will constrain an industry's potential for advancement and upgrading.

But the points of the diamond are also self-reinforcing: they constitute a system. Two elements, domestic rivalry and geographic concentration, have especially great power to transform the diamond into a system—domestic rivalry because it promotes improvement in all the other determinants and geographic concentration because it elevates and magnifies the interaction of the four separate influences.

The role of domestic rivalry illustrates how the diamond operates as a self-reinforcing system. Vigorous domestic rivalry stimulates the development of unique pools of specialized factors, particularly if the rivals are all located in one city or region: the University of California at Davis has become the world's leading center of wine-making research, working closely with the California wine industry. Active local rivals also upgrade domestic demand in an industry. In furniture and shoes, for example, Italian consumers have learned to expect more and better products because of the rapid pace of new product development that is driven by intense domestic rivalry among hundreds of Italian companies. Domestic rivalry also promotes the formation of related and supporting industries. Japan's world-leading group of semiconductor producers, for instance, has spawned world-leading Japanese semiconductor-equipment manufacturers.

The effects can work in all directions: sometimes world-class suppliers become new entrants in the industry they have been supplying. Or highly sophisticated buyers may themselves enter a supplier industry, particularly when they have relevant skills and view the new industry as strategic. In the case of the Japanese robotics industry, for example, Matsushita and Kawasaki originally designed robots for internal use before beginning to sell robots to others. Today they are strong competitors in the robotics industry. In Sweden, Sandvik moved from specialty steel into rock drills, and SKF moved from specialty steel into ball bearings.

Another effect of the diamond's systemic nature is that nations are rarely home to just one competitive industry; rather, the diamond creates an environment that promotes *clusters* of competitive industries. Competitive industries are not scattered helter-skelter throughout the economy but are usually linked together through vertical (buyer-seller) or horizontal (common customers, technology, channels) relationships. Nor are clusters usually scattered physically; they tend to be concentrated geographically. One competitive industry helps to create another in a mutually reinforcing process. Japan's strength in consumer electronics, for example, drove its success in semiconductors toward the memory chips and integrated circuits these products use. Japanese strength in laptop computers, which contrasts to limited success in other segments, reflects the base of strength in other compact, portable products and leading expertise in liquid-crystal display gained in the calculator and watch industries.

Once a cluster forms, the whole group of industries becomes mutually supporting. Benefits flow forward, backward, and horizontally. Aggressive rivalry in one industry spreads to others in the cluster, through spin-offs, through the exercise of bargaining power, and through diversification by established companies. Entry from other industries within the cluster spurs upgrading by stimulating diversity in R&D approaches and facilitating the introduction of new strategies and skills. Through the conduits of suppliers or customers who have contact with multiple competitors, information flows freely and innovations diffuse rapidly. Interconnections within the cluster, often unanticipated, lead to perceptions of new ways of competing and new opportunities. The cluster becomes a vehicle for maintaining diversity and overcoming the inward focus, inertia, inflexibility, and accommodation among rivals that slows or blocks competitive upgrading and new entry.

The Role of Government

In the continuing debate over the competitiveness of nations, no topic engenders more argument or creates less understanding than the role of the government. Many see government as an essential helper or supporter of industry, employing a host of policies to contribute directly to the competitive performance of strategic or target industries. Others accept the "free market" view that the operation of the economy should be left to the workings of the invisible hand.

Both views are incorrect. Either, followed to its logical outcome, would lead to the permanent erosion of a country's competitive capabilities. On one hand, advocates of government help for industry frequently propose policies that would actually hurt companies in the long run and only create the demand for more helping. On the other hand, advocates of a diminished government presence ignore the legitimate role that government plays in shaping the context and institutional structure surrounding companies and in creating an environment that stimulates companies to gain competitive advantage.

Government's proper role is as a catalyst and challenger; it is to encourage—or even push—companies to raise their aspirations and move to higher levels of competitive performance, even though this process may be inherently unpleasant and difficult. Government cannot create competitive industries; only companies can do that. Government plays a role that is inherently partial, that succeeds only when working in tandem with favorable underlying conditions in the diamond. Still, government's role of transmitting and amplifying the forces of the diamond is a powerful one. Government policies that succeed are those that create an environment in which companies can gain competitive advantage rather than those that involve government directly in the process, except in nations early in the development process. It is an indirect, rather than a direct, role.

Japan's government, at its best, understands this role better than anyone— including the point that nations pass through stages of competitive development and that government's appropriate role shifts as the economy progresses. By stimulating early demand for advanced products, confronting industries with the need to pioneer frontier technology through symbolic cooperative projects, establishing prizes that reward quality, and pursuing other policies that magnify the forces of the diamond, the Japanese government accelerates the pace of innovation. But like government officials anywhere, at their worst Japanese bureaucrats can make the same mistakes: attempting to manage industry structure, protecting the market too long, and yielding to political pressure to insulate inefficient retailers, farmers, distributors, and industrial companies from competition.

It is not hard to understand why so many governments make the same mistakes so often in pursuit of national competitiveness: competitive time for companies and political time for governments are fundamentally at odds. It often takes more than a decade for an industry to create competitive advantage; the process entails the long upgrading of human skills, investing in products and processes, building clusters, and penetrating foreign markets. In the case of the Japanese auto industry, for instance, companies made their first faltering steps toward exporting in the 1950s—yet did not achieve strong international positions until the 1970s.

But in politics, a decade is an eternity. Consequently, most governments favor policies that offer easily perceived short-term benefits, such as subsidies, protection, and arranged mergers—the very policies that retard innovation. Most of the policies that would make a real difference either are too slow and require too much patience for politicians or, even worse, carry with them the sting of short-term pain. Deregulating a protected industry, for example, will lead to bankruptcies sooner and to stronger, more competitive companies only later.

Policies that convey static, short-term cost advantages but that unconsciously undermine innovation and dynamism represent the most common and most profound error in government industrial policy. In a desire to help, it is all too easy for governments to adopt policies such as joint projects to avoid "wasteful" R&D that undermine dynamism and competition. Yet even a 10% cost saving through economies of scale is easily nullified through rapid product and process improvement and the pursuit of volume in global markets—something that such policies undermine.

There are some simple, basic principles that governments should embrace to play the proper supportive role for national competitiveness: encourage change, promote domestic rivalry, stimulate innovation. Some of the specific policy approaches to guide nations seeking to gain competitive advantage include the following:

Focus on specialized factor creation. Government has critical responsibilities for fundamentals like the primary and secondary education systems, basic national infrastructure, and research in areas of broad national concern such as health care. Yet these kinds of generalized efforts at factor creation rarely produce competitive advantage. Rather, the factors that translate into competitive advantage are advanced, specialized, and tied to specific industries or industry groups. Mechanisms such as specialized apprenticeship programs, research efforts in universities connected with an industry, trade association activities, and, most important, the private investments of companies ultimately create the factors that will yield competitive advantage.

Avoid intervening in factor and currency markets. By intervening in factor and currency markets, governments hope to create lower factor costs or a favorable exchange rate that will help companies compete more effectively in international markets. Evidence from around the world indicates that these policies—such as the Reagan administration's dollar devaluation—are often counterproductive. They work against the upgrading of industry and the search for more sustainable competitive advantage.

The contrasting case of Japan is particularly instructive, although both Germany and Switzerland have had similar experiences. Over the past 20 years, the Japanese have been rocked by the sudden Nixon currency devaluation shock, two oil shocks, and, most recently, the yen shock—all of which forced Japanese companies to upgrade their competitive advantages. The point is not that government should pursue policies that intentionally drive up factor costs or the exchange rate. Rather, when market forces create rising factor costs or a higher exchange rate, government should resist the temptation to push them back down.

Enforce strict product, safety, and environmental standards. Strict government regulations can promote competitive advantage by stimulating and upgrading domestic demand. Stringent standards for product performance, product safety, and environmental impact pressure companies to improve quality, upgrade technology, and provide features that I respond to consumer and social demands. Easing standards, however tempting, is counterproductive.

When tough regulations anticipate standards that will spread internationally, they give a nation's companies a head start in developing products and services that will be valuable elsewhere. Sweden's strict standards for environmental protection have promoted competitive advantage in many industries. Atlas Copco, for example, produces quiet compressors that can be used in dense urban areas with minimal disruption to residents. Strict standards, however, must be combined with a rapid and streamlined regulatory process that does not absorb resources and cause delays.

Sharply limit direct cooperation among industry rivals. The most pervasive global policy fad in the competitiveness arena today is the call for more cooperative research and industry consortia. Operating on the belief that independent research by rivals is wasteful and duplicative, that collaborative efforts achieve economies of scale, and that individual companies are likely to underinvest in R&D because they cannot reap all the benefits, governments have embraced the idea of more direct cooperation. In the United States, antitrust laws have been modified to allow more cooperative R&D; in Europe, mega-projects such as ESPRIT, an information-technology project, bring together companies from several countries. Lurking behind much of this thinking is the fascination of Western governments with—and fundamental misunderstanding of—the countless cooperative research projects sponsored by the Ministry of International Trade and Industry (MITI), projects that appear to have contributed to Japan's competitive rise.

But a closer look at Japanese cooperative projects suggests a different story. Japanese companies participate in MITI projects to maintain good relations with MITI, to preserve their corporate images, and to hedge the risk that competitors will gain from the project—largely defensive reasons. Companies rarely contribute their best scientists and engineers to cooperative projects and usually spend much more on their own private research in the same field. Typically, the government makes only a modest financial contribution to the project.

The real value of Japanese cooperative research is to signal the importance of emerging technical areas and to stimulate proprietary company research. Cooperative projects prompt companies to explore new fields and boost internal R&D spending because companies know that their domestic rivals are investigating them.

Under certain limited conditions, cooperative research can prove beneficial. Projects should be in areas of basic product and process research, not in subjects closely connected to a company's proprietary sources of advantage. They should constitute only a modest portion of a company's overall research program in any given field. Cooperative research should be only indirect, channeled through independent organizations to which most industry participants have access. Organizational structures, like university labs and centers of excellence, reduce management problems and minimize the risk to rivalry. Finally, the most useful cooperative projects often involve fields that touch a number of industries and that require substantial R&D investments.

Promote goals that lead to sustained investment. Government has a vital role in shaping the goals of investors, managers, and employees through policies in various areas. The manner in which capital markets are regulated, for example, shapes the incentives of investors and, in turn, the behavior of companies. Government should aim to encourage sustained investment in human skills, in innovation, and in physical assets. Perhaps the single most powerful tool for raising the rate of sustained investment in industry is a tax incentive for long-term (five years or more) capital gains restricted to new investment in corporate equity. Long-term capital gains incentives should also be applied to pension funds and other currently untaxed investors, who now have few reasons not to engage in rapid trading.

Deregulate competition. Regulation of competition through such policies as maintaining a state monopoly, controlling entry into an industry, or fixing prices has two strong negative consequences: it stifles rivalry and innovation as companies become preoccupied with dealing with regulators and protecting what they already have; and it makes the industry a less dynamic and less desirable buyer or supplier. Deregulation and privatization on their own, however, will not succeed without vigorous domestic rivalry—and that requires, as a corollary, a strong and consistent antitrust policy.

Enforce strong domestic antitrust policies. A strong antitrust policy— especially for horizontal mergers, alliances, and collusive behavior—is fundamental to innovation. While it is fashionable today to call for mergers and alliances in the name of globalization and the creation of national champions, these often undermine the creation of competitive advantage. Real national competitiveness requires governments to disallow mergers, acquisitions, and alliances that involve industry leaders. Furthermore, the same standards for mergers and alliances should apply to both domestic and foreign companies. Finally, government policy should favor internal entry, both domestic and international, over acquisition. Companies should, however, be allowed to acquire small companies in related industries when the move promotes the transfer of skills that could ultimately create competitive advantage.

Reject managed trade. Managed trade represents a growing and dangerous tendency for dealing with the fallout of national competitiveness. Orderly marketing agreements, voluntary restraint agreements, or other devices that set quantitative targets to divide up markets are dangerous, ineffective, and often enormously costly to consumers. Rather than promoting innovation in a nation's industries, managed trade guarantees a market for inefficient companies.

Government trade policy should pursue open market access in every foreign nation. To be effective, trade policy should not be a passive instrument; it cannot respond only to complaints or work only for those industries that can muster enough political clout; it should not require a long history of injury or serve only distressed industries. Trade policy should seek to open markets wherever a nation has competitive advantage and should actively address emerging industries and incipient problems.

Where government finds a trade barrier in another nation, it should concentrate its remedies on dismantling barriers, not on regulating imports or exports. In the case of Japan, for example, pressure to accelerate the already rapid growth of manufactured imports is a more effective approach than a shift to managed trade. Compensatory tariffs that punish companies for unfair trade practices are better than market quotas. Other increasingly important tools to open markets are restrictions that prevent companies in offending nations from investing in acquisitions or production facilities in the host country—thereby blocking the unfair country's companies from using their advantage to establish a new beachhead that is immune from sanctions.

Any of these remedies, however, can backfire. It is virtually impossible to craft remedies to unfair trade practices that avoid both reducing incentives for domestic companies to innovate and export and harming domestic buyers. The aim of remedies should be adjustments that allow the remedy to disappear.

The Company Agenda

Ultimately, only companies themselves can achieve and sustain competitive advantage. To do so, they must act on the fundamentals described above. In particular, they must recognize the central role of innovation—and the uncomfortable truth that innovation grows out of pressure and challenge. It takes leadership to create a dynamic, challenging environment. And it takes leadership to recognize the all-too-easy escape routes that appear to offer a path to competitive advantage, but are actually short-cuts to failure. For example, it is tempting to rely on cooperative research and development projects to lower the cost and risk of research. But they can divert company attention and resources from proprietary research efforts and will all but eliminate the prospects for real innovation.

Competitive advantage arises from leadership that harnesses and amplifies the forces in the diamond to promote innovation and upgrading. Here are just a few of the kinds of company policies that will support that effort:

Create pressures for innovation. A company should seek out pressure and challenge, not avoid them. Part of strategy is to take advantage of the home nation to create the impetus for innovation. To do that, companies can sell to the most sophisticated and demanding buyers and channels; seek out those buyers with the most difficult needs; establish norms that exceed the toughest regulatory hurdles or product standards; source from the most advanced suppliers; treat employees as permanent in order to stimulate upgrading of skills and productivity.

Seek out the most capable competitors as motivators. To motivate organizational change, capable competitors and respected rivals can be a common enemy. The best managers always run a little scared; they respect and study competitors. To stay dynamic, companies must make meeting challenge a part of the organization's norms. For example, lobbying against strict product standards signals the organization that company leadership has diminished aspirations. Companies that value stability, obedient customers, dependent suppliers, and sleepy competitors are inviting inertia and, ultimately, failure.

Establish early-warning systems. Early-warning signals translate into early-mover advantages. Companies can take actions that help them see the signals of change and act on them, thereby getting a jump on the competition. For example, they can find and serve those buyers with the most anticipatory needs; investigate all emerging new buyers or channels; find places whose regulations foreshadow emerging regulations elsewhere; bring some outsiders into the management team; maintain ongoing relationships with research centers and sources of talented people.

Improve the national diamond. Companies have a vital stake in making their home environment a better platform for international success. Part of a company's responsibility is to play an active role in forming clusters and to work with its home-nation buyers, suppliers, and channels to help them upgrade and extend their own competitive advantages. To upgrade home demand, for example, Japanese musical instrument manufacturers, led by Yamaha, Kawai, and Suzuki, have established music schools. Similarly, companies can stimulate and support local suppliers of important specialized inputs—including encouraging them to compete globally. The health and strength of the national cluster will only enhance the company's own rate of innovation and upgrading.

In nearly every successful competitive industry, leading companies also take explicit steps to create specialized factors like human resources, scientific knowledge, or infrastructure. In industries like wool cloth, ceramic tiles, and lighting equipment, Italian industry associations invest in market information, process technology, and common infrastructure. Companies can also speed innovation by putting their headquarters and other key operations where there are concentrations of sophisticated buyers, important suppliers, or specialized factor-creating mechanisms, such as universities or laboratories.

Welcome domestic rivalry To compete globally, a company needs capable domestic rivals and vigorous domestic rivalry. Especially in the United States and Europe today, managers are wont to complain about excessive competition and to argue for mergers and acquisitions that will produce hoped-for economies of scale and critical mass. The complaint is only natural—but the argument is plain wrong. Vigorous domestic rivalry creates sustainable competitive advantage. Moreover, it is better to grow internationally than to dominate the domestic market. If a company wants an acquisition, a foreign one that can speed globalization and supplement home-based advantages or offset home-based disadvantages is usually far better than merging with leading domestic competitors.

Globalize to tap selective advantages in other nations. In search of "global" strategies, many companies today abandon their home diamond. To be sure, adopting a global perspective is important to creating competitive advantage. But relying on foreign activities that supplant domestic capabilities is always a second-best solution. Innovating to offset local factor disadvantages is better than outsourcing; developing domestic suppliers and buyers is better than relying solely on foreign ones. Unless the critical underpinnings of competitiveness are present at home, companies will not sustain competitive advantage in the long run. The aim should be to upgrade home-base capabilities so that foreign activities are selective and supplemental only to over-all competitive advantage.

The correct approach to globalization is to tap selectively into sources of advantage in other nations' diamonds. For example, identifying sophisticated buyers in other countries helps companies understand different needs and creates pressures that will stimulate a faster rate of innovation. No matter how favorable the home diamond, moreover, important research is going on in other nations. To take advantage of foreign research, companies must station high-quality people in overseas bases and mount a credible level of scientific effort. To get anything back from foreign research ventures, companies must also allow access to their own ideas—recognizing that competitive advantage comes from continuous improvement, not from protecting today's secrets.

Use alliances only selectively Alliances with foreign companies have become another managerial fad and cure-all: they represent a tempting solution to the problem of a company wanting the advantages of foreign enterprises or hedging against risk, without giving up independence. In reality, however, while alliances can achieve selective benefits, they always exact significant costs: they involve coordinating two separate operations, reconciling goals with an independent entity, creating a competitor, and giving up profits. These costs ultimately make most alliances short-term transitional devices, rather than stable, long-term relationships.

Most important, alliances as a broad-based strategy will only ensure a company's mediocrity, not its international leadership. No company can rely on another outside, independent company for skills and assets that are central to its competitive advantage. Alliances are best used as a selective tool, employed on a temporary basis or involving non-core activities.

Locate the home base to support competitive advantage. Among the most important decisions for multinational companies is the nation in which to locate the home base for each distinct business. A company can have different home bases for distinct businesses or segments. Ultimately, competitive advantage is created at home: it is where strategy is set, the core product and process technology is created, and a critical mass of production takes place. The circumstances in the home nation must support innovation; otherwise the company has no choice but to move its home base to a country that stimulates innovation and that provides the best environment for global competitiveness. There are no half-measures: the management team must move as well.

The Role of Leadership

Too many companies and top managers misperceive the nature of competition and the task before them by focusing on improving financial performance, soliciting government assistance, seeking stability, and reducing risk through alliances and mergers.

Today's competitive realities demand leadership. Leaders believe in change; they energize their organizations to innovate continuously; they recognize the importance of their home country as integral to their competitive success and work to upgrade it. Most important, leaders recognize the need for pressure and challenge. Because they are willing to encourage appropriate—and painful—government policies and regulations, they often earn the title "statesmen," although few see themselves that way. They are prepared to sacrifice the easy life for difficulty and, ultimately, sustained competitive advantage. That must be the goal, for both nations and companies: not just surviving, but achieving international competitiveness.

And not just once, but continuously.

Appendix A

Patterns of National Competitive Success

To investigate why nations gain competitive advantage in particular industries and the implications for company strategy and national economies, I conducted a four-year study of ten important trading nations: Denmark, Germany, Italy, Japan, Korea, Singapore, Sweden, Switzerland, the United Kingdom, and the United States. I was assisted by a team of more than 30 researchers, most of whom were natives of and based in the nation they studied. The researchers all used the same methodology.

Three nations—the United States, Japan, and Germany—are the world's leading industrial powers. The other nations represent a variety of population sizes, government policies toward industry, social philosophies, geographical sizes, and locations. Together, the ten nations accounted for fully 50% of total world exports in 1985, the base year for statistical analysis.

Most previous analyses of national competitiveness have focused on single nation or bilateral comparisons. By studying nations with widely varying characteristics and circumstances, this study sought to separate the fundamental forces underlying national competitive advantage from the idiosyncratic ones.

In each nation, the study consisted of two parts. The first identified all industries in which the nation's companies were internationally successful, using available statistical data, supplementary published sources, and field interviews. We defined a nation's industry as internationally successful if it *possessed competitive advantage relative to the best worldwide competitors.* Many measures of competitive advantage, such as reported profitability, can be misleading. We chose as the best indicators the presence of substantial and sustained exports to a wide array of other nations and/or significant outbound foreign investment based on skills and assets created in the home country. A nation was considered the home base for a company if it was either a locally owned, indigenous enterprise or managed autonomously although owned by a foreign company or investors. We then created a profile of all the industries in which each nation was internationally successful at three points in time: 1971, 1978, and 1985. The pattern of competitive industries in each economy was far from random: the task was to explain it and how it had changed over time. Of particular interest were the connections or relationships among the nation's competitive industries.

In the second part of the study, we examined the history of competition in particular industries to understand how competitive advantage was created. On the basis of national profiles, we selected over 100 industries or industry groups for detailed study; we examined many more in less detail. We went back as far as necessary to understand how and why the industry began in the nation, how it grew, when and why companies from the nation developed international competitive advantage, and the process by which competitive advantage had been either sustained or lost. The resulting case histories fall short of the work of a good historian in their level of detail, but they do provide insight into the development of both the industry and the nation's economy.

We chose a sample of industries for each nation that represented the most important groups of competitive industries in the economy. The industries studied accounted for a large share of total exports in each nation: more than 20% of total exports in Japan, Germany, and Switzerland, for example, and more than 40% in South Korea. We studied some of the most famous and important international success stories—German high-performance autos and chemicals, Japanese semiconductors and VCRs, Swiss banking and pharmaceuticals, Italian footwear and textiles, U.S. commercial aircraft and motion pictures—and some relatively obscure but highly competitive industries—South Korean pianos, Italian ski boots, and British biscuits. We also added a few industries because they appeared to be paradoxes: Japanese home demand for Western-character typewriters is nearly nonexistent, for example, but Japan holds a strong export and foreign investment position in the industry. We avoided industries that were highly dependent on natural resources: such industries do not form the backbone of advanced economies, and the capacity to compete in them is more explicable using classical theory. We did, however, include a number of more technologically intensive, natural-resource-related industries such as newsprint and agricultural chemicals.

The sample of nations and industries offers a rich empirical foundation for developing and testing the new theory of how countries gain competitive advantage. The accompanying article concentrates on the determinants of competitive advantage in individual industries and also sketches out some of the study's overall implications for government policy and company strategy. A fuller treatment in my book, *The Competitive Advantage of Nations,* develops the theory and its implications in greater depth and provides many additional examples. It also contains detailed descriptions of the nations we studied and the future prospects for their economies.

Appendix B

What is National Competitiveness?

National competitiveness has become one of the central preoccupation of government and industry in every nation. Yet for all the discussion, debate, and writing on the topic, there is still not persuasive theory to explain national competitiveness. What is more, there is not even an accepted definition of the term "competitiveness" as applied to a nation. While the notion of a competitive company is clear, the notion of competitive nation is not.

Some see national competitiveness as a macro-economic phenomenon, driven by variables such as exchange rates, interest rates, and government deficits. But Japan, Italy, and South Korea have all enjoyed rapidly rising living standards despite budget deficits; Germany and Switzerland despite appreciating currencies; and Italy and Korea despite high interest rates.

Others argue that competitiveness is a function of cheap and abundant labor. But Germany, Switzerland, and Sweden have all prospered even with high wages and labor shortages. Besides, shouldn't a nation seek higher wages for its workers as a goal of competitiveness?

Another view connects competitiveness with bountiful natural resources. But how, then, can one explain the success of Germany, Japan, Switzerland, Italy, and South Korea—countries with limited natural resources?

More recently, the argument has gained favor that competitiveness is driven by government policy: targeting, protection, import promotion, and subsidies have propelled Japanese and South Korean auto, steel, shipbuilding, and semiconductor industries into global preeminence. But a closer look reveals a spotty record. In Italy, government intervention has been ineffectual—but Italy has experienced a boom in world export share second only to Japan. In Germany, direct government intervention in exporting industries is rare. And even in Japan and South Korea, government's role in such important industries as facsimile machines, copiers, robotics, and advanced materials has been modest; some of the most frequently cited examples, such as sewing machines, steel, and shipbuilding, are now quite dated.

A final popular explanation for national competitiveness is differences in management practices, including management-labor relations. The problem here, however, is that different industries require different approaches to management. The successful management practices governing small, private, and loosely organized Italian family companies in footwear/textiles, and jewelry, for example, would produce a management disaster if applied to German chemical or auto companies, Swiss pharmaceutical makers, or American aircraft producers. Nor is it possible to generalize about management-labor relations. Despite the commonly held view that powerful unions undermine competitive advantage, unions are strong in Germany and Sweden-and both countries boast internationally preeminent companies.

Clearly, none of these explanations is fully satisfactory; none is sufficient by itself to rationalize the competitive position of industries within a national border. Each contains some truth; but a broader, more complex set of forces seems to be at work.

The lack of a clear explanation signals an even more fundamental question. What is a "competitive" nation in the first place? Is a "competitive" nation one where every company or industry is competitive? No nation meets this test. Even Japan has large sectors of its economy that fall far behind the world's best competitors.

Is a "competitive" nation one whose exchange rate makes its goods price competitive in international markets? Both Germany and Japan have enjoyed remarkable gains in their standards of living—and experienced sustained periods of strong currency and rising prices. Is a "competitive" nation one with a large positive balance of trade? Switzerland has roughly balanced trade; Italy has a chronic trade deficit—both nations enjoy strongly rising national income. Is a "competitive" nation one with low labor costs? India and Mexico both have low wages and low labor costs—but neither seems an attractive industrial model.

The only meaningful concept of competitiveness at the national level is *productivity*. The principal goal of a nation is to produce a high and rising standard of living for its citizens. The ability to do so depends on the productivity with which a nation's labor and capital are employed. Productivity is the value of the output produced by a unit of labor or capital. Productivity depends on both the quality and features of products (which determine the prices that they can command) and the efficiency with which they are produced. Productivity is the prime determinant of a nation's long-run standard of living; it is the root cause of national per capita income. The productivity of human resources determines employee wages; the productivity with which capital is employed determines the return it earns for its holders.

A nation's standard of living depends on the capacity of its companies to achieve high levels of productivity-and to increase productivity over time. Sustained productivity growth requires that an economy continually *upgrade itself.* A nation's companies must relentlessly improve productivity in existing industries by raising product quality, adding desirable features, improving product technology, or boosting production efficiency. They must develop the necessary capabilities to compete in more and more sophisticated industry segments, where productivity is generally high. They must finally develop the capability to compete in entirely new, sophisticated industries.

International trade and foreign investment can both improve a nation's productivity as well as threaten it. They support rising national productivity by allowing a nation to specialize in those industries and segments of industries where its companies are more productive and to import where its companies are less productive. No nation can be competitive in everything. The ideal is to deploy the nation's limited pool of human and other resources into the most productive uses. Even those nations with the highest standards of living have many industries in which local companies are uncompetitive.

Yet international trade and foreign investment also can threaten productivity growth. They expose a nation's industries to the test of international standards of productivity. An industry will lose out if its productivity is not sufficiently higher than foreign rivals' to offset any advantages in local wage rates. if a nation loses the ability to compete in a range of high-productivity/high-wage industries, its standard of living is threatened.

Defining national competitiveness as achieving a trade surplus or balanced trade per se is inappropriate. The expansion of exports because of low wages and a weak currency, at the same time that the nation imports sophisticated goods that its companies cannot produce competitively, may bring trade into balance or surplus but lowers the nation's standard of living. Competitiveness also does not mean jobs. It's the *type* of jobs, not just the ability to employ citizens at low wages, that is decisive for economic prosperity.

Seeking to explain "competitiveness" at the national level, then, is to answer the wrong question. What we must understand instead is the determinants of productivity and the rate of productivity growth. To find answers, we must focus not on the economy as a whole but on *specific industries and industry segments.* We must understand how and why commercially viable skills and technology are created, which can only be fully understood at the level of particular industries. It is the outcome of the thousands of struggles for competitive advantage against foreign rivals in particular segments and industries, in which products and processes are created and improved, that underpins the process of upgrading national productivity.

When one looks closely at any national economy, there are striking differences among a nation's industries in competitive success. International advantage is often concentrated in particular industry segments. German exports of cars are heavily skewed toward high-performance cars, while Korean exports are all compacts and subcompacts. In many industries and segments of industries, the competitors with true international competitive advantage are *based in only a few nations.*

Our search, then, is for the decisive characteristic of a nation that allows its companies to create and sustain competitive advantage in particular fields—the search is for the competitive advantage of nations. We are particularly concerned with the determinants of international success in technology—and skill-intensive segments and industries, which underpin high and rising productivity.

Classical theory explains the success of nations in particular industries based on so-called factors of production such as land, labor, and natural resources. Nations gain factor-based comparative advantage in industries that make intensive use of the factors they possess in abundance. Classical theory, however, has been overshadowed in advanced industries and economies by the globalization of competition and the power of technology.

A new theory must recognize that in modern international competition, companies compete with global strategies involving not only trade but also foreign investment. What a new theory must explain is why a nation provides a favorable *home base* for companies that compete internationally. The home base is the nation in which the essential competitive advantages of the enterprise are created and sustained. It is where a company's strategy is set, where the core product and process technology is created and maintained, and where the most productive jobs and most advanced skills are located. The presence of the home base in a nation has the greatest positive influence on other linked domestic industries and leads to other benefits in the nation's economy. While the ownership of the company is often concentrated at the home base, the nationality of shareholders is secondary.

A new theory must move beyond comparative advantage to the competitive advantage of a nation. It must reflect a rich conception of competition that includes segmented markets, differentiated products, technology differences, and economies of scale. A new theory must go beyond cost and explain why companies from some nations are better than others at creating advantages based on quality, features, and new product innovation. A new theory must begin from the premise that competition is dynamic and evolving; it must answer the questions: Why do some companies based in some nations innovate more than others? Why do some nations provide an environment that enables companies to improve and innovate faster than foreign rivals?

Appendix C
How the Diamond Works: The Italian Ceramic Tile Industry

In 1987, Italian companies were world leaders in the production and export of ceramic tiles, a $10 billion industry. Italian producers, concentrated in and around the small town of Sassuolo in the Emilia-Romagna region, accounted for about 30% of world production and almost 60% of world exports. The Italian trade surplus that year in ceramic tiles was about $1.4 billion.

The development of the Italian ceramic tile industry's competitive advantage illustrates how the diamond of national advantage works. Sassuolo's sustainable competitive advantage in ceramic tiles grew not from any static or historical advantage but from dynamism and change.

Sophisticated and demanding local buyers, strong and unique distribution channels, and intense rivalry among local companies created constant pressure for innovation. Knowledge grew quickly from continuous experimentation and cumulative production experience. Private ownership of the companies and loyalty to the community spawned intense commitment to invest in the industry.

Tile producers benefited as well from a highly developed set of local machinery suppliers and other supporting industries, producing materials, services, and infrastructure. The presence of world-class, Italian-related industries also reinforced Italian strength in tiles. Finally, the geographic concentration of the entire cluster supercharged the whole process. Today foreign companies compete against an entire subculture. The organic nature of this system represents the most sustainable advantage of Sassuolo's ceramic tile companies.

The Origins of the Italian Industry

Tile production in Sassuolo grew out of the earthenware and crockery industry, whose history traces back to the thirteenth century. Immediately after World War II, there were only a handful of ceramic tile manufacturers in and around Sassuolo, all serving the local market exclusively.

Demand for ceramic tiles within Italy began to grow dramatically in the immediate postwar years, as the reconstruction of Italy triggered a boom in building materials of all kinds. Italian demand for ceramic tiles was particularly great due to the climate, local tastes, and building techniques.

Because Sassuolo was in a relatively prosperous part of Italy, there were many who could combine the modest amount of capital and necessary organizational skills to start a tile company. In 1995, there were 14 Sassuolo area tile companies; by 1962, there were 102.

The new tile companies benefited from a local pool of mechanically trained workers. The region around Sassuolo was home to Ferrari, Maserati, Lamborghini, and other technically sophisticated companies. As the tile industry began to grow and prosper, many engineers and skilled workers gravitated to the successful companies.

The Emerging Italian Tile Cluster

Initially, Italian tile producers were dependent on foreign sources of raw materials and production technology. In the 1950s, the principal raw materials used to make tiles were kaolin (white) clays. Since there were red- but no white-clay deposits near Sassuolo, Italian producers had to import the clays from the United Kingdom. Tile-making equipment was also imported in the 1950s and 1960s: kilns from Germany, America, and France; presses for forming tiles from Germany. Sassuolo tile makers had to import even simple glazing machines.

Over time, the Italian tile producers learned how to modify imported equipment to fit local circumstances: red versus white clays, natural gas versus heavy oil. As process technicians from tile companies left to start their own equipment companies, a local machinery industry arose in Sassuolo. By 1970, Italian companies had emerged as world-class producers of kilns and presses; the earlier situation had exactly reversed: they were exporting their red-clay equipment for foreigners to use with white clays.

The relationship between Italian tile and equipment manufacturers was a mutually supporting one, made even more so by close proximity. In the mid-1980s, there were some 200 Italian equipment manufacturers; more than 60% were located in the Sassuolo area. The equipment manufacturers competed fiercely for local business, and tile manufacturers benefited from better prices and more advanced equipment than their foreign rivals.

As the emerging tile cluster grew and concentrated in the Sassuolo region, a pool of skilled workers and technicians developed, including engineers, production specialists, maintenance workers, service technicians, and design personnel. The industry's geographic concentration encouraged other supporting companies to form, offering molds, packaging materials, glazes, and transportation services. An array of small, specialized consulting companies emerged to give advice to tile producers on plant design, logistics, and commercial, advertising, and fiscal matters.

With its membership concentrated in the Sassuolo area, Assopiastrelle, the ceramic tile industry association, began offering services in areas of common interest: bulk; purchasing, foreign-market research, and consulting on fiscal and legal matters. The growing tile cluster stimulated the formation of a new, specialized factor-creating institution: in 1976, a consortium of the University of Bologna, regional agencies, and the ceramic industry association founded the Centro Ceramico di Bologna, which conducted process research and product analysis.

Sophisticated Home Demand

By the mid-1960s, per-capita tile consumption in Italy was considerably higher than in the rest of the world. The Italian market was also the world's most sophisticated. Italian customers, who were generally the first to adopt new designs and features, and Italian producers, who constantly innovated to improve manufacturing methods and create new designs, progressed in a mutually reinforcing process.

The uniquely sophisticated character of domestic demand also extended to retail outlets. In the 1960s, specialized tile showrooms began opening in Italy. By 1985, there were roughly 7,600 specialized showrooms handling approximately 80% of domestic sales, far more than in other nations. In 1976, the Italian company Piemme introduced tiles by famous designers to gain distribution outlets and to build brand name awareness among consumers. This innovation drew on another related industry, design services, in which Italy was world leader, with over $10 billion in exports.

Sassuolo Rivalry

The sheer number of tile companies in the Sassuolo area created intense rivalry. News of product and process innovations spread rapidly, and companies seeking technological, design, and distribution leadership had to improve constantly.

Proximity added a personal note to the intense rivalry. All of the producers were privately held, most were family run. The owners all lived in the same area, knew each other, and were the leading citizens of the same towns.

Pressures to Upgrade

In the early 1970s, faced with intense domestic rivalry, pressure from retail customers, and the shock of the 1973 energy crisis, Italian tile companies struggled to reduce gas and labor costs. These efforts led to a technological breakthrough, the rapid single-firing process, in which the hardening process, material transformation, and glaze-fixing all occurred in one pass through the kiln. A process that took 225 employees using the double-firing method needed only 90 employees using single firing roller kilns. Cycle time dropped from 16 to 20 hours to only 50 to 55 minutes.

The new, smaller, and lighter equipment was also easier to export. By the early 1980s, exports from Italian equipment manufacturers exceeded domestic sales; in 1988, exports represented almost 80% of total sales.

Working together, tile manufacturers and equipment manufacturers made the next important breakthrough during the mid- and late 1970s: the development of materials-handling equipment that transformed tile manufacture from a batch process to a continuous process. The innovation reduced high labor costs—which had been a substantial selective factor disadvantage facing Italian tile manufacturers.

The common perception is that Italian labor costs were lower during this period than those in the United States and Germany. In those two countries, however different jobs had widely different wages. In Italy, wages for different skill categories were compressed, and work rules constrained manufacturers from using overtime or multiple shifts. The restriction proved costly: once cool, kilns are expensive to reheat and are best run continuously. Because of this factor disadvantage, the Italian companies were the first to develop continuous, automated production.

Internationalization

By 1970, Italian domestic demand had matured. The stagnant Italian market led companies to step up their efforts to pursue foreign markets. The presence of related and supporting Italian industries helped in the export drive. Individual tile manufacturers began advertising in Italian and foreign home-design and architectural magazines, publications with wide global circulation among architects, designers, and consumers. This heightened awareness reinforced the quality image of Italian tiles. Tile makers were also able to capitalize on Italy's leading world export positions in related industries like marble, building stone, sinks washbasins, furniture, lamps, and home appliances.

Assopiastrelle, the industry association, established trade-promotion offices in the United States in 1980, in Germany in 1984, and in France in 1987. It organized elaborate trade shows in cities ranging from Bologna to Miami and ran sophisticated advertising. Between 1980 and 1987 the association spent roughly $8 million to promote Italian tiles in the United States.

—Michael J. Enright and Paolo Tenti

Michael J. Enright, a doctoral student in business economics at the Harvard Business School, performed numerous research and supervisory tasks for The Competitive Advantage of Nations. Paolo Tenti was responsible for the Italian part of research undertaken for the book. He is a consultant in strategy and finance for Monitor Company and Analysis BA.—Milan.

Table 3-1. Estimated Number of Japanese Rivals in Selected Industries

Estimated Number of Japanese Rivals in Selected Industries

Air Conditioners	13	Motorcycles	4
Auto Equipment	25	Musical Instruments	4
Automobiles	9	Personal Computers	16
Cameras	15	Semiconductors	34
Car Audio	12	Sewing Machines	20
Carbon Fibers	7	Shipbuilding[14]	33
Construction Equipment[15]	15	Steel[16]	5
Copiers	14	Synthetic Fibers	8
Facsimile Machines	10	Television Sets	15
Large-scale Computers	6	Truck and Bus Tires	5
Lift Trucks	8	Trucks	11
Machine Tools	112	Typewriters	14
Microwave Equipment	5	Videocassette Recorders	10

[14] Six companies had annual production exports in excess of 10,000 tons.

[15] The number of companies varied by product area. The smallest number, 10, produced bulldozers. Fifteen companies produced shovel trucks, truck cranes, and asphalt-paving equipment. There were 20 companies in hydraulic excavators, a product area where Japan was particularly strong.

[16] Integrated companies.

Sources: Field interviews; *Nippon Kogyo Shinbun, Nippon Kogyo Nenkan*, 1987; Yano Research, *Market Share Jitan*, 1987; researchers' estimates.

4.   NEW MODEL: DEBATE

Debates over the Diamond Model:
Determinants of National Competitiveness
Hwy-Chang Moon

Conflicting Perspectives
Diamond in the Rough
Porter Takes the Wrong Turn
Response by Porter and Armstrong
Counter-Response by Rugman
Evaluation on the Debates

Summary and Key Points

Since Porter published his book (1990) and the report on Canada's competitiveness (1991), debates have continued over the diamond model and its application in the real world. This chapter summarizes the pros and cons of the Porter model, and highlights the debate between Porter and Rugman. An overall evaluation on the debates will then be provided.

In his first article, "Diamond in the Rough," Rugman argues that Porter's single diamond has two flaws. First, multinational activity is not properly incorporated. Second, the government's role is understated. While he talks primarily about conceptual issues of the diamond model in his previous article, Rugman discusses more policy issues in his second article, "Porter Takes the Wrong Turn."

Porter and Armstrong respond that Rugman fails to distinguish between the geographic scope of competition (for example, North American or global) and the geographic locus of competitive advantage as reflected in the diamond. For example, competition in the automobile industry is global, but Japanese firms use a strong local diamond. Rugman counter-responds that Porter and Armstrong's alleged dichotomy between scope and locus is operationally meaningless. Rugman argues that the appropriate size of the diamond need not be national; it is determined by the strategy of the firm.

The debate in this Chapter, like that in Chapter 2, is sometimes very acute. However, they do not criticize each other personally—just what they say about competitiveness. Anyway, there is no perfect theory. Porter's single diamond model has been extended to the double diamond model (Rugman & D'Cruz), the generalized double diamond model (Moon, Rugman & Verbeke) and the nine-factor model (Cho). We will discuss these extended models in Chapters 5 and 6.

CONFLICTING PERSPECTIVES

Porter introduced the diamond model when he conducted a four-year study covering 10 nations and 100 industries. The results are documented in *The Competitive Advantage of Nations*, a densely written, 855-page book published in 1990. Here are some quotes about this book.

☐ As its title suggests, the book is meant to be a contemporary equivalent of *The Wealth of Nations*, and the Free Press is marketing the volume as the new-forged version of Adam Smith's world-transforming thunderbolt (Ryan 1990).
☐ This book is long and tough to read. Nevertheless, it is absolutely mandatory. If you read only one book on business this year this should be it (Thain 1990).
☐ This book is read by aspiring intellectuals and despairing politicians everywhere and has projected Porter into a stratosphere. (Economist, October 8, 1994).

Since he published the book *Competitive Strategy* (1980), Porter has been the most famous scholar and is frequently sought by managers and policy makers. Here are some quotes about Porter.

☐ Business school professors tend to be an anonymous breed, and their research is often denigrated as a blend of big words and small ideas. Yet Michael Porter of the Harvard Business School stands out as a genuine star. When he speaks, people in business and government listen— frequently paying handsomely to do so (*New York Times*, September 19, 1992).
☐ Professor Porter's extensive contributions to the competitive strategy literature and his unique holistic way of applying economic and strategic concepts to corporate and national strategy have made him an undisputed leader in competitive strategy (Harvard Business School Bulletin, abstracted from *Business Quarterly*, Spring 1992, 12).
☐ Porter is probably the only business academic to have graced the cover of a major magazine—*Fortune* in November 1987. Indeed, if you were

to do a survey of outstanding academics, it would be hard to come up with another name like Porter's (*Management Today*, August 1989).

However, there are criticisms on Porter.

☐ Some people complain that he is forever producing laundry lists of "forces" and "factors" and passing them off as explanations. Others add that his lists, though they are invariably exhaustive, are not always particularly original (*Economist*, October 8, 1994).
☐ Porter argues that geographically concentrated clustering can play a significant role for competitiveness. However, Italian tile industry (an example taken by Porter) became internationally competitive using imported machinery. Moreover, any attempt to define which sectors are clustered together is inevitably judgmental and subjective (Ryan 1990).
☐ Almost all of Canada's large multinationals rely on sales in the United States and other triad markets. Indeed, it could be argued that the U.S. diamond is likely to be more relevant for Canada's industrial multinationals than is Canada's own diamond, since, on average over 70 percent of their sales take place there... This weakness in Porter's model would not only apply to Canadian-based firms but to multinationals from all small open economies, that is, over 90 percent of the world's nations potentially cannot be modelled by the Porter diamond (Rugman 1991).

The principle of the diamond may still hold good—but its geographical constituency has to be established on very different criteria (Dunning 1993). In particular, Porter's single diamond is not much relevant in small economies because their domestic variables are very limited. For example, in the case of Canada, an integrated North American diamond (including both Canada and the United States), not just a Canadian one, is more relevant (Rugman 1991). Moon and Lee (1995) showed that this is true even in the case of large economies such as the United States. They found that international variables such as international rivalry and foreign markets are important for the competitiveness of U.S. software firms. The double diamond framework, developed by Rugman and D'Cruz (1993) suggests that managers build upon both domestic and foreign diamonds to become globally competitive in terms of survival, profitability, and growth. Although the Rugman/D'Cruz North American diamond framework fits well for Canada, it does not apply well to other small nations such as Korea. Thus,

Moon, Rugman, and Verbeke (1995, 1998) developed the framework further, improving its use in analyzing small economies as well as large economies.[17]

The main purpose of this chapter is to compare and contrast debates over the Porter diamond model so that we can correctly understand determinants of international competitiveness in an era of globalization. In particular, the debate between Porter and Rugman will be highlighted. Rugman first criticizes Porter's work, Porter and Armstrong respond, Rugman counter-responds. An overall evaluation on the debates will then be provided.

CRITIC 1: DIAMOND IN THE ROUGH

In his article, "Diamond in the Rough," Rugman criticizes Porter's work along four dimensions.

The Economic Size

Porter's work is superficial and plain wrong when applied in Canadian situation. His work needs to be modified in order to analyze the issue of Canada's international competitiveness. Canada is only one-tenth the economic size of the U.S. Since Canada is relatively small, almost all of Canada's large multinationals rely on sales in the U.S. and other triad markets. Indeed, it could be argued that the U.S. diamond is likely to be more relevant for Canada's industrial multinationals than is Canada's own diamond, since, on average over 70 percent of their sales take place there. The Canada-U.S. free trade agreement reinforces this point. This weakness in Porter's model would not only apply to Canadian-based firms but to multinationals from all small open economies, that is, over 90% of the world's nations potentially cannot be modeled by the Porter diamond.

---

[17] The summary of pros and cons of the Porter model is abstracted from Moon, Rugman, and Verbeke (1997). For more information about the debates between Porter and Rugman, see Winter 1991 (pp. 61-64), Winter 1992 (pp. 59-64), Spring 1992 (pp. 6-10), and Summer 1992 (pp. 7-10) issues of *Business Quarterly*.

Foreign Direct Investment

The major conceptual problem with Porter's model is due to the narrow definition that he applies to foreign direct investment (FDI). Porter defines only outward FDI as being valuable in creating competitive advantage. He then states that foreign subsidiaries are not sources of competitive advantage and that inward FDI is "not entirely healthy." He also states that foreign subsidiaries are importers, and that this is a source of competitive disadvantage. All of these statements are questionable and have long ago been refuted by Canadian-based scholars. All have demonstrated that the research and development undertaken by foreign-owned firms is not significantly different from that of Canadian-owned firms. The largest 20 U.S. subsidiaries in Canada export virtually as much as they import. (The ratio of exports to sales is 25% while that of imports to sales is 26%).

The Economic Stage

Porter's lack of knowledge of Canada tends to devalue the application of his core model to Canada. Porter's focus on Canada's "home country" diamond cannot explain Canadian competitiveness. Whereas Canada's successful clusters are resource-based, they have value added in them. Porter's statements in his book, to the effect that Canada is a stage one "factor-driven" economy simply is inaccurate and dangerously misleading as policy advice to Canadians. The views expressed by Porter on the role of natural resources are old fashioned and misguided. He argues that reliance on natural resources is as bad as reliance on unskilled labor or simple technology. In fact, Canada has developed a number of successful mega firms that have turned our comparative advantage in natural resources into proprietary firm-specific advantages in resource processing and further refining. These are sources of sustainable competitive advantage. Canada's successful multinationals such as Alcan, Noranda and Nova, illustrate the methods by which value added has been introduced by the managers of these resource-based companies. Over time, Canada's resource-based industries do, in fact, have sustainable advantages.

Two Outside Forces

The Porter model is based on four country-specific determinants and two external variables: chance and government. Porter's four determinants and two outside forces interact in the diamond of competitive advantage, with the nature of a country's international competitiveness depending upon the type and quality of these interactions. Porter's two outside forces, chance and government, present interesting contrasts. Government is clearly of critical importance as an influence on a home nation's competitive advantage. For example, to penalize foreign firms, government can use tariffs as a direct entry barrier, or it can use subsidies as an indirect vehicle. In both cases domestic firms benefit from short-run competitive advantages. These discriminatory government actions can lead to shelter for domestic firms, where shelter actually prevents the development of sustainable long-run competitive advantages.

According to Rugman, the most serious problem of the Porter model is that it does not incorporate the true significance of multinational activity. However, even Rugman is not sure yet how to incorporate the multinational activity. He says, "It is questionable if multinational activity can actually be added into any, or all, of the four determinants, or included as a third exogenous variable."

CRITIC 2: PORTER TAKES THE WRONG TURN

While he talks primarily about conceptual issues of the diamond model in his previous article, Rugman discusses more policy issues in his second article on Porter. Rugman's arguments are summarized as follows.

Incompatible Policy Recommendations

The key result of the Porter/Monitor study is the finding that Canada's home "diamond" is weak and leads to an inability of Canadian-based businesses to develop sustainable global competitive advantages, except in resources. But Porter states that resource-based industries are an essential part of Canada's "old economic order", which Porter thinks has no future. He says, in effect, that Canada's diamond is broken and that it needs to be upgraded to improve Canada's lack of international competitiveness. Most of Porter's policy recommendations are sound, especially his call to reduce the budget deficit, upgrade worker and management skills and improve business-labor-government relations. Yet these policy recommendations are actually incompatible with his analysis. This incompatibility arises because Porter insists on applying his home base diamond analysis to Canada, whereas a much more relevant concept for Canadian managers is that of a North American diamond. This approach, developed by Joe D'Cruz and me in 1991,[18] suggests that to become globally competitive, Canadian managers need to design strategies across both the U.S. and Canadian diamonds. They need to benchmark decisions on a North American basis, not just a Canadian one.

Old-Fashioned Policy Recommendations

Porter's view that multinationals can only succeed with a strong home country base may still be true for the U.S., but it is out of date for Canada. Porter's old-fashioned, naive and politically mischievous viewpoint is inconsistent with Canada's support of the free trade agreement, tax reform, constitutional renewal and other economic, social and political measures aimed at improving the climate for doing business in a Canadian economy that is interdependent with that of the U.S. It is as if Porter/Monitor had never heard of, or participated in, the divisive free trade election in Canada in 1988. In this the forces of economic nationalism were narrowly defeated by the economic realism and sovereignty considerations underlying the free trade agreement. Porter's strategy would have been suitable in the 1890s, but it is wrong for the 1990s. Instead, to become globally competitive a North American mindset is required for Canadian business decisions.

Misleading Policy Recommendations

After Canadian managers have read Porter's study they should ask the following questions. First, does Canada need an industrial strategy to mend the broken Canadian diamond? Second, should Canada give up on its resource-based industries and replace them by innovation-driven industries? Third, does Canada need to keep out foreign-owned firms that do not develop product lines using Canada as a home base? The reason these questions are important is that Porter says that Canada's lack of international

---

[18] Rugman, Alan M. and Joseph D'Cruz, *Fast Forward: Improving Canada's International Competitiveness*, Toronto: Kodak Canada, 1991. It should be noted that Porter does not cite this study correctly in Chapter 3 of his report; instead he cites the study referenced here as number 10.

competitiveness is due to problems in these areas. Yet his analysis fails to provide logical support for his recommendations.

According to Rugman, in sum, Porter's policy recommendations are incompatible, old-fashioned, and misleading. Rugman concludes that Porter took a wrong turning when he crossed the border.

RESPONSE BY PORTER AND ARMSTRONG

Since Porter and the Monitor company published the report, *Canada at the Crossroads: The Reality of a New Competitive Environment,* there has been a continuing debate on the diamond model among the scholars. After they briefly evaluate several scholars' comments on the validity of the diamond model, Porter and Armstrong highlight their response to Rugman's criticism on Porter. They criticize Rugman along the following points.

Geographic Scope and Geographic Locus

Rugman is preoccupied with the North American model and has a lack of understanding of the diamond model. Rugman fails to distinguish between the geographic scope of competition (for example, North American or global) and the geographic locus of competitive advantage, as reflected in the diamond. Competition in the automobile industry is global, but that does not mean there is a 'world diamond' for automobile manufacturing and firms based in all nations are equally positioned. The striking competitiveness of Japanese-based firms belies this view. Their success has been fueled by a strong local (Japanese) diamond in which rivalry has been intense, customers demanding and related and supporting industries well developed.

Different Levels of Analysis

Regions and even cities register striking differences in economic prosperity. For example, the standard of living within the U.S. varies sharply, and differences have persisted. This refutes any notion that Canada's standard of living is secured by proximity to the U.S. States in the U.S. have different per capita incomes precisely because of differences in their local diamonds. Whereas U.S. states have much in common, their differences are sufficient to strongly influence competitive and income patterns. On a similar note, there are many similarities between Canada and the U.S., but there are also significant differences in institutions, history, culture, government structures and policies, and economic circumstances. Such differences create distinct Canadian diamonds in industries. An example of how competitive fortunes have differed even on opposite sides of the border is provided by the software industries in Vancouver and Seattle. The industry in Seattle is booming. In Vancouver—just 225 kilometers to the north—the industry is far smaller.

Building Domestically or Outsourcing Abroad

Most disturbing about Rugman's North American diamond view is that it apparently leads him to believe that the critical problems we see in Canada in areas of education, training, science and technology, can be ignored because Canadian firms can source these skills elsewhere. Indeed, Rugman stated in an interview reported in the University of Toronto Bulletin that Canada should look outside its own borders to develop the economy in global context, and not, as we suggest, concentrate first on building up its skills. Canadians must be vitally concerned with the state of their home environment. The Canadian standard of living depends on the particular activities that take place in Canada. The issue is where the most highly productive economic activities, and those that most benefit upgrading in other industries, will be located. These, in turn, will determine the wages that Canadian jobs command and the returns to capital invested there.

Porter and Armstrong conclude that Rugman significantly distorts their views on Canada's competitiveness.

COUNTER-RESPONSE BY RUGMAN

Rugman is invited to counter-respond to Porter and Armstrong. He focuses on the key question of the practical relevance of Porter's single diamond model versus the "double diamond" approach. His response is as follows.

Geographic Scope and Geographic Locus

Porter and Armstrong state that, "Rugman fails to distinguish between the geographic scope of competition (for example, North American or global) and the geographic locus of competitive advantage as reflected in the diamond." Two examples are given to illustrate this point. First, that "competition in the automobile industry is global", but that "Japanese-based firms" use a strong local diamond. Second, that "regions and even countries register striking differences in economic prosperity", which "refutes any notion that Canada's standard of living is secured by proximity to the U.S." Further, "U.S. states...have differences in their local diamonds"... and the software industry in Seattle is booming whereas that in Vancouver is not. Paradoxically, both of these Porter-Armstrong examples offer more support for a double diamond framework than a single diamond. First, Canada's successful auto industry is fully integrated with the one across the U.S. border; the auto pact is an institutionalized double diamond that has worked well for a quarter of a century. Canada is not like Japan with an isolated single diamond; instead the advantages of geography and the economics of the auto pact have let Canada escape from the disadvantages of its own small local diamond. Second, the smaller size of the software industry in Vancouver compared to Seattle is largely explained by Boeing being in Seattle. The real issue is: what U.S. diamond conditions explain Boeing? Why is Boeing in Seattle and not in Vancouver? But this is not a very useful question to ask about the competitiveness of B.C., which surely requires some analysis of forest products and the new, emerging, high tech industries. From the viewpoint of global competitive strategy the locus for Canadian-based businesses must be broader than the national diamond.

Different Levels of Analysis

The only point in dispute is the size of the diamond. Does it always have to be a nation? Porter and Armstrong themselves admit that diamonds can go down to state levels. I agree; these are sub-national diamonds. But Porter and Armstrong cannot seem to make a symmetrical logical step and visualize a double diamond that goes up across national borders. Yet for purposes of global strategy, in smaller nations like Canada and New Zealand, this is common. Even in Britain, the E.C. diamond is now impossible to ignore; there is a double diamond for U.K. firms, just as there is for Canadian ones operating in the U.S. The appropriate size of the diamond need not be national; it is determined by the strategy of the firm. The relevant focus is indeed the locus of corporate strategy; for international business, it is an international locus. Multinational firms compete globally, not nationally.

Porter and Armstrong's alleged dichotomy between scope and locus is operationally meaningless.

Building Domestically or Outsourcing Abroad

Porter and Armstrong also state that "Rugman's North American diamond view ... apparently leads him to believe that the actual problems we see in Canada in areas of education, training, science and technology, can be ignored because Canadian firms can source these skills elsewhere." Wrong again. The whole point of the double diamond is that it has two diamonds! Therefore I believe very strongly that the elements of the Canadian diamond must be upgraded—they are half of the North American diamond! I have never suggested that Canadian policies for upgrading be ignored; indeed, I wrote that I agree with the Porter report and its recommendations in these cases. It is their analysis that is the subject of dispute. Porter and Armstrong seem to think that my North American diamond is an American-only diamond; it is not—there are two integral and linked components. Having market access to the U.S. for business purposes need not constrain Canadian sovereignty or the need for public policy to upgrade the Canadian diamond. But a limited focus on Canada's diamond alone will fail to lead to the development of globally competitive Canadian businesses.

Rugman concludes, "My articles do not criticize Porter personally—just what he says about Canada; Porter's fame and reputation at Harvard are not in question but his scholarly work on Canada is."

EVALUATION ON THE DEBATES

In a Dialogue section Business Quarterly (Winter, Spring, and Summer 1992) published several articles of pros and cons on Porter's report, *Canada at the Crossroads*. In particular, the debate between Michael Porter and Alan Rugman has called for significant attention both in the business and academic communities. Porter and Rugman are both worldwide distinguished scholars in their own field—Porter in strategic management and Rugman in international business. Exchange of different views will enrich these two academic fields, and may lead to marrying these two areas into international strategic management. Some of their insights are keen enough to demand widespread attention. This topic, i.e., the determinants of competitiveness, is a very important issue among scholars and policy makers. Although the debate focuses on the Canadian case, this is a worldwide topic. The inclusion of the New Zealand case is thus appropriate. Business Quarterly should welcome other cases, too. The experience of other countries will benefit Canadian policy makers.

In the debate, Porter appears to be somewhat upset with the provocative articles of Rugman (1991, 1992). However, Porter (1990, especially Chapter One) is also quite provocative in criticizing the existing economic theories on this issue. The provocative nature of both Porter and Rugman has probably made them the great scholars they are today.

It is noteworthy that there is an important difference in the basic approaches of Porter and Rugman. This difference will help understand their current and future debate. As indicated in the titles of his best selling books such as *Competitive Strategy* and *The Competitive Advantage of Nations*, Porter's approach focuses on competition-based corporate and national strategies. On the other hand, Rugman's basic approach is to understand the rational behavior of multinational firms rather than just to beat the competitors (for example, see Rugman, 1981). According to Rugman, multinational firms frequently utilize foreign markets and resources. Rugman believes that the border for a multinational firm is no longer the nation state. Rugman and other international business scholars may thus feel very uneasy with Porter's diamond model, in which the competitive determinants are fixed on a national level.

Porter (1990) says that nations are most likely to succeed in industries or industry segments where the national "diamond" is the most favorable. The diamond has four broad elements—(1) factor conditions, (2) demand conditions, (3) related and supporting industries, and (4) firm strategy, structure, and rivalry. In his criticisms on the Porter model, Rugman (1991) argues that while most of Porter's analysis would work for large economies such as the U.S., it may not adequately explain small economies such as Canada. The double diamond approach of Rugman (and D'Cruz) says that a Canadian manager needs to consider the U.S. diamond as well as the Canadian and should design across the two diamonds (Rugman, 1992).

The key point of the debate in determining the competitiveness of Canada appears to be whether the diamond is single or double. However, the critical difference between Porter and Rugman on this issue is whether international activities should be included in the model or not. Rugman's point is that Porter's original model should be extended to encompass international activities. Porter also realizes the importance of international or global activities. However, he refuses to incorporate them, by distinguishing the geographic scope of competition and the geographic locus of competitive advantage (Porter and Armstrong, Dialogue 1992).

The difference now appears to be pedagogic and minimal, but in fact it is real. In particular, it can have a major impact on policy implications. One extreme example is that if Porter is right, the diamond must be fixed through an appropriate industrial policy; if Rugman is correct, Canada should pursue the North American diamond, and economic integration with the U.S. must be even more aggressively focused (Ballinger, Dialogue 1992). In which direction should Canada go? If the Porter model is taken literally, opportunities would be eliminated because world-class demand and world-class competition do not exist in the national diamond (Stewart, Dialogue 1992).

Another limitation of the single diamond is its poor predictive ability. Cartwright (Dialogue 1992) says that his New Zealand study cast considerable doubt on the ability of the Porter diamond theory to predict or prescribe the nature of internationally competitive industries that are export-dependent and land-based. Cartwright (Dialogue 1992) explains that the home-base diamond model is inadequate because it omits variables that explain international competitiveness.

While criticizing Rugman, Thain (Dialogue 1992) also recognizes the importance of international activities, in saying that what we really need to understand is that all national diamonds overlap more or less, and are inextricably linked in a global system. If everybody recognizes the important role of international business in today's global economy, why don't we explicitly incorporate it into the model? The extension and even correction of Porter's original model does not reduce the value of Porter. As long as everybody is talking about his model, Porter remains a big shot. Porter might be surprised to see how his original model could be improved in the future. Still, he has provided the foundation.

Porter's single diamond is not the final answer. Rugman may agree that the double diamond is not, either. In social sciences no theory may survive without being revised and corrected. There will be multiple diamond, Triad diamond, and even global diamond. Rugman sparked an intelligent and constructive debate that would serve all of us well (Nankivell, Dialogue 1992). The potential value of his ideas will stir up considerable controversy and debate on the issues (Ballinger, Dialogue 1992).

There may be several other areas for further discussion. First, how can we operationalize the model? In other words, how can we practically measure the relative competitiveness of each determinant? Second, the need for internationalization may be different among the determinants. Stewart, for example, argues that two determinants (factor conditions and related industries) may be national, while the other two determinants (demand and rivalry) should be international. However, some multinational firms exploit foreign factors and utilize foreign related industries. This may vary across industries and countries. A more comprehensive discussion can thus be provided. In any case, Stewart has provided another ground for discussion.

Another area of further discussion concerns Porter's two exogenous factors, i.e., chance and government. In particular, the government factor may be integrated into the new model; thus, the shape of the model may be "pentagon" rather than "diamond". Porter (1990, pp.126-127) says that this is not correct because the government's real role in national competitive advantage is in influencing the four determinants. However, all the factors influence one another (see Porter, 1990, Figure 4-1 through Figure 4-4 in Chapter 4). Or government can be placed in the center of the diamond. In any case, it may not be adequate to treat the government merely as an exogenous factor.

Thain (Dialogue 1992) suggests that any further debate should focus on the practical realities of how Porter's recommendations can be put into practice. Implementation is very important. However, policy recommendations of Porter's study are based on the single diamond model. If the model is flawed, then the recommendations may not be sound. Here, Rugman has made another important point. Most of Porter's policy recommendations based on it may be sound, but they are incompatible with his analysis (Rugman, 1992, p.59). We need to continue the analytical debate if the model is still controversial and may be inconsistent with recommendations. Further debate will benefit both scholars and practitioners.

REFERENCES

Cho, D. S. 1994. A dynamic approach to international competitiveness: The case of Korea. *Journal of Far Eastern Business*, 1(1): 17-36.

Dialogue. 1992. Canada at the crossroads. *Business Quarterly* (Winter, Spring, and Summer).

Dunning, J.H. 1993. Internationalizing Porter's diamond. *Management International Review*, 33 (2): 7-15.

Economist. 1994. Professor Porter Ph.D., October 8: 75.

Management Today. 1989. Guru on the riverbank (August): 52-56.

Moon, H.C. and K.C. Lee. 1995. Testing the diamond model: Competitiveness of U.S. software firms. *Journal of International Management,* 1 (4): 373-387.

Moon, H.C., A.M. Rugman, and A. Verbeke. 1995. The generalized double diamond approach to international competitiveness. In Research in Global Strategic Management, 5: 97-114, edited by A. M. Rugman. Greenwich, CT: JAI Press.

Moon, H.C., A. M. Rugman, and A. Verbeke. 1997. The new global competitiveness of Korea and the generalized double diamond approach. *The Korean Economic and Business Review* (Fall): 48-57.

Moon, H.C., A.M. Rugman, and A. Verbeke. 1998. The generalized double diamond approach to global competitiveness of Korea and Singapore. *International Business Review,* 7: 135-150.

New York Times. 1992. Economic analyst says U.S. needs long-term investments (September 7).

Porter, M. E. 1980. *Competitive strategy: Techniques for analyzing industries and companies.* New York: Free Press.

Porter, M. E. 1990. *The competitive advantage of nations.* New York: Free Press.

Porter, M. E. and the Monitor Company. 1991. *Canada at the crossroads: The reality of a new competitive environment.* Ottawa: Business Council on National Issues and Minister of Supply and Services of the Government of Canada.

Porter, M. E. and J. Armstrong. 1992. Canada at the Crossroads: Dialogue. *Business Quarterly* (Spring): 6-10.

Rugman, Alan M., 1981. *Inside the multinationals.* New York: Columbia University Press, 1981.

Rugman, A. M. 1991. Diamond in the Rough. *Business Quarterly* (Winter): 61-64.

Rugman, A. M. 1992. Porter Takes the Wrong Turn. *Business Quarterly* (Winter): 59-64.

Rugman, A. M. and J. R. D'Cruz. 1993. The "Double diamond" model of international competitiveness: The Canadian experience. *Management International Review* 33 (2): 17-39.

Ryan, R. 1990. A grand disunity. *National Review* (July 9): 46-47.

Thain, D. H. 1990. The war without bullets. *Business Quarterly* (Summer): 13-19.

5.   EXTENDED MODEL (1)

The Generalized Double Diamond Model
Moon, Rugman & Verbeke, 1998

Summary and Key Points

Porter (1990) proposed the diamond model, and Rugman (1991) pointed out two problems with regard to multinational activity and government. Rugman and D'Cruz (1993) developed a double diamond model. Although this model fits well for Canada, it may not fit well for other nations. Moon, Rugman, and Verbeke (1995) extended it to a generalized double diamond that works well for all countries. This generalized model appropriately incorporates multinational activity and government.

In considering multinational activity, Moon, Rugman, and Verbeke (1995) emphasized two elements. First, sustainable value added in a country results from both domestically owned and foreign owned firms. Second, sustainability requires a value added configuration spread over many countries. Thus, multinational activity, whether inbound or outbound, is important for a nation's competitiveness. Since multinational activity affects all the determinants of the diamond, it is not appropriate to treat this variable as one of the determinants. Instead, they incorporate this variable by doubling the diamond.

To test the validity of these two models this chapter evaluates relevant data for both domestic and international variables in the case of Korea and Singapore. The results generally support the generalized double diamond model. Korea has a "larger" domestic diamond than Singapore, but Singapore has a much "larger" international diamond than Korea. This result implies that Korea is more competitive than Singapore when only domestic determinants are considered, but less competitive than Singapore when both domestic and international determinants are considered. According to several parameters such as productivity and managers' perception, Korea is less competitive than Singapore. This leads to the conclusion that both domestic and international determinants are important to the competitiveness of Korea and Singapore.

Source:
Moon, H. Chang, Alan M. Rugman, and Alain Verbeke, 1998. A generalized double diamond approach to the international competitiveness of Korea and Singapore. *International Business Review*, 7: 135-150.

INTRODUCTION

In his famous book, *The Competitive Advantage of Nations,* Porter [1990] studied eight developed countries and two newly industrialized countries (NICs). The latter two are Korea and Singapore. Porter is quite optimistic about the future of the Korean economy. He argues that Korea may well reach true advanced status in the next decade [p. 383]. In contrast, Porter is less optimistic about Singapore. In his view, Singapore will remain a factor-driven economy [p. 566] which reflects an early stage of economic development. Since the publication of Porter's work, however, Singapore has been more successful than Korea, as will be discussed in this paper. This difference in performance raises important questions regarding the validity of Porter's diamond model of a nation's competitiveness.

Porter has used the diamond model when consulting with the governments of Canada [Porter and the Monitor Company 1991] and New Zealand [Crocombe, Enright and Porter 1991]. While the variables of Porter's diamond model are useful terms of reference when analysing a nation's competitiveness, a weakness of Porter's work is his exclusive focus on the "home base" concept. In the case of Canada, Porter did not adequately consider the nature of multinational activities [Rugman 1991]. In the case of New Zealand, the Porter model could not explain the success of export-dependent and resource-based industries [Cartwright 1993]. Therefore, applications of Porter's home-based diamond require careful consideration and appropriate modification.

In Porter's single home-based diamond approach, a firm's capabilities to tap into the location advantages of other nations are viewed as very limited. Rugman [1992: 59] has demonstrated that a much more relevant concept prevails in small, open economies, namely the "double diamond" model. For example, in the case of Canada, an integrated North American diamond (including both Canada and the United States), not just a Canadian one, is more relevant. The double diamond model, developed by Rugman and D'Cruz [1993], suggests that managers build upon both domestic and foreign diamonds to become globally competitive in terms of survival, profitability, and growth. While the Rugman and D'Cruz North American diamond framework fits well for Canada and New Zealand, it does not carry over to all other small nations, including Korea and Singapore. Thus, Moon,

Rugman, and Verbeke [1995] adapted the double diamond framework to a generalized double diamond which works well for analysing all small economies. The main purpose of the present paper is to assess the global competitiveness of Korea and Singapore using this new, generalized double diamond framework. It should be emphasized that the comparison between the single diamond approach and the generalized double diamond will be performed at the macro level rather than the level of individual industries. In this context, it should be remembered that Porter himself made statements about Korea and Singapore at the macro level.

This paper consists of three sections. The first section reviews Porter's [1990] original diamond model and contrasts it with a new framework, the generalized double diamond model [Moon, Rugman, and Verbeke 1995]. The second section presents data and analyses the variables. In the subsequent section, the results are discussed.

SINGLE OR DOUBLE DIAMONDS?

Porter [1990: 1] raises the basic question of international competitiveness: "Why do some nations succeed and others fail in international competition?" As its title suggests, the book is meant to be a contemporary equivalent of The Wealth of Nations, a new-forged version of Adam Smith's opus [Ryan, 1990: 46]. Porter argues that nations are most likely to succeed in industries or industry segments where the national "diamond" is the most favourable. The diamond has four interrelated components; (1) factor conditions, (2) demand conditions, (3) related and supporting industries, and (4) firm strategy, structure, and rivalry, and two exogenous parameters (1) government and (2) chance, as shown in Figure 5-1.

This model cleverly integrates the important variables determining a nation's competitiveness into one model. Most other models designed for this purpose represent subsets of Porter's comprehensive model. However, substantial ambiguity remains regarding the signs of relationships and the predictive power of the "model" [Grant 1991]. This is mainly because Porter fails to incorporate the effects of multinational activities in his model. To solve this problem, Dunning [1992], for example, treats multinational activities as a third exogenous variable which should be added to Porter's model. In today's global business, however, multinational activities represent much more than just an exogenous variable. Therefore, Porter's original diamond model has been extended to the generalized double diamond model [Moon, Rugman, and Verbeke 1995] whereby multinational activity is formally incorporated into the model.

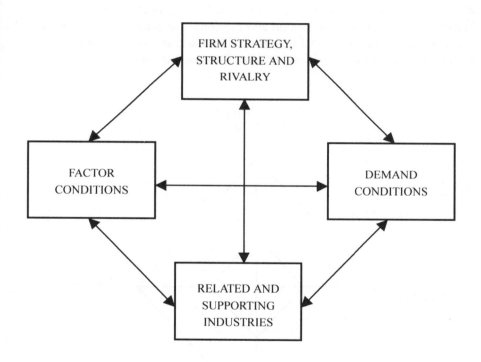

Figure 5-1. The Home-Based Single Diamond

Firms from small countries such as Korea and Singapore target resources and markets not just in a domestic context, but also in a global context.[19] Therefore, a nation's competitiveness depends partly upon the domestic diamond and partly upon the "international" diamond relevant to its firms. Figure 5-2 shows the generalized double diamond where the outside one

---

[19] Global targeting also becomes very important to firms from large economic systems such as the United States.

represents a global diamond and the inside one a domestic diamond. The size of the global diamond is fixed within a foreseeable period, but the size of the domestic diamond varies according to the country size and its competitiveness. The diamond of dotted lines, between these two diamonds, is an international diamond which represents the nation's competitiveness as determined by both domestic and international parameters. The difference between the international diamond and the domestic diamond thus represents international or multinational activities. The multinational activities include both outbound and inbound foreign direct investment (FDI).

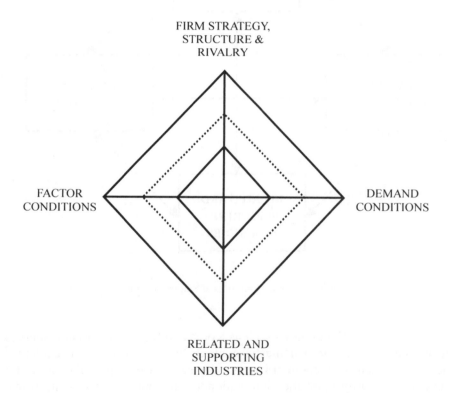

Figure 5-2. The Generalized Double Diamond

In the generalized double diamond model, national competitiveness is defined as the capability of firms engaged in value added activities in a specific industry in a particular country to sustain this value added over long periods of time in spite of international competition. Theoretically, two methodological differences between Porter and this new model are important. First, sustainable value added in a specific country may result from both domestically owned and foreign owned firms. Porter, however, does not incorporate foreign activities into his model as he makes a distinction between geographic scope of competition and the geographic locus of competitive advantage [Porter and Armstrong 1992]. Second, sustainability may require a geographic configuration spanning many countries, whereby firm specific and location advantages present in several nations may complement each other. In contrast, Porter [1986, 1990] argues that the most effective global strategy is to concentrate as many activities as possible in one country and to serve the world from this home base. Porter's global firm is just an exporter and his methodology does not take into account the organizational complexities of true global operations by multinational firms [Moon 1994].

Porter's narrow view on multinational activities has led him to underestimate the potential of Singapore's economy. Porter [1990: 566] argues that Singapore is largely a production base for foreign multinationals, attracted by Singapore's relatively low-cost, well-educated workforce and efficient infrastructure including roads, ports, airports, and telecommunications. According to Porter, the primary sources of competitive advantage of Singapore are basic factors such as location and unskilled/semi-skilled labour which are not very important to national competitive advantage. In actual fact, Singapore has been the most successful economy among the NICs. Singapore's success is mainly due to inbound FDI by foreign multinational enterprises in Singapore, as well as outbound FDI by Singapore firms in foreign countries. The inbound FDI brings foreign capital and technology; whereas outbound FDI allows Singapore to gain access to cheap labour and natural resources. It is the combination of domestic and international diamond determinants that leads to a sustainable competitive advantage in many Singaporean industries.

Multinational activities are also important in explaining Korea's competitiveness. The most important comparative advantage of Korea is its human resources which have been inexpensive and well-disciplined. However, Korea has recently experienced severe labour problems. Its labour is no longer cheap and controllable. Major increases in the wages in Korea were awarded to a newly militant labour force in 1987-1990, which lifted average earnings in manufacturing by 11.6 per cent in 1987, 19.6 per cent in 1988, 25 per cent in 1989 and 20.2 per cent in 1990 [The Economist Intelligence Unit 1992]. Korea's wage level is now comparable to that of the United Kingdom, but the quality of its products has not kept pace. For the last several years, Korea's wage increases have been significantly higher than those in other NICs and three or four times as high as those in other developed countries [Chungang Daily Newspaper February 25, 1995]. Faced with a deteriorating labour advantage, Korean firms have two choices: (1) go abroad to find cheap labour; (2) enhance their production capabilities by introducing advanced technology from developed countries. In both cases, the implementation of these choices requires the development of multinational activities.

To sum up, multinational activities are very important when analysing the global competitiveness of Korea and Singapore. In fact the most important difference between the single diamond model [Porter 1990] and the generalized double diamond model [Moon, Rugman and Verbeke 1995] is the successful incorporation of multinational activities in the latter. In the next section, we will assess the Porter versus the generalized double diamond models using data for both domestic and international determinants in the cases of Korea and Singapore.

DIAMOND VARIABLES AND DATA

Dependent Variables

The dependent variable of the diamond model is a nation's competitiveness. Porter [1990] argues that the only meaningful concept of competitiveness at the national level is national productivity [p. 6], although he uses exports and outbound FDI as proxies for competitiveness [p. 25]. In our view, the two latter variables should be regarded as explanatory variables and not as proxy for the dependent variable. Table 5-1 lists possible proxy variables for the dependent variable of the diamond model in the cases of Korea and Singapore. Productivity variables include output per capita and output per unit of energy consumption. Managers' perception variables include the strength of the general economy and manufacturing base. While these variables are used for illustrative purposes only, they suggest that Singapore is more competitive than Korea.

Table 5-1. Dependent Variables of the Diamond Model

	Korea	Singapore
Productivity		
GNP per capita ($), 1993	7,660	19,850
GDP per energy kg (oil equil) ($), 1993	2.6	3.6
Managers' Perception		
Strong economy as a whole (% agreed), 1992	14.1	58.8
Strong manufacturing base (% agreed), 1992	27.1	57.5

Sources:
International Monetary Fund. 1996. *International Financial Statistics*. February.
The World Bank. 1995. *World Development Report 1995*.
IMD. 1992. *The World Competitiveness Report*. Lausanne, Switzerland.

Independent Variables

As discussed, the most important debate over the diamond model is whether the international variables should be incorporated into the model or not. We will assess the model, first with the domestic variables only, and then with both the domestic and international variables. Table 5-2 lists the domestic independent variables and Table 5-3 lists the international independent variables. These variables do not constitute a full set of all relevant parameters but represent acceptable proxies to illustrate the "value added" of incorporating international elements in the diamond model.

Table 5-2. Domestic Independent Variables of the Diamond Model

	Korea	Singapore
Factor Conditions		
Basic	Wages in manufacturing (USA = 100.0), 1994	
	37.0	37.0
Advanced	Scientists & technicians (1,000 persons), 1986-1991	
	45.9	22.9
Demand Conditions		
Size	Average annual growth (%), 1980-1993	
	8.2	6.1
Sophistication	Education index (literacy + schooling), 1992	
	2.6	2.1
Related & Supporting Industries		
Transportation	Paved roads (km/million persons), 1992	
	1,090.0	993.0
Communication	Telephones (per 100 persons), 1990-1992	
	41.4	39.2
Firm Strategy, Structure & Rivalry		
Rivalry	Unequal treatment of foreigners (% agreed), 1992	
	43.7	37.2

Sources:
U.S. Department of Commerce. 1995. *Statistical Abstract of the United States* 1995. September.
United Nations Development Programme. 1994. *Human Development Report* 1994.
The World Bank. 1995. *World Development Report* 1995.
IMD. 1992. *The World Competitiveness Report*. Lausanne, Switzerland.

Table 5-3. International Independent Variables of the Diamond Model

		Korea	Singapore
Factor Conditions			
Basic	Outbound FDI per capita ($), 1994	56.7	743.0
Advanced	Inbound FDI per capita ($), 1994	18.2	1,907.2
Demand Conditions			
Size	Export dependency (% of GNP), 1994	25.5	140.5
Sophistication	Export diversification (% of exp. without top 3), 1992	53.5	58.6
Related & Supporting Industries			
Transportation	Good air transport system (% agreed), 1992	70.6	97.8
Communication	International telex traffic (outgoing traffic in minutes per capita), 1990	0.2	7.7
Firm Strategy, Structure & Rivalry			
Rivalry	Openness to foreign products (% agreed), 1992	57.5	87.7

Sources:
International Monetary Fund. 1996. *International Financial Statistics*. February.
Europa Publications Limited. 1995. *The Europa World Year Book 1995*. London, England.
IMD. 1992. *The World Competitiveness Report*. Lausanne, Switzerland.

1. Factor Conditions

Porter distinguishes between basic factors and advanced factors. Basic factors include natural resources, climate, location, unskilled and semiskilled labour, and debt capital. Advanced factors include modern communications infrastructure and highly educated personnel such as engineers and scientists. Porter [1990: 77] argues that advanced factors are now the most significant ones for competitive advantage. Since Korea and Singapore are not yet fully developed countries, however, basic factors remain important for their competitiveness. In this study, we choose to measure basic factors by wages in manufacturing and advanced factors are measured by the number of the technical staff per 1,000 persons as shown in Table 5-2 which reports domestic independent variables.[20] Since wages are rapidly increasing in these countries, Korea and Singapore are investing in other countries such as China and the Southeast Asian countries where labour is cheap. Yet Korea and Singapore still need to attract multinational firms from advanced countries, as this may be one way to obtain access to modern technologies. In short, both inbound and outbound FDI are important in enhancing these countries' factor conditions. These international determinants are reported as international independent variables in Table 5-3.

2. Demand Conditions

The rate of growth of home demand can be more important to competitive advantage than its absolute size. Rapid domestic growth leads a nation's firms to adopt new technologies faster, with less fear that such technologies would make existing investments redundant, and to build large, efficient facilities with the confidence that they will be utilized [Porter 1990: 94]. In addition, a nation's firms gain competitive advantage if domestic buyers are sophisticated and demanding as regards the product or service [Porter 1990: 89]. It can be hypothesized that a higher level of education of the consumers increases demand sophistication. The size and sophistication of demand conditions are measured by average annual growth and an education index, respectively in Table 5-2.[21]

---

[20] Both Korea and Singapore are natural resource-poor countries. Therefore, only labour, but not natural resources, is considered as a determinant for the state of the factor conditions.

[21] See United Nations Development Programme [1994: 108] for the calculation of the education index.

For both Korea and Singapore, however, domestic markets are relatively small so global economies of scale cannot be achieved. The most successful firms in these countries target international, rather than domestic markets.[22] The export market measured as a percentage of GNP can serve as a proxy for the relative importance of international demand. If a country's exports depend on just a few foreign countries, however, its export markets are not diversified and are thus not sophisticated. The diversification of export markets serves a proxy for the sophistication of international demand faced by a nation's firms. It is hypothesized that a high ratio of exports, excluding the top three destination countries, vis-à-vis total exports, reflects a more diversified and more sophisticated international demand. These data for proxies for international demand are shown in Table 5-3.

3. Related and Supporting Industries

Related and supporting industries are those whereby firms coordinate or share activities in the value chain or those which involve products that are complementary to the firms of a given nation. These industries may have strong backward and forward linkages with the firms in a given sector. Since we are testing the competitiveness of manufacturing industries in general in Korea and Singapore, however, the information on general infrastructure such as transportation and communication is important. Transportation is measured by paved roads (km/million persons) and communication is measured by telephone lines (per 100 persons) as shown in Table 5-2. We recognize that modern physical infrastructure could be regarded as an advanced factor, but we did not incorporate it in our earlier section on factor conditions as we believe that it is better to incorporate physical infrastructure as a related and supporting industry.

Again, both Korea and Singapore depend heavily on international business. In today's global business, it is neither efficient nor desirable to rely solely on home-based related and supporting industries.[23] The infrastructure for international business is important. The infrastructure for

---

[22] For example, Korea's export market at the beginning of internationalization was larger than the domestic market [Cho, Choi & Yi 1994]

[23] Porter [1990: 103] argues that foreign suppliers (and related industries) rarely represent a valid substitute for home-based ones. However, when a firm cannot compensate for the disadvantages (e.g. technology) in the home country, the firm will seek this factor in the foreign country [Moon and Roehl 1993].

international transportation is measured by the extent to which international air transport infrastructure meets business requirements. The infrastructure for international communication is measured by the international telex traffic in terms of traffic in minutes per capita. The relevant data reflecting these variables are shown in Table 5-3. We recognize that other proxy variables could be used, such as seaport infrastructure, but we have chosen these proxies for convenience of illustration.

4. Firm Strategy, Structure, and Rivalry

The final determinant of a nation's competitiveness reflects the context in which firms are created, organized, and managed. National advantage may result from a good match among these variables. However, Porter [1990] finds that no one managerial system is universally appropriate [p. 108]. Instead, he expresses a strong preference in favour of vigorous domestic rivalry for creating and sustaining competitive advantage in an industry [p. 117]. In this study we attempt to measure whether rivalry, as well as strategy and structure, is domestically oriented or not. This is difficult to do and we choose to measure it by the extent to which foreigners are treated unequally as compared to domestic citizens as shown in Table 5-2. It is hypothesized that a high level of unequal treatment of foreigners is xenophobic and it is correlated with a high domestic orientation of rivalry and firm strategy and structure.

Porter [1990: 117] argues that domestic rivalry is superior to rivalry with foreign competitors. This argument may be true in large economies such as the United States, but not in small economies such as Canada [Rugman 1990], Korea and Singapore. The successful firms in Korea and Singapore are more concerned about international rivalry than about domestic rivalry. International rivalry can be measured by the openness to foreign products which is the extent to which national protectionism does not prevent competitive products from being imported as shown in Table 5-3.

EMPRIRICAL RESULTS OF THE DIAMOND TESTS

The data for domestic independent variables in Table 5-2 and international independent variables in Table 5-3 are transformed into "competitiveness indices" in Table 5-4. It should again be emphasized that these are used for illustrative purposes only, as indications that Porter's single diamond model lead to wrong conclusions. To calculate the competitiveness index, for each variable, a maximum value "100" is given to the country which has the higher value and a relative ratio in terms of percentage is given to the other country which has the lower value. If a variable is measured by two elements, one half weight is given to each element. For example, in Table 5-2, both of Korea's basic and advanced factor conditions have equal or higher values than those of Singapore so that maximum value "100" is given to each of the two factor conditions of Korea. Thus, the competitive index of Korea's domestic factor conditions is

$$100/2 + 100/2 = 100.0$$

Singapore's basic factor condition has the same value (37.0) as that of Korea. The maximum value "100" is given to Singapore for this element. However, Singapore's advanced factor has the value (22.9) which represents 49.9% of that (45.9) of Korea's advanced factor. Thus, the competitive index of Singapore's domestic factor conditions is

$$100/2 + 49.9/2 = 75.0$$

Table 5-4. Competitiveness Index of the Diamond Model

	Korea	*Singapore*
Factor Conditions		
Domestic Variables	100.0	75.0
International Variables	4.3	100.0
Demand Conditions		
Domestic Variables	100.0	77.6
International Variables	54.7	100.0
Related & Supporting Industries		
Domestic Variables	100.0	92.9
International Variables	37.4	100.0
Firm Strategy, Structure & Rivalry		
Domestic Variables	100.0	85.1
International Variables	65.6	100.0

Table 5-4 shows that for all four determinants of the diamond model Korea has higher competitive indices for domestic variables, but Singapore has higher competitive indices for international variables. This difference is clearly visualized in Figure 5-3 and Figure 5-4. Korea's domestic diamond consisting of solid lines and its international diamond consisting of dotted lines are shown in Figure 5-3. Similarly, Singapore's domestic and international diamonds are shown in Figure 5-4. The international diamond is constructed by adding the international competitiveness index to the domestic competitiveness index for each variable. In Figure 5-3, for example, domestic competitiveness index (D1d) for factor conditions is "100.0" By adding the international competitiveness index "4.3" to this value, the coordinate "D1i" represents "104.3". Therefore, the international diamond represents domestic plus international determinants. It can thus be said that the difference between the international diamond and domestic diamond is the international or multinational determinants of the nation's competitiveness.

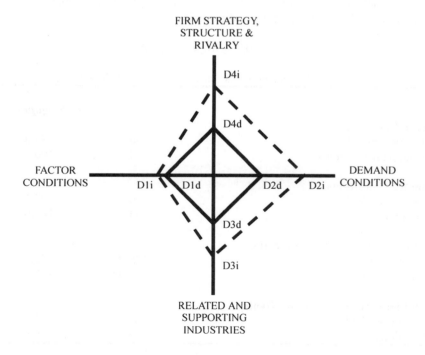

Figure 5-3. The Competitiveness of Korea

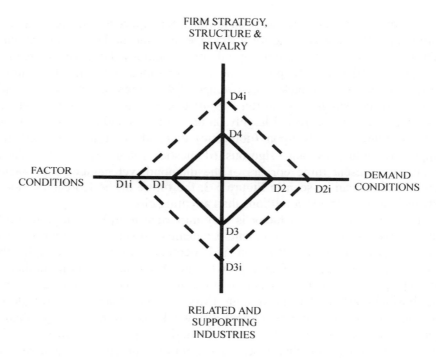

Figure 5-4. The Competitiveness of Singapore

Three interesting points can be made when comparing the domestic and international diamonds in Figure 5-3. and Figure 5-4. First, Korea has a "larger" domestic diamond than Singapore, but Singapore has a "larger" international diamond than Korea.[24] This result implies that Korea is more competitive than Singapore when considering only domestic determinants, but less competitive than Singapore when considering both domestic and international determinants. As shown in Table 5-1, Korea is less competitive than Singapore according to several parameters. This leads to the conclusion that both domestic and international determinants are important to the competitiveness of Korea and Singapore.

Second, compared with that of Singapore, Korea's international diamond appears to be almost identical to its domestic one with respect to factor conditions. This implies that Korea is relatively weak as regards the

---

[24] Figure 5-3 and Figure 5-4 are drawn on the same scale.

international portion of the factor conditions. Singapore has actively pursued outbound FDI to compensate for a shortage of domestic labour and inbound FDI to obtain access to foreign capital and technology. However, Korea has not been as active as Singapore in these multinational activities. In contrast, Porter's work reflects a lack of knowledge of the Korean economy and leads to an incorrect suggestion. Porter [1990] claims that Korea's competitive advantage has thus far rested largely on basic factor conditions [p. 477], but that its future depends upon (domestic) demand conditions, related and supporting industries, and vigorous (domestic) rivalry [p. 479].[25] These variables represent three corners of the diamond, yet neglect one—factor conditions. As can be seen in Figure 5-3, the future of the Korean economy depends more on factor conditions than anything else.

Third, the government factor is very important in influencing a nation's competitive advantage. Governments frequently pursue interventionist trade and industrial strategies [Rugman and Verbeke 1990]. For example, the thirty years of Korea's economic growth have been marked by a number of different phases and in each period government intervention in economic and business affairs has been high [Moon 1992]. Facing a new global environment, the Korean government is now taking various steps to enhance Korea's competitiveness. For related and supporting industries, the government brings together research institutions, universities, and private companies in a joint effort to create science parks.[26] As regards demand conditions, Korea pushes global demand because of the relatively small size of its domestic market. The government also emphasizes globalization in the area of firm strategy, structure, and rivalry. Korea has unveiled plans to privatize or merge many state-funded companies. Recent efforts to alleviate entry barriers against foreign companies are also examples of public effort to achieve a globalization of industry structure and rivalry.

---

[25] In 1994, one of Korea's leading business newspapers, *Mae-il-kyung-jai* [Daily Economic Review], invited several world-famous scholars to express their opinions on Korea's competitiveness. Porter received special attention, thanks to his diamond model. Porter [1994] suggested a similar policy to this, but neglected a possible solution to the problem of factor conditions through multinational activities.

[26] For example, Daedok Science town includes 13 government institutes, 3 private research institutes, and 3 universities on its 53 square kilometres. The primary goal of the science parks is to develop their own indigenous technologies. These parks are also playing major roles in the transfer of technology from the West. For a comparison of science parks of NICs, see Gwynne [1993].

Yet as shown in Figure 5-3, the most important determinant of Korea's global competitiveness lies in factor conditions. Korean firms are no longer cost competitive in overseas markets because the Southeast Asian countries have cheaper sources of labour. On the other hand, Korean firms' technology does not match that of developed countries such as the United States and Japan. The implications for Korea's competitiveness are now clear: to find cheap labour and to increase technological capability. In order to obtain access to cheap labour, Korean firms need to invest in Southeast Asian countries and China. For technological improvement, Korean firms need to invest more in R&D and specialize in the most competitive sectors. However, this is a risky and very long-term strategy. The most practical means of compensating for the country's lack of advanced technology is to import foreign technology. To conclude, both inbound and outbound FDI are important to maintain Korea's competitive edge regarding factor conditions. At the current stage of economic development, the crucial role of the Korean government is to relax various regulations and to provide a favourable environment for both inbound and outbound FDI.

CONCLUSION

The concept of globalization has become both a buzzword and a crucial long-term goal in many small economies such as Korea and Singapore. Globalization represents both a challenge and an opportunity for these countries. However, this concept is extremely complex and it is not clear how to increase global competitiveness. Porter's diamond model is a good starting paradigm for analysing important determinants of global competitiveness. However, Porter's original diamond model is incomplete, mainly because he did not adequately incorporate multinational activities.

A new model, the generalized double diamond model, developed and extended in this paper, has led to three important extensions to Porter's original framework. First, the new model explicitly incorporates multinational activities, whereas Porter's original diamond considers mainly the impact of traditional home-based activities. Second, the new approach easily allows us to operationalize the competitiveness paradigm, whereas Porter's original approach is hard to operationalize. In the generalized double diamond approach, a comparison of the sizes and shapes of the domestic and international diamonds reveals major strategic differences.

Third, the new model includes government, not as an exogenous parameter, but as an important variable which influences the four determinants of the diamond model.

All of these three extensions are important when analysing the global competitiveness of Korea and Singapore. First, as discussed above, both outbound and inbound FDI, i.e., multinational activities, are crucial to a nation's competitiveness. Second, by comparing the sizes and shapes of both domestic and international diamonds of Korea and Singapore, the most important variable requiring policy intervention can be identified (i.e., factor conditions in the case of Korea). Third, the government factor in small economies such as Korea and Singapore is more important than anything else in affecting the other variables. This does not mean that the government should intervene in every aspect of business affairs, but that the government should be very careful when intervening, considering its potentially large impact on competitiveness.

Table 5-5. Information Sources of the Variables

Dependent variables

Productivity

GNP per capita ($), 1993	WB, p. 163
GDP per energy kg (oil equil) ($), 1993	WB, p. 171
Managers' Perception	
Strong economy as a whole (% agreed), 1992	IMD, p. 1.26
Strong manufacturing base (% agreed), 1992	IMD, p. 1.28

Independent Variables	*Domestic*	*International*
Factor Conditions		
Basic	USDC, p. 865	IMF, p. 344, 508
Advanced	UNDP, p. 138	IMF, p. 344, 508
Demand Conditions		
Size	WB, p. 163	IMF, p. 344, 508
Sophistication	UNDP, p. 129	EPL, p. 1789, 2697
Related & Supporting Industries		
Transportation	WB, p. 225	IMD, p. 5.20
Communication	UNDP, p. 160	IMD, p. 5.27
Firm Strategy, Structure & Rivalry		
Rivalry	IMD, p. 2.39	IMD, p. 2.37

Sources:

International Monetary Fund (IMF). 1996. *International Financial Statistics.* February.

The World Bank (WB). 1995. *World Development Report 1995.*

IMD. 1992. *The World Competitiveness Report.* Lausanne, Switzerland.

U.S. Department of Commerce (USDC). 1995. *Statistical Abstract of the United States 1995.*

United Nations Development Programme (UNDP). 1994. *Human Development Report 1994.*

Europa Publications Limited (EPL). 1995. *The Europa World Year Book 1995*

From Adam Smith to Michael Porter

REFERENCES

Cartwright, Wayne R. 1993. Multiple linked diamonds: New Zealand's experience. *Management International Review*, 33 (2): 55-70.

Cho, Dong-Sung, Jinah Choi & Youjae Yi. 1994. International advertising strategies by NIC multinationals: The case of a Korean firm. *International Journal of Advertising*, 13: 77-92.

Chungang Daily Newspaper. 1995. Wages of Korea and other major countries. February 25.

Crocombe, F. T., M .J. Enright & M. E. Porter. 1991. *Upgrading New Zealand's competitive advantage.* Auckland: Oxford University Press.

Dunning, J.H. 1992. "The Competitive Advantage of Countries and the Activities of Transnational Corporations." *Transnational Corporations* l(l):135-168.

The Economist Intelligence Unit. 1992. South Korea 1992-93: Annual survey of political and economic background. *EIU Country Profile.*

Europa Publications Limited. 1995. *The Europa world year book 1995.* London, England.

Grant, R.M. 1991. "Porter's Competitive Advantage of Nations: An Assessment." *Strategic Management Journal* 12(7):535-548.

Gwynne, Peter. 1993. Directing technology in Asia's dragons. *Research Technology Management*, March/April 32(2): 12-15.

IMD. 1992. *The world competitiveness report.* Lausanne, Switzerland.

International Monetary Fund. 1996. *International financial statistics*, February.

Moon, H. Chang. 1992. New challenges for Korean conglomerates. In Thomas Chen, Young B. Choi and Sung Lee, eds. *Economic and political reforms in Asia.* New York: St. John's University Press.

Moon, H. Chang. 1994. A revised framework of global strategy: Extending the coordination-configuration framework. *The International Executive*, 36(5): 557-574.

Moon, H. Chang & Thomas W. Roehl. 1993. An imbalance theory of foreign direct investment. *Multinational Business Review*, Spring: 56-65.

Moon, H. Chang, Alan M. Rugman & Alain Verbeke. 1995. The generalized double diamond approach to international competitiveness. In Alan Rugman, Julien Van Den Broeck & Alain Verbeke, eds. *Research in global strategic management: volume 5: Beyond the diamond.* Greenwich, CT: JAI Press: 97-114.

Porter, Michael E. 1986. Competition in global industries: A conceptual framework. In Michael E. Porter, ed. *Competition in global industries.* Boston: Harvard Business School Press.

Porter, Michael E. 1990. *The competitive advantage of nations.* New York: Free Press.

Porter, Michael E. 1994. Competitiveness of the Korean economy. *Mae-il-kyung-jai* [Daily Economic Review], January 4, 5, 6.

Porter, Michael E. & John Armstrong. 1992. Canada at the crossroads: Dialogue. *Business Quarterly*, Spring: 6-10.

Porter, Michael E. & the Monitor Company. 1991. *Canada at the crossroads: The reality of a new competitive environment*. Ottawa: Business Council on National Issues and Minister of Supply and Services of the Government of Canada.

Rugman, A.M. 1990. *Multinationals and Canada-United States Free Trade*. Columbia: University of South Carolina Press.

Rugman, A.M. 1991. "Diamond in the Rough." *Business Quarterl* 55(3):61-64.

Rugman, A.M. 1992. "Porter Takes the Wrong Turn." *Business Quarterly 56(3):59-64.*

Rugman, Alan M. & Joseph R. D'Cruz. 1993. The double diamond model of international competitiveness: Canada's experience. *Management International Review*, 33 (2): 17-39.

Rugman, A.M. and A. Verbeke. 1990. *Global Corporate Strategy and Trade Policy*. London/New York: Croom Helm/ Routledge.

Ryan, Richard. 1990. A Grand Disunity. *National Review*, July 9, 42(13): 46-47.

Spring, D. 1992. An international marketer's view of Porter's New Zealand study. *Business Quarterly* 56(3): 65-69.

United Nations Development Programme. 1994. *Human development report 1994*.

United States Department of Commerce. 1995. *Statistical abstract of the United States 1995*.

The World Bank. 1995. *World development report* 1995.

Wu, F. 1991. The ASEAN Economies in the 1990s and Singapore's regional role. *California Management Review* 34(1):103-114.

6. EXTENDED MODEL (2)

The Nine-Factor Model
Cho, 1994

Summary and Key Points

Cho (1994) also argues that Porter's original model is limited in its application to developing countries such as Korea. He emphasizes different groups of human factors and different types of physical factors in explaining a nation's competitiveness. Human factors include workers, politicians/bureaucrats, entrepreneurs, and professionals. Physical factors include endowed resources, domestic demand, related and supporting industries, and other business environment. An external factor, chance, is added to these eight internal factors to make a new paradigm, the nine-factor model.

The differences between the nine-factor model and Porter's diamond model are in the division of factors, and in the addition of new factors. The diamond model includes both natural resources and labor in factor conditions, but the nine-factor model places natural resources under endowed resources, while labor is included within the category of workers. Human factors mobilize the physical factors, and people combine and arrange the physical factors with the aim of obtaining international competitiveness.

So far, we have discussed determinants for a nation's competitiveness. Another important point is that competitiveness is meaningful only among the nations endowed with similar comparative advantages competing in similar industries. In other words, the relative competitive position among similar countries in a certain stage of economic development, but not among all the countries in the world, is an important element for a nation's competitiveness. So, we need stage models for economic development. We will discuss this in Chapter 7 and Chapter 8.

Source:
Cho, Dong-Sung. 1994. A dynamic approach to international competitiveness: The case of Korea. *Journal of Far Eastern Business*. 1(1): 17-36.

INTRODUCTION

Michael Porter's recent work helps explain the sources of international competitiveness possessed by the economies of advanced nations, but has a limited application when it comes to explaining the levels and dynamic changes of economies in less developed or developing countries. The experience of Korea's economic development in the past three decades reveals how groups of well-educated, motivated, and dedicated people have played a central role in not only shaping the nation's competitiveness but also moving the nation dynamically from a less developed stage to an advanced one. If we modify Porter's diamond model to take account of the Korean experience, we are left with a new paradigm of international competitiveness. It divides sources of international competitiveness into two broad categories: 'physical' factors and 'human' factors. By 'physical' factors, we refer to endowed resources, the business environment, related and supporting industries, and domestic demand, which together determine the level of international competitiveness of a given nation at a given time. Human factors include workers, politicians and bureaucrats, entrepreneurs, and professional managers and engineers. By creating, motivating and controlling the four physical elements, these human factors drive the national economy from one stage of international competitiveness to the next. An external factor of pure chance is added to these eight internal factors to make the new paradigm a nine-factor model. As we shall see, this new framework can elucidate the sources of economic growth in less developed countries as well as those dynamic changes in international competitiveness that are associated with economic growth. The relative importance of each of the eight physical and human factors changes as the national economy moves from a less developed stage to a developing stage, to a semi-developed stage, and, finally, to a fully developed stage.

When a nation's trade balance swings from surplus to deficit, its people begin to worry about an economic decline and associate it with a diminution in the nation's international competitiveness. Governments can point to uncontrollable, or external factors such as a slowdown in the international economy or high exchange rates as the cause of trade deficits and weakened international competitiveness. Businessmen would take advantage of this occasion to demand tax cuts and the imposition of import barriers as corrective measures. However, trade balance and international competitiveness are not the same. There are nations which suffer from weak international competitiveness, whilst possessing balanced trade accounts or even, as a result of import controls, trade surpluses. Some nations have demonstrable international competitiveness, but reveal occasional trade deficits. Lastly, international competitiveness is not determined by external factors alone. Under the same global economic environment, some nations gain market share at the expense of others. In this paper the term 'international competitiveness' is defined in a way that systematically explains the long-term resilience of a nation's economy. Next, a new paradigm is formulated, and it is composed of the nine factors which determine the international competitiveness of a nation as it moves from a less developed stage to a developing stage, to a semi-developed stage, and finally to a developed stage. Then, the model is applied to Korea and to the development of its four major industries at different stages of international competitiveness. The final part of this paper looks at policies to improve international competitiveness.

THE THEORETICAL BACKGROUND TO INTERNATIONAL COMPETITIVENESS

A Definition of International Competitiveness

One misconception of international competitiveness is based on the notion that it depends on a plentiful supply of labor, capital and natural resources at low prices.[27] This economic theory mistakenly links a nation's international competitiveness to its factor endowments. Endowed resources are only a part of many determinant factors. There are countries with plentiful resources but a weak economy. In a world in which raw materials, capital and even labor move across national borders, the possession of endowed resources alone does not determine international competitiveness. Another misconception is to measure a nation's international competitiveness by its share of world

---

[27] M.E. Porter, 'The Competitive Advantage of Nations', *Harvard Business Review* (March-April 1990), pp.84-5.

markets.[28] While a useful indicator, it is often misleading because a nation's share of world markets can rise regardless of its international competitiveness. A nation may arbitrarily raise its market share by lowering export prices below production costs, sometimes through government subsidies, but its international competitiveness is not necessarily strengthened. As we have seen, trade balances have limited value in this debate.[29] Some nations register large temporal trade deficits, despite their maintaining competitiveness when they are confronted with political or international difficulties. A good illustration is the Federal Republic of Germany in the early 1990s which had to carry trade deficits while undergoing unification with East Germany. On the other hand, Middle East nations showed extravagant trade surpluses during the energy crises of the 1970s, but their industries generally lacked international competitiveness. Trading accounts are inappropriate indicators, at least in the short term, of industrial strength. One widespread misconception is to divide international competitiveness into two categories: price competitiveness, such as nominal wages, exchange rates and labor productivity; and non-price competitiveness, such as quality, marketing, service and market differentiation.[30] In order to gauge price competitiveness, export price, production cost, and consumer or wholesale price indices are used. Rising prices are seen as weakening a nation's international competitiveness. In reality there are cases in which nations with strong international competitiveness can and do raise the price of their products. Quality status, durability, design and consumer satisfaction are used to evaluate non-price competitiveness, but there are no empirical studies to prove their influence. Price and non-price factors are not the causes but the results of a nation's international competitiveness.

In summary, traditional views cover only a part of many factors determining the level of international competitiveness, or mistake results for causes.[31] A new definition of international competitiveness is required and it should include all of the major factors in a holistic, systematic manner if the

---

[28] C . Brown and T. D . Sheriff, 'De-industrialization: A Background Paper, in F. Blackaby (ed.), *De-industrialization* (London: Heinemann,1978).

[29] HMSO, Report from the Select Committee of the House of Lords on Overseas Trade, The Aldington Report, 1985.

[30] A. Francis and P.K.M. Tharakan (eds.), *The Competitiveness of European Industry* (London and NY: Routledge,1989), pp.5-20.

[31] M. J. Baker and S.J. Hart, *Marketing and Competitive Success* (Philip Allan,1989), pp.5-8.

causal relations between the factors and the resulting level of a nation's competitiveness are to be discovered. The international competitiveness of a national industry can be defined by its having a superior market position through high profits and constant growth when compared to competitors. A country cannot possess international competitiveness simply because it has one or two successful industries. Sri Lanka has a well-developed trade in tea growing and processing, and Iceland is the center of a strong fish processing industry, yet few would argue that these two nations have international competitiveness. A nation needs to have a multitude of industries with strong competitiveness. Nor can a nation be regarded as internationally competitive if her industries are strong because of some external factors. The United States, in the 1945-70 period, enjoyed an uncontested position in most of the industries which were reliant upon high levels of technology and vast domestic markets. A nation needs the sources of competitiveness which can be applied to a number of industries. A nation, then, is internationally competitive when it has many industries with competitive advantage based on common domestic sources of competitiveness.

Existing Studies on Determinants of International Competitiveness

Studies on determinants of international competitiveness are mostly predicated on theories of international trade which focus on the comparative cost of production, natural resources, and technologies.[32] Since each nation has different comparative advantages, scholars have not succeeded in finding a general theory that can explain the economic fortune of countries with a small number of generic, universally applicable factors. In the early 1960s, economists began to recognize how a nation's international competitiveness could be affected not only by its trade, but also by overseas direct investment undertaken by multinational enterprises. Theories of FDI subsequently proliferated. Concepts of monopolistic advantages have identified ownership-specific advantages such as technology, marketing know-how, management skills, financial resources, and scale economies as the sources of competitiveness uniquely possessed by multinationals.[33] On the other hand, industrial organization theory has demonstrated market imperfections

---

[32] W. Leontief, 'Factor Proportions and Structure of American Trade: Further Theoretical and Empirical Analysis', *Review of Economics and Statistics*, Vol.38.

[33] C.P. Kindleberger, *American Business Abroad* (New Haven: Yale University Press, 1969), p.13.

or failures to be the main spur of FDI and the origins of the advantages exercised by multinational enterprises.[34] By concentrating on a particular type of business organization both approaches failed to explain the sources of national competitive advantage in a comprehensive and systematic manner. Dunning integrated these independently evolved theories in order to explain comprehensively all the advantages possessed of multinational enterprises. He outlined the changing investment patterns which a nation may undergo as it moves from one stage of development to the next. But he does not deal with the importance of international competitiveness in relation to stages of national development.[35] Buckley and Casson have discussed the evolving role of specific factors which determine the success of multinational enterprises operating in foreign markets, but their discussion is limited to issues of geography and entrepreneurial culture.[36] In answer to these shortcomings new more systematic studies on international competitiveness have been produced by Kogut, Goldsmith and Clutterbuck, and Yamazawa. They have presented the determinants of international competitiveness at the level of individual companies, but they do not show how these develop into the macro-level advantages of a nation or industry.[37]

The link was first demonstrated by Porter. He pointed out that classical trade theories based on comparative advantage did not satisfactorily explain

---

[34] P.J. Buckley and M. Casson, *The Future of the Multinational Enterprise* (MacMillan, 1976), pp.33-65.

[35] See J.H. Dunning, International Production and the Multinational Enterprise (London: George Allen&Unwin, 1981),Table 4.2 'The Eclectic Theory of International Production', on pp.80-81, and Ch.5, 'Explaining the International Direct Investment Position of Countries: Towards a Dynamic or Developmental Approach', on pp. 109-37. See also J. H. Dunning, Explaining International Production (London: Unwin Hyman Ltd ., 1988), Ch.5, 'The Investment Development Cycle and Third World Multinationals', pp.140-65.

[36] P.J. Buckley and M.C. Casson, Ch.2, 'Multinational Enterprises in Less Developed Countries: Cultural and Economic Interactions', in P.J. Buckley and J. Clegg (eds.), Multinational Enterprises in Less Developed Countries (London: MacMillan, 1991), pp.27-55.

[37] B. Kogut, 'Designing Global Strategies: Comparative and Competitive Value-Added Chains', Sloan Management Review (Summer 1985), pp.15-28; W. Goldsmith and D. Clutterbuck, The Winning Streak: Britain's Top Companies Reveal Their Formulas for Success (Weidenfeld&Nicolson,1984); I. Yamazawa, 'Intensity Analysis of World Trade Flow', Hitotsubashi Journal of Economics (1970), pp.61-90.

the trade patterns of resource-poor countries like Japan. Then he presented his model of international competitiveness, based on the 'diamond'.[38] The model is composed of four determinants: factor conditions; firm strategy, structure, and rivalry; related and supporting industries; and demand conditions. Besides these four, Porter cites chance and government as additional factors. In essence, this model shows how an industry can maintain international competitiveness when these determinants are in place, but it must be said that Porter's theory primarily explains the economies of advanced nations. His model needs to be modified for it to be applied to developing or less developed nations, because the countries have to create international competitiveness without necessarily having any of the four determinants in place. Porter's analysis cannot explain the success which Korea and Taiwan have achieved in the second half of the twentieth century. A new model will serve two objectives: one is better to evaluate which elements have contributed to the international competitiveness of less developed economies; the other is to show how a nation can improve its national advantage.

A NEW MODEL OF INTERNATIONAL COMPETITIVENESS FOR LESS DEVELOPED COUNTRIES

The Nine-Factor Model

In order to assess Korea's international competitiveness, two major considerations should be addressed. Government and businesses had to introduce capital and technology from foreign countries or create resources and other factors influencing economic growth from their initial stages. The key engine of Korea's economic growth has been an abundant and diverse group of people with generally high levels of education, motivation and dedication to work. Korea's population can be grouped into four: workers; politicians and bureaucrats who formulate and implement economic plans; entrepreneurs who make investment decisions despite high risks; and professional managers who are in charge of operations and engineers who

---

[38] M.E. Porter, *The Comparative Advantage of Nations* (NY: The Free Press, 1990), pp.69-130.

implement new technologies. To appreciate their contribution to Korea's development, a nine-factor model is required. There are four physical determinants of international competitiveness, namely endowed resources, the business environment, related and supporting industries and domestic demand; there are also four human factors namely workers, politicians and bureaucrats, entrepreneurs and professional managers and engineers. External chance events should be noted as the ninth factor (see Figure 6-1).

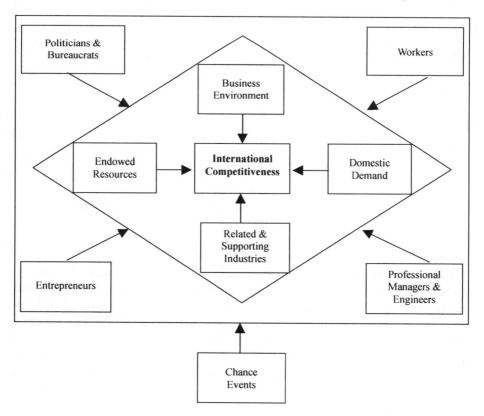

Figure 6-1. A New Paradigm of International Competitiveness
(The Nine Factor Model)

The difference between the new model and Porter's diamond model is to be found as much in the division of factors as in the addition of new ones. The diamond included both natural resources and labor in factor conditions, but the nine factor model places natural resources under endowed resources, while labor is included within the category of workers. A detailed investigation of the nine factors of international competitiveness is needed.

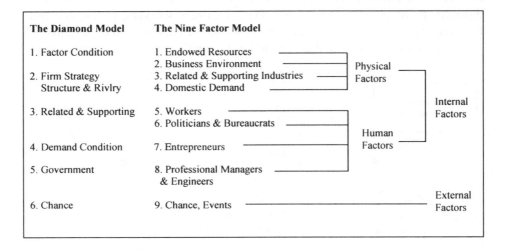

Figure 6-2. Comparison of the Diamond and the Nine Factor Model

(i) Physical Factors

(a) *Endowed resources* can be divided into mineral, agricultural, forestry, fishery and environmental resources. Mineral resources are depletable, and energy resources such as coal, oil and natural gas can be distinguished from non-energy resources such as iron ore, gold and silver. Agriculture, forests and fish stocks are renewable and environmental factors are composed of land, weather, water and other natural advantages.[39] All these resources can form inputs into economic activities, and they may add to a nation's international competitiveness.

(b) *Business environment.* The business environment should be viewed at the levels of nation, industry and company. At the national level, there are visible and invisible components: the first includes roads, ports,

---

[39] Uh Sun Shin, *Resource Economics* (Park-Young Sa, 1988), pp.9-11.

telecommunications and other forms of infrastructure; the second is concerned with the people's acceptance of competitive values and market mechanisms and the commitment of producers, merchants, consumers and other participants in the economy to the legitimacy and obligations of commercial deals and credit. At an industrial level, the business environment is determined by the number and size of competitors, the type and height of entry barriers, the degree of product differentiation, and other factors shaping the nature of rivalry and economic activity. At a company level, the strategy and organization of businesses and the attitudes and behavior of individuals and groups within enterprises are major considerations.[40]

(c) *Related and supporting industries.* Related industries can be divided into vertically related industries and horizontally related industries. While one encompasses the influence of upstream and downstream stages of production, the other is concerned with industries that use the same technology, raw materials, distribution networks or marketing activities. Supporting industries include financial, insurance, information, transportation and other service sectors.[41]

(d) *Domestic demand* includes both quantitative and qualitative aspects. The size of domestic market determines minimum economies of scale for indigenous companies, as well as the stability of demand. The home economy acts as a test market for products that can be shipped overseas, and the risks of international commerce are reduced. Greater benefits can be gained from the qualitative dimensions. The expectations of consumers can stimulate competitiveness, and, in a nation where consumers have sophisticated and strict standards on product quality in addition to a high degree of consumerism, its businesses can accrue international advantages in the course of satisfying demanding home conditions.[42]

(ii) Human Factors

It is the human factors which mobilize the above-mentioned physical factors. People combine and arrange the physical factors with the aim of obtaining international competitiveness. Workers, politicians and bureaucrats,

---

[40] M. E. Porter, op. cit., pp.107-24.

[41] Ibid., pp.100-06.

[42] Ibid., pp.86-100.

entrepreneurs, and professional managers and engineers have to be considered.

(a) *Workers*. The most easily identified measure of the worth of workers is the wage level, yet it is only one of the many attributes which directly or indirectly affect labor productivity. Others are levels of education, a sense of belonging to an organization, acceptance of authority, a work ethic, and the size of the labor pool. The traditional explanation of Korea's comparative advantage in cheap labor from the 1960s to the mid-1980s overlooked more fundamental factors such as high education levels, discipline and the work ethic.

(b) *Politicians and bureaucrats*. Politicians seek to win and maintain power, and economic development is one of the many routes they can choose for achieving their primary objective. Nations governed by politicians that are committed to growth and success can assist in the creation of international competitiveness. China in the late 1980s and 1990s is a manifestation of how a national economy can benefit from leaders that appreciate the value of economic development, even under a Communistic system. In general, an efficient and non-corrupt bureaucracy can assist the application of state policy, and can make a substantial addition to international competitiveness.

(c) *Entrepreneurs*. As entrepreneurs venture on new businesses despite a high degree of risk, they are distinct from ordinary businessmen. They are essential to any nation at an early stage of economic development. Over time, a country's competitiveness is strengthened by their efforts to diminish risks and maximize returns.

(d) *Professional managers and engineers*. When international competition necessitates fierce price cutting and a search for enhanced service, risk-taking attitude alone will not bring deeply entrenched competitiveness. The dedicated work of professional managers in reducing production costs by even small fractions and the cutting of delivery times determines the future of nations as well as individual businesses.

(iii) The External Factor: Chance Events

Chance events are unpredictable changes in the environment, often unassociated with the international business system. They include unexpected breakthroughs in new technologies or products, oil shocks, sharp fluctuations in world capital markets or foreign exchange rates, changes in the policies of foreign governments, movements in international demands, and the outbreak of war. Physical and human factors have in many cases to be reconfigured if a nation is to maintain competitiveness, or take the opportunity to improve competitive advantage.

THE LIFE CYCLE OF NATIONAL COMPETITIVENESS

We can evaluate a nation's international competitiveness by judging the influence which the nine factors may have, and we can similarly begin to understand its development. A nation's economic status is determined by its international competitiveness and the nine factors have varying weights as a country moves from a less-developed stage to a developing stage, then to a semi-developed stage, and finally to a developed stage.[43] A model framework of the life cycle of national competitiveness is shown in Figure 6-3, and a review of the characteristics prevalent in each stage and the major sources of competitive advantage at each juncture will be valuable.

(i) Less Developed Stage

Countries prior to economic development have only limited endowed and labor resources, and they tend to lack the management know-how and technology which can put these assets into production processes that can generate value-added. It follows that they lack international competitiveness, and nations with a per capita income of less than US$500 in 1990 are to be found in this category, a number of African and Southwest Asian nations being exemplary. Although most of the Central and South American nations have per capita incomes of more than $500, a few do belong to this group. These nations cannot implement stable economic policies because of

---

[43] The per capita GNP standard measuring each nation's economic status differs from one scholar to another. In this research, the standards dividing less-developed nations, developing nations, semi-developed nations and developed nations were set at US$500, US$3,000 and US$15,000. Please refer to W.J. Keegan, Global Marketing Management (4th ed., Englewood Cliffs, NJ: Prentice-Hall,1989), pp.86-9 for further details.

frequent changes of power and other political uncertainties, although they do possess considerable natural resources and quite sizable labor pools.

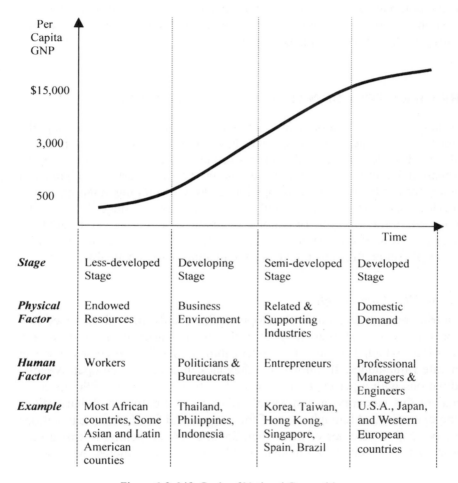

Stage	Less-developed Stage	Developing Stage	Semi-developed Stage	Developed Stage
Physical Factor	Endowed Resources	Business Environment	Related & Supporting Industries	Domestic Demand
Human Factor	Workers	Politicians & Bureaucrats	Entrepreneurs	Professional Managers & Engineers
Example	Most African countries, Some Asian and Latin American counties	Thailand, Philippines, Indonesia	Korea, Taiwan, Hong Kong, Singapore, Spain, Brazil	U.S.A., Japan, and Western European countries

Figure 6-3. Life Cycle of National Competitiveness

(ii) Developing Stage

The developing stage, when a nation is at the early period of development, sees the inertia of a less developed economy being overcome by politicians beginning to fulfill political ambition through policies of growth and construction. In the process, they mobilize bureaucrats to carry out industrial policies, and enhance the business environment through the creation of financial markets and social infrastructures. Sometimes, endowed resources and available workforces are channeled into government-run enterprises, and a nation has its first opportunity to strengthen international competitiveness. Businesses tend to introduce production technology from foreign countries and they also depend on foreign markets for the sale of products. As a result, a nation's international competitiveness in this stage largely rests on changes in the international business environment, including foreign exchange rates and the prices of raw materials. Because businesses are still establishing organizational capacity and facing strong competition in world markets, the government frequently allocates scarce resources to one or two companies in each industry. Most industries at this stage of development are monopolized by a single or a few enterprises.

The process of founding international competitiveness through collaboration between politicians and bureaucrats can be seen in the case of Korea during the 1960s. President Park Chung-Hee, who assumed power as a result of a military coup, had to cope with the abrupt suspension of economic assistance from the United States, which disapproved of his military regime. Park believed that to keep power he had to reduce huge trade deficits. He formulated and implemented a series of Five-Year Economic Development Plans from 1962 onwards, designed to invest resources in selected strategic industries, and, in order to improve the business environment, highways, ports, subways and other essential social infrastructure were built. Companies were encouraged to develop manufacturing facilities in textiles, footwear, steel, electronics, machinery and automobiles, and received financial support and payment guarantees from the government. Nations at the developing stage show a per capita income of between US$500 and US$3,000, and include Korea and Taiwan in the 1960s through to the early 1970s, and Thailand, Malaysia, Indonesia, and the Philippines in the 1990s.

(iii) Semi-Developed Stage

As economic development passes the early period, a capitalist system may allow entrepreneurs to make bold investments despite associated high risks, and they begin to reduce their dependence on the government. In other words, monopoly rents do not accrue only to state-supported enterprises, and the business environment has become favorable to the process of active investment. Entrepreneurs are prepared to invest and seek to achieve economies of scale. If necessary, they borrow resources from overseas. While nations with abundant natural resources will take advantage of them, those at a semi-developed stage may secure essential in-puts at low prices through long-term contracts or direct resource development. As a result of these efforts, the latter's international competitiveness can become stronger than that of the former. The human factors which form the main source of international competitiveness include risk-taking entrepreneurs. An oligopolistic pattern of competition appears amongst businesses at the semi-developed stage, and companies tend to diversify into new areas from their initial, successful base, resulting in the further development of related and supporting industries. The international competitiveness of industries is enhanced by the strengthening of these linkages. Nations at this stage have a per capita income in the range of US$3,000 to US$15,000, and are evidenced by Japan in the 1960s and the so-called newly industrializing economies of Korea, Taiwan, Hong Kong and Singapore in the 1990s.

(iv) Developed Stage

Following the innovation of manufacturing processes, products and business organizations in the semi-developed stage, the connections among horizontally and vertically related and supporting industries are further enhanced. The goods and services of these industries can enter competitive international markets on equal terms with those from advanced countries. Manufacturing processes become more sophisticated, product quality is improved and a balanced development between upstream and downstream areas is achieved. The role of entrepreneurs becomes less important, as professional managers and engineers develop their businesses and increase efficiency. Sectors that are horizontally and vertically related to initially successful industries become internationally competitive, and government controls such as the artificial allocation of funds, market protection and the payment of subsidies, are gradually phased out. The wage pressures from workers do intensify, as does competition from innovations in marketing, product quality and sales service. As income levels rise, consumers make more demands for better quality and services. Per capita incomes of more than US$15,000 are apparent in developed nations, which comprise the United States, Japan, Germany and other West European countries.

THE LIFE CYCLE OF INDUSTRIAL COMPETITIVENESS

As can be seen from the above analysis, international competitiveness is determined by four physical factors—endowed resources, the business environment, related and supporting industries and domestic demand and these are created, mobilized and controlled by the four human factors—workers, politicians and bureaucrats, entrepreneurs, and professional managers and engineers. These eight factors play different roles in the different stages of a nation's economic development. Each nation's economy also consists of primary, secondary and tertiary sectors, and the balance of activity between them differs between different stages of development. The stage and speed of each industry's development differs according to the nation's overall business environment. In order to appreciate each nation's international competitiveness more fully an analysis of industries is needed to supplement the macro-perspective. An industry's international competitiveness is strengthened or weakened according to changes in the business environment and the specific responses of human actors. A static approach using the nine factors requires a dynamic analysis based on the life cycle of industrial competitiveness. Industries move from an early stage to a growth stage, to a maturing stage, and finally to a declining stage.[44] The physical and human factors of international competitiveness have varying influences as each industry passes through different phases.

(i) Early Stage

In general, an industry is at an early stage if its sources of competition are limited to endowed resources, such as abundant mineral resources, and ample and fertile land. Despite their availability, some countries cannot utilize their given attributes due to insufficient know-how and technology. An industry gains growth potential by making lower priced products and using unprocessed resources and labor.

---

[44] Please refer to J . E . Smallwood, 'The Product Life Cycle: A Key to Strategic Marketing Planning', in B.A. Weitz and R. Wensley (ed.), *Strategic Marketing: Planning Implementation and Control* (Boston, MA: Kent Publishing Company, 1984), pp.184-92 for further details.

(ii) Growth Stage

To transfer from the early stage to a growth stage, industries need politicians and bureaucrats who are willing to support businesses systematically. Politicians and bureaucrats create a business environment favorable to active investment, select certain industries for advancement, provide administrative and financial support, tax credits, insurance and information services and payment guarantees to chosen entrepreneurs. They sometimes protect particular industries until enough demand becomes captive or until access to foreign technology has been won. The market is organized on monopolistic or oligopolistic lines.

(iii) Maturing Stage

Innovation occurs in manufacturing processes, product development, and business organization. Connections among horizontally and vertically related industries become stronger at this stage, and businesses which pursue a balanced development in both downstream and upstream areas remain competitive in international markets. Entrepreneurs take a leading role in a system reliant on active investment. This stage comes at a time when an industry's international competitiveness is extended to horizontally and vertically related industries, and government measures, such as the artificial allocation of investment capital, market protection and the payment of subsidies, are phased out. Industries embrace full competition from both domestic and foreign firms and the ensuing competition stimulates product development and quality improvements.

(iv) Declining Stage

An industry that passes through the maturing stage and fails to maintain innovation naturally enters a declining stage. Markets are saturated at this point and consumers' expectations for product quality are high. Production costs rise if businesses try to meet sophisticated consumer demands, resulting in a fast decline in their international competitiveness. Industries can correct these problems if professional managers and engineers cooperate to achieve organizational and technological innovations.[45]

---

[45] Japanese shipbuilding industry provides an example. Japanese shipbuilding industry fell into a declining stage in the early 1980s due in the main to the cost leadership possessed by developing countries such as Korea and Brazil. Since the

CASE STUDIES: KOREA'S MAJOR INDUSTRIES

Figure 6-4 illustrates the above-mentioned life cycle of industrial competitiveness as applied to Korean industries which have had, presently possess, or are expected to achieve international competitiveness. The four cases studied were made to represent each stage of the industry life cycle: semiconductors belong to the early stage; automobiles to the growth stage, steel to a maturing stage, and apparel to a declining stage.

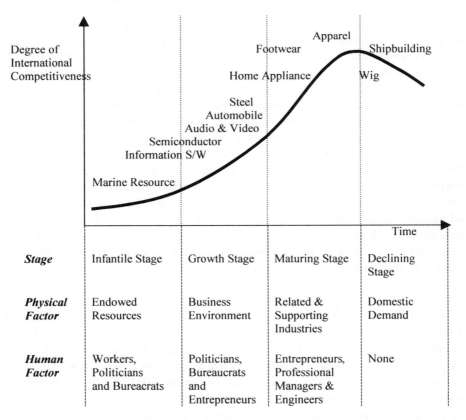

Stage	Infantile Stage	Growth Stage	Maturing Stage	Declining Stage
Physical Factor	Endowed Resources	Business Environment	Related & Supporting Industries	Domestic Demand
Human Factor	Workers, Politicians and Bureacrats	Politicians, Bureaucrats and Entrepreneurs	Entrepreneurs, Professional Managers & Engineers	None

Figure 6-4. Life Cycle of Industrial Competitiveness

mid-1980s, however, Japan has drastically changed the nature of the industry by introducing robotization into manufacturing processes, thereby recovering their cost competitiveness.

The Semiconductor Industry

Korea's semiconductor industry began in 1965 with the establishment of a joint venture called Komy Semiconductor. The string of factories established by US or Japanese firms to assemble simple transistors performed simple assembly processes requiring little technological input.[46] The only source of international competitiveness at this early phase was various labor attributes such as low wages, work discipline, and an abundant supply of skilled manpower. Many workers had been previously employed and trained by companies in the apparel and home electronics industries, and they quickly adapted to semiconductors. Various tax incentive schemes and direct financial support from government attracted foreign investment in this sector. In the growth period since 1978, Korea's semiconductor industry has been assisted by a variety of advantages: basic technologies were made available through joint ventures with foreign companies; Korean engineers, educated and trained in the United States and other advanced countries, returned; the government designated the industry to be strategically important, and provided companies with incentives for expansion and for research and development. Byung-Cheol Lee of the Samsung Group initiated a major investment in the industry at a time when nobody was sure of its success; and the spirit of rivalry amongst Samsung, Hyundai and Goldstar prompted additional developments in production and technology. The temporary shortage of electronic parts during the energy crisis of 1979 and the opportunities opened by the US-Japan Semiconductor Agreement in the US market benefited Korean semiconductor makers.

The Automobile Industry

Korea's automobile industry was founded in 1962 with a complete knockdown or kit mode of production with parts supplied by Honda and Toyota, and it reached a semi-knock-down stage in 1967. Soon, General Motors moved into Korea with a local assembly plant to tap the growing Korean market. Major sources of international competitiveness during this early stage were the skilled labor force, geographic proximity to the Japanese companies which Korean firms were emulating, and industrial policies banning the importation of assembled cars and providing indigenous exporters with tax incentives. In essence, Korea's automobile industry

---

[46]   Korea Electronic Industries Promotion Institute, 'Prospect for Long-term Development of Electronic Industries',1989. 9.

gained its growth potential through the correct combination of foreign capital and technologies, joint international ventures, and government industrial policy. In 1975, a new company entered the industry. It was the Hyundai Motor Company which chose a strategy very different from the existing manufacturers. Instead of depending on the foreign capital and technology being offered through a joint venture proposed by Ford, Chairman Ju-Young Chung of the Hyundai Group decided that the company should construct its own plant with the money earned from construction and shipbuilding. It was a bold attempt with high risks, but in return it provided the company with the invaluable asset of independence and autonomy at a point when it was beginning to penetrate overseas markets. Unlike Mazda and Ford-affiliated Kia or GM-affiliated Daewoo, Hyundai could move into and export to any part of the world. In the 1980s, Hyundai made an inroad into the American and European markets and firmly established itself as one of the major automobile makers of the world.

Major sources of competitive advantage in the growth stage since the mid-1970s came from Chung's aggressive investment in production facilities and overseas marketing, the integration of subcontractors into the Hyundai family business and the development of indigenous technologies and original models. Although the government in 1980 disrupted the automobile industry by unsuccessfully mandating a merger between Hyundai and Daewoo and the closing of Kia, it later provided generous assistance in research and development and continued to protect the domestic market from an invasion of Japanese models. Other major factors underpinning expansion included the concurrent development of related industries such as steel, electric, electronic and machinery, as well as a growth in aggregate domestic demand.[47]

The Steel Industry

The history of Korea's steel industry has been the history of Pohang Iron and Steel Co. (POSCO). The industry's foundations are to be found before the First Five-Year Economic Development Plan in 1962, but it was not until the first phase of steel mill construction was completed in Ulsan in 1973 that the industry was firmly established. From that point, POSCO moved rapidly through the early stage. The industry was developed through an abundant labor force possessing skills and work discipline, foreign capital, the transfer

---

[47] KIET, 'Future Picture of Automobile Industries', Series of Future Industries,1987.

of technologies from Western European countries, and government assistance as exemplified most notably by the Steel Industry Promotion Law. The increase in steel demand was induced by the series of economic development plans, and the then President, Park Chung-Hee, was convinced that the industry was fundamental to a number of related industries like automobiles, shipbuilding, electrics and electronics, and machinery. Chairman T.J. Park of POSCO was another important influence in his company's and industry's success.

The growth stage began after the second phase of construction at the Ulsan steel mill in 1978, when advanced steel-making countries were reducing their production capacities and modernizing facilities. Major sources of international competitiveness during this stage were state industrial policies, the rise in domestic demand, and relative cost increases in US and Japanese firms. Most importantly, it was Chairman Park's leadership that drove POSCO's continued expansion, including the second steel plant at Kwangyang Bay, and he was determined to create a globally renowned company committed to product quality and managerial excellence. The maturing stage started in 1988 when major competitors in Japan, the US and Europe had completed their rationalization programs and concentrated on high value-added steel products. Korea sustained its international competitiveness in basic steel products, but its position in special steel categories was weakened. In response, POSCO increased efficiency and developed more expensive goods. Diversification strategies into telecommunications and other related and non-related industries were led by professional managers of POSCO in an attempt to broaden the company's commercial base.

The Apparel Industry

The apparel industry was one of Korea's earliest successful industries, and, in its early stage in the 1950s, major sources of competitiveness were found in a plentiful, cheap and dexterous labor force, post-war reconstruction projects by the government, state support for foreign loans and technology imports, and the knowledge already possessed in long-established firms. As the industry entered its growth stage in the 1960s, sources of advantage shifted to the high education levels of workers and their ability to adapt to new technologies, export-driven industrial policies, financial and tax benefits through the Textile Industry Promotion Law, investment and construction by entrepreneurs, and the growth in original engineering manufacture-based exports. Apparel makers transformed themselves into general trading companies such as Sunkyong, Hyosung, and Hanil,[48] and they assisted the penetration of foreign markets. A developing petrochemical industry then supplied high-quality artificial materials at competitive prices.

In the maturing stage of the 1980s, the United States enforced quotas on apparel imports, and the Korean government shifted priorities from light goods industries to heavy machinery, chemicals, and electronics. Wage levels increased in the course of Korea's rapid economic growth. The apparel industry had to face full and open competition, and mergers and acquisitions occurred. Independently or in partnership with general trading companies, manufacturers moved their plants to East Asian countries and the Caribbean islands, where production costs were lower and barriers to the US market could be avoided. Marketing subsidiaries were established overseas to facilitate and diversify export markets, and managerial policies have sustained the industry's competitiveness in the 1990s. Yet there are three areas of weakness: most sophisticated textile machines have to be imported; many closely related industries such as dyeing and fashion design are not internationally competitive; and, as a consequence, technologies and know-how in the manufacturing of top-quality apparel are lacking. Unless these deficiencies are remedied, the apparel industry will enter the declining stage.

CONCLUSION

A Comparison of Four Industries

If we compare the historical evolution of four industries, it is possible to identify the fact that major sources of competitiveness were identical at each stage of the industrial life cycle regardless of industry type. Major sources of advantage in the early stage of all four industries were the workers and politicians and bureaucrats. In the semiconductor industry, it was the labor content of production that persuaded foreign investors to establish a whole industry. In automobiles, it was the skilled workers and state industrial policies that attracted overseas interest and, in the steel industry, it was employee skills and disciplines and the commitment of the political leader. In apparel, an abundant supply of cheap and dexterous labor and the

---

[48] Hanil Synthetic Fiber Co. Ltd. lost the title of general trading company in 1981.

government's reconstruction objectives were determinant. The state remains a major source of competitiveness in the growth stage, but entrepreneurs become more influential than workers. In the semiconductor industry, the government designated it to be strategically important, providing incentives and subsidies for research and development, while the leadership of Chairman Lee of Samsung was critical. In automobiles, Japanese automobiles faced import barriers, and Chairman Chung established the Hyundai Motor as a major international producer. Government's policies and the management of Chairman Park turned POSCO into a global leader. In the apparel industry, the government provided financial assistance through an export promotion policy, while a number of entrepreneurs like Chairman Chey of Sunkyong created general trading companies.

As an industry moves to a maturing stage, the entrepreneurs continue to be crucial sources of strength, but government is less determinant than professional managers and engineers. The professional managers of POSCO slowly but steadily enhanced efficiency and diversified the business, while engineers led the development of high value-added products. In apparels, professional managers also brought about diversification in export markets, invested abroad, and penetrated local markets.

Implications for the Korean Economy

The Korean economy possesses international competitiveness because it has a number of industries in the growth and maturing stages and common sources of advantage. In the life cycle of national competitiveness, it can be placed in the semi-developed stage category (see Figure 6-3), moving toward a developed stage. Nevertheless, Korea has been experiencing a major crisis in recent years, because the real wage level has more than doubled in just four years, the trade balance has evolved into a big deficit since 1989, and the rate of economic growth has slowed from a ten per cent level to less than six per cent in 1992. Koreans are very concerned about their economy deterioration before it reaches a par with advanced nations. What is the model telling us about Korea and its ability to reach a developed phase?

Workers and politicians and bureaucrats—the main forces of economic growth until now—should enable entrepreneurs and professional managers and engineers to take a lead. As the sources of economic growth moved from workers to government, and from government to entrepreneurs, Korea has been transformed from a less developed country into a developing country and then into a semi-developed country. In becoming a developed country, wages will inevitably be raised until they meet the marginal cost of capital needed to automate production processes, and, as democracy develops, government cannot so definitively promote certain industries at the expense of others. Korean companies cannot compete with counterparts from advanced nations by venturing into risky investments, because increased competition has lowered industry-wide marginal profits and major losses are more likely. So, if Korea is to become an advanced nation, professional managers and engineers must have a prominent role, yet workers too will have to cooperate with efforts to improve productivity. The government needs to stabilize the business environment so that planning can be conducted with greater certainty, and entrepreneurs and powerful family-business groups must bestow responsibilities and authority on corporate managers.

Implications for Other Nations

This analysis has indicated the roles which workers, politicians and technocrats, entrepreneurs, and professional managers and engineers must perform if international competitiveness is to be strengthened. Industries at an early stage of development need to invest in endowed resources; those at a growth stage must improve the business environment; those at a maturing stage must build synergy with related and supporting industries. Governments should determine their policies towards different industries based on the proper understanding of their level of international competitiveness. A comprehensive industrial policy should reinforce mutually supportive links between industries, but governments should appreciate when its active engagement is desirable and when it becomes less beneficial. Entrepreneurs, professional managers and engineers should also appreciate their varying roles in an industry's life cycle, and the organization of firms and the setting of policy have to adjust.

Limitations of the Study and Suggestions for Future Research

This research attempted to analyze the international competitiveness of a nation from static and dynamic perspectives, by using the nine-factor and the life cycle models. Caution is needed in the generalization of the nine-factor model because it has only been to Korea and the industrial life cycle approach has been tested against four Korean industries. The findings in this study need to be validated by similar and parallel work on other nations and industries.

7.   STAGE MODEL (1)

Comparison of Stage Models for Economic Development
Dong-Sung Cho

The Stages of Society   Adam Smith, 1976 (1776)
The Theory of Modern History   Karl Marx, 1951
The Stages of Economic Growth   Walt Rostow, 1971
The Third Wave   Alvin Toffler, 1980
The Competitive Development   Michael Porter, 1990
   of National Economies
Integration

Summary and Key Points

National economies are anything but static. Upgrading in an economy is the movement toward more sophisticated sources of competitive advantage and toward positions in higher productivity segments and industries. Porter extended the diamond theory to consider the national economy as a whole, and provided ways of thinking about how entire national economies progress. Porter's stage model is the newest and most rigorous. Notwithstanding, it is still useful to compare and contrast other stage models with the Porter model. This chapter deals with the stage models of Adam Smith, Karl Marx, Walt Rostow, Alvin Toffler, and Michael Porter.

Porter's theory suggests four distinct stages of national competitive development: factor-driven, investment-driven, innovation-driven, and wealth-driven stages. The first three stages involve successive upgrading of a nation's competitive advantages and are normally associated with progressively rising economic prosperity. The fourth stage is one that ultimately leads to decline. These stages provide one way of understanding how economies develop or decline.

The stage model of economic development provides a better understanding of a nation's competitiveness by further considering different development stages, and thereby should be used together with the diamond model of competitiveness. Porter recognized this need and made another contribution to this area with the introduction of a new stage model. However, the Porter stage model has some problems, which will be discussed in the next chapter.

INTRODUCTION

There are two schools of thought toward the development of human history---those who believe in stage models and those who do not. We believe that stage models do provide us with a powerful explanatory device to depict major characteristics of certain periods of human history, albeit their inherent danger is that the history is viewed as a discrete function.

Among the scholars who belong to the stage model school, Adam Smith, Karl Marx, Walt Rostow, Alvin Toffler, and Michael Porter stand up as most notable. This is because of the scientific rigor to which each of these scholars adhered. They respectively developed a paradigm or a proposition as a criterion to separate one stage from another. Furthermore, the paradigm or proposition that they respectively chose in developing their own stage model was the product of their long and hard research and insights from history.

Let us review their respective stage models and underlying paradigms or propositions, and see how they compare with one another in terms of explanatory power of human history. Only the models based on a sound paradigm or proposition will possess the explanatory power of the past, present, and future.

ADAM SMITH

According to Adam Smith, economic prosperity of a nation was a natural consequence of specialization in production through division of labor and the resulting expansion of trade. Thus he believed that the growth of a nation would halt when serious bottlenecks and limitations to specialization in production emerged. A typical example of such conditions, he argued, was the emergence of mercantilist policies in international trade. He condemned the mercantilists who were eager to accumulate gold through surpluses in international trade, on the ground that they would hamper orderly growth of free market and restrict division of labor.

In the subsequent part of the argument, Smith stated the basic principles behind the origin of government. He then showed the way in which the outlines of society and government would vary, by classifying four stages of socio-economic types: the hunting stage, the pasture stage, the agriculture stage, and the commercial stage.

The first stage is the primitive stage such as "we find it among the native tribes of North America." In this case, life is maintained through gathering the spontaneous fruits of the soil, and the dominant activities are hunting and fishing. This is the rudest way of acquiring subsistence. The communities in this stage are characterized by small size and a high degree of personal liberty. Because there is virtually no private property, disputes between different members of the community are minor. There is seldom any established administration of justice. Universal poverty establishes universal equality.

The second stage is that of pasture, a more advanced state of society such as Smith found it among the Tartars and Arabs. The use of cattle is the dominant economic activity and life tends to be nomadic. The communities are larger in size than those in the previous stage. Most dramatically, the appropriation of cattle introduces an inequality of fortune, which gives rise to regular administration or government. Property can be accumulated and transmitted from one generation to another, thus giving a great authority to those who possess it. Authority and subordination are more perfectly established. The authority of an Arabian scherif was very great; that of a Tartar khan despotical.

The third stage is agricultural society. People acquire some idea of agriculture, and the form of productive activity is changed from cattle to land. As in the previous stage, those who do not have the means of subsistence can acquire it only through the exchange of personal service. They must obey their lord for the same reason that soldiers must obey the prince who pays them. Societies become self-governing cities paying a "rent certain" to the king. The trade and manufacturers of the cities also have a significant impact on the society.

The final stage is that of commerce, where goods and services command a price, thus diminishing the power which is directly derived from the ownership of property. Most significantly, commerce is a new source of wealth which can be more widely distributed than previously, and which shifts the power from the old landed aristocracy towards a new mercantile class. As a result of a change in the mode of earning subsistence, individuals gain independence. The ancient nobility is gradually undermined and the privileges of the people are extended in the same proportion.

KARL MARX

Marx agreed with the classical growth theory that postulated the importance of market expansion for the economic growth of a nation. However, what he agreed with was not the universal law of market mechanism. Instead, he considered the importance of market mechanism applicable only in a certain stage of the human history, i.e., the capitalistic stage. He strongly believed in the evolution of the human history. Along that line, he thought of capitalism as one of the inevitable stages that the humankind must face after feudalism, but before socialism. Naturally, he argued that market mechanism would work only under capitalism.

He developed a very systematic, and at the same time, persuasive paradigm as a means to explain what was going on in the transitory period from one stage to another. In a word, his argument was such that human history becomes nothing but a series of conflicts between production power and production structure, and that the history would grow in an orderly fashion, in between the hegemonic conflicts. Here, production power is the amount of time that human beings can spend for production of goods and services at a certain point in time, while production structure is how this time of human beings can be used to produce tangible results.

He applied his logic to the historic evolution of the human race. His observation of human history started with primitive communism, in which people would form a tribe and roam around. They would typically gather berries and fruit when the weather was good. When they found animals, they would form a circle around them and squeeze so that the animals could not escape from them. Yet, without having appropriate tools for killing the animals, they apparently had enormous difficulty in catching the animals. Some used sticks to irritate the animals, while others pinched and poked them with stones and other devices. Some members of the tribe would get killed in the process. Since it was so difficult for them to make a living in such a harsh environment, they had to form a team that enabled them to produce together, possess together, and consume together. So, co-production or communism was the most natural form of production structure that the human race could ever conceive of. Nevertheless, the primitive form of communism was not efficient enough to produce more than what the people could consume. Without production surplus, communism in its early stage did not allow anybody to be away from the production structure.

In the latter stage of primitive communism, people began to use various tools and vehicles such as stone spears and knives, which in turn brought about surpluses from the production structure. People began to produce more than they could consume. These surpluses were then stored away, in preparation for future uncertainties. Noticing the surpluses of the neighboring tribes, however, some tribal groups began to find smarter ways of production. Instead of laboring hard and facing the risk of jeopardizing human lives in the midst of catching wild animals, they captured the neighboring tribes with surplus goods by surprise, robbed them of these surpluses, and enslaved them. As far as slaves produced more than they consumed, masters enjoyed surpluses as the fruits of the newly found production structure, the slavery system.

This slavery system was later changed into feudalism as the masters with large pools of slaves could not efficiently handle and control them. In other words, production power became simply too big for the existing production structure to accommodate. The early stage masters became kings, and they distributed slaves and land among generals who greatly contributed to the kings' successful possession of slaves and lands. Thus kings were turned into feudal lords, while slaves were turned into serfs and tenants. On appearance, the status of slaves was improved. Yet, the exploitative relation between the haves and the have-nots, or between the bourgeois class and the proletariat class, continued. The surpluses of production, i.e., the output above and beyond the consumption of those who produced them, remained positive. And those with power were able to take advantage of these surpluses, and accumulate wealth through the processes.

As a new form of production emerged in factories, cities embracing these facilities started to lure the serfs and tenants away from feudal manors. Feudal manors had to give way to a new production structure that would be able to swallow large pools of labor. As the people flocked into cities, however, they found no place other than firms that provided them with basic means for living in exchange for their labor. Again, surpluses of production went into the hands of the capitalists, and so capitalism boomed. Again, Capitalism showed somewhat different relations between managers and laborers, yet, the fundamental nature of their relations remained the same as before, an exploitative one.

Marx harshly criticized the capitalistic structure for its inherent contradictions. He argued that firms, which were major players in capitalism, were dominated by managers, who were only interested in exploiting the helpless laborers. However, these laborers were the most important constituents of the market. Thus their weakened power would result in the collapse of the market system, which was the very foundation of the firm.

Speculating this phenomenon, Marx argued the eventual downfall of the capitalistic society.

Marx further argued that a new production structure should be able to replace the opportunistic behavior of managers in the capitalistic era with better and more equality-oriented planners. He envisioned the arrival of socialism as the next step, in which production would be carried out by a state-owned enterprises.

Eventually, however, Marx argued that the emergence of the communistic structure of production, in which all the people would possess and share the wealth of the nation and the production structure through the communistic party and its elite leaders. Marx further argued that the eventual destination of the human history would be the restoration of the primitive communism with higher level of consumption so that all the people would be freed from the world of materialistic limitations. He called this state the communistic utopia.

In essence, Karl Marx showed the evolution of human history through his own perspective—primitive communism, slavery, feudalism, capitalism, socialism, and finally communistic utopia. According to Marx, people got astray through a series of exploitative alternatives such as slavery, feudalism and capitalism, then finally restored their balance by returning to the communistic utopia.

WALT ROSTOW

Rostow's thesis for growth stages was based on his belief of the nation-state as a major influencer of the nation's economic growth. According to Rostow, every society goes through five stages: traditional society, preconditions for take-off, take-off, the drive to maturity, and the age of high mass-consumption.

Traditional society indicates pre-Newtonian society where people would depend on a traditional way of production rather than exploring new frontiers or learning newly emerging sciences. Newton is used here as a symbol for that watershed in history when men came to believe that the external world is subject to a few knowable laws, and can be manipulated for systematic production. The central fact about traditional society is that a ceiling exists on the level of attainable output per head. This ceiling results from the fact that the potentialities, which flow from modern science and technology, are neither available nor systematically applied. In this society, people believe that the present would not be different from the past, and so would the future be not much different from the present. As far as people do not change their mindsets, there is no chance for social evolution or development.

With the precondition of scientific civilization, the emergence of a strong leadership from the central government let people begin to appreciate potentials for growth. New firms emerge and mobilize savings to invest in new ventures characterized by high risks associated with high returns. The preconditions for take-off were initially developed in Western Europe in the late seventeenth and early eighteenth centuries as the insights of modern science began to be translated into new production functions in both agriculture and industry. The more general case in modern history, however, saw the stage of preconditions arise not endogenously but from some external intrusion by more advanced societies. Although there has been some improvement, society is still characterized by traditional low-productivity methods, and old social structure and values.

In the third stage of take-off, the entire society is now ready to make a quantum leap toward industrialization and economic growth. Cities expand, and the industrial composition of a nation radically changes to higher value-added sectors. Societal and political structures also change, allowing further growth of the national economy. During the take-off new industries expand rapidly, yielding profits, a large proportion of which are reinvested in new plant; and these new industries, in turn, stimulate other sectors. The whole process of expansion in the modern sector yields an increase of income in the hands of those who not only save at high rates but place their savings at the disposal of those engaged in modern sector activities. The economy exploits hitherto unused natural resources and methods of production.

In the fourth stage of drive to maturity, the rapid transformation of traditional industries spreads around all sectors of the economy. New industries and technologies pop up, and overall productivity leaps and bounds. Some 10-20 percent of the national income is steadily invested, permitting output regularly to outstrip the increase in population. The makeup of the economy changes unceasingly as technique improves, new industries accelerate, older industries level off. The economy, focused during the take-off around a relatively narrow complex of industry and technology, extends its range into more refined and oftern more technologically complex processes.

In the final stage of high mass-consumption, people reap the benefit of the advanced economy. Diverse products and high-quality services are readily available. The leading sectors shift towards durable consumers' goods and services. For the United States, the turning point was, perhaps, Henry Ford's moving assembly line of 1913-1914; but it was in the 1920s, and again in the post-war decade, 1946-1956, that this stage of growth was pressed to its logical conclusion. In addition to these economic changes, society becomes more interested in welfare and economic security rather than simplistic economic growth. It is in this post-maturity stage, for example, that, through the political process, Western societies have chosen to allocate increased resources to social welfare and security. The emergence of the welfare state is one manifestation of a society's moving beyond technical maturity.

Rostow put a heavier emphasis on the third stage of take-off as the most pivotal in a nation's process for growth. The take-off requires all three conditions: (a) a high-growth rate of productive investment, say, 5 percent or less to over 10 percent of national income; (b) a high-growth rate of one or more substantial manufacturing sectors; and (c) the quick emergence of a new elite class and institutional framework that exploit the impulses to expansion in the modern sector and help an ongoing development toward the modern industrial society.

ALVIN TOFFLER

Although Toffler is not a scholar *per se*, his intuition as a futurist outshines all his contemporaries. Using 'source of production power' as a key word, he divides the human history into four stages: the nomadic era, the agricultural era, the industrial era, and the newly emerging information age.

When nomadic tribes roamed around in the primitive stage, the most important source of production was raw human power. Then people were swept by the first wave circa ten thousand years ago, from which they found ways to engage in agriculture by utilizing repetitive arrivals of similar weather every 365 days. In this era, land substituted human power as the most critical source of production, and the manors became the center of economic activities.

The second wave in the mid-eighteenth century allowed people to make a huge leap in productivity through industrialization. In the first wave, wealth was land; in the second wave, wealth diversified into three factors of production: land, labor, and capital. In this period, however, capital was the most important factor and substituted land as the key factor of production. Money was infused into the economic system as capital to the firms, which replaced the manors as the most important economic institution.

The third wave in the mid 1970s was even more profound in its impact upon the lives of people. With the advent of computer and telecommunication technologies, physical and time gaps between different groups of people were greatly reduced. Old paradigms of economic principles based on the scarcity of resources lost their appeal. Instead, the new economy is poised for predicting the future world, which is not necessarily bound by resource limitations. At the center of this profound transformation lies the information, which is, unlike in the old days of production, pollution-free and free of resource depletion.

Although Toffler is still fond of using the third wave as a means to explain the present phenomena, he reckons that this wave is perhaps the first of its kind in human history in terms of the power of impact upon human lives and economic activities. Toffler says that the dawn of this new civilization is the single most explosive fact of our lifetimes. We are not totally in Toffler's third wave but still in transition between the second and third waves. This is why the implications of the transformation are not immediately obvious.

In the third wave, good ideas can come from anywhere and anyone. Just as knowledge is replacing material and manpower, the old role of producer and consumer are blurring. Toffler calls this blurred role, "prosumer." Consumers are no longer a passive market upon which firms sell standardized goods but a part of the whole process in which they design products and services from their own imagination. In this new wave, there are greater demands for freedom and individualism

MICHAEL PORTER

In addition to the diamond model, Porter introduced a new stage model and provided some ways of thinking about how entire national economies progress in competitive terms. Each stage involves different industries and industry segments as well as different company strategies. Unlike previous studies, Porter focused on the postwar development of nations. The Porter model has four stages of national competitive development: factor-driven, investment-driven, innovation-driven, and wealth-driven.

In the first factor-driven stage, a nation's international competitive advantage derives solely from basic factors of production such as natural resources, favorable growing conditions for certain crops, or an abundant and inexpensive semi-skilled labor pool. In the diamond of national competitiveness, therefore, only factor conditions are an advantage. A nation's indigenous firms in such an economy compete solely on the basis of price in industries that require either little product or process technology. Nearly all developing nations and virtually all centrally planned economies are at this stage. Some prosperous nations with bountiful resources such as Canada and Australia are also at this stage.

The investment-driven stage, as its name indicates, is one where the ability and willingness to invest is the principal advantage rather than the ability to offer unique products. In this stage, there is a gradual improvement in factor conditions, demand conditions, and firm strategy, structure and rivalry. Factors are upgraded from basic to more advanced with the creation of a modern infrastructure. Home demand is largely unsophisticated but growing. Firms are highly motivated and there is a growing rivalry in some industries. However, related and supporting industries are largely undeveloped in the nation at this stage. In the postwar period, only Japan and more recently Korea have succeeded. Taiwan, Singapore, Hong Kong, Spain, and to a lesser extent Brazil are showing signs of achieving this stage. However, they are still lacking important elements, whether they are capable indigenous firms, in-house abilities to improve product and process technology, international marketing channels controlled by the nation's firms, and so on.

In the innovation stage, all the determinants of the diamond are at work and their interactions are at their strongest. This stage is called innovation-driven because firms not only appropriate and improve technology from other nations but also create them. Instead of factor cost advantages, selective factor disadvantages stimulate innovations that advance product and process technology. Consumer demand becomes increasingly sophisticated because of rising incomes, higher levels of education, and the invigorating role of domestic rivalry. World-class related and supporting industries develop in the important clusters. Firms compete with self-contained global strategies and possess their own international marketing and service networks along with growing brand reputations abroad. There is significant outbound foreign direct investment.

The final, wealth-driven stage is one that ultimately leads to decline. In this stage, the country begins to lose competitive advantage in all the determinants of the diamond. Factor advantages are not from innovative but from old ones such as brand loyalty (for example, cigarettes). Personal income begins to fall behind that in other advanced nations, eroding the quality and sophistication of home demand. Industries are characterized by falling motivation and ebbing rivalry because of more attention to preserving position than to enhancing it. Industry clusters are also thinning. In this stage, foreign firms that possess the true competitive advantage begin to acquire the nation's firms and integrate them into global strategies with the home base elsewhere. Foreign subsidiaries then erode shares for domestic competitors. Outbound foreign direct investment may be substantial despite these problems in the nation. However, the nature of foreign investment changes from technology transfer to purely financial investment.

INTEGRATION

We have reviewed paradigms or propositions of five eminent scholars on human history in this chapter: Adam Smith, Karl Marx, Walt Rostow, Alvin Toffler, and Michael Porter. The stage models that these scholars have developed can be divided into two broad categories: stage models with linear progression and stage models with circular progression.

The linear stage models postulate the development of human history from one extreme to the other, usually from an underdeveloped stage to a most developed stage in civilization and culture. Those that belong to this category are Adam Smith's model from the primitive stage to that of commerce, Walt Rostow's model from the traditional society to high mass-consumption, and Alvin Toffler's model from the nomadic era to the information age.

The circular stage models also postulate that human history starts from a certain original point or situation and goes through a series of different stages before moving to a final stage. Unlike the linear stage models, however, these circular stage models show that the final stage is either similar to the original point, or likely to be linked to a certain stage within the model. In this regard, the circular stage models suggest that history repeats itself or goes through a spring-shaped evolutionary process in the long run. Those that belong to this category are Karl Marx's model from primitive communism to communist utopia, and Michael Porter's model from the factor-driven stage to the wealth-driven stage.

Although Marx's and Porter's models belong to the same category, the nature of their models is quite different. Through his circular stage model, Marx in effect argued that human history was making a big circle before it should return to the communistic world where nobody would unduly take advantage of others. On the other hand, Porter argued that the wealth-driven stage is neither the final destination nor the most desirable stage. Instead, Porter suggested that the wealth-driven stage is the beginning of decline, and that nation in this stage must be prepared to move back to factor-driven, investment-driven, or innovation-driven stages according to each nation's special circumstances, and ready to jump-start another round of development.

The circular stage models have a distinctive advantage over the linear stage models in explaining future stages beyond the final stage described in the models respectively. In particular, Porter's model enables us to understand why and how once-advanced nations such as the United Kingdom retreat to the status of declining economy before emerging as a new global force with its investment-driven policy.

REFERENCES

Marx, Karl. 1962 (1894). *Capital: A critique of political economy*. In Vol, 3, F. Engels, editor. Moscow: Foreign Languages Publishing.

Porter, Michael E. 1990. *The competitive advantage of nations*, New York: The Free Press.

Rostow, Walt W., 1971. *The stages of economic growth.* Cambridge: Oxford University Press.

Smith, Adam. 1976 (1776). *An inquiry into the nature and causes of the wealth of nations*, Oxford: Clarendon Press.

Toffler, Alvin, 1980, *The Third Wave*, New York : Morrow.

8.   STAGE MODEL (2)

A New Stage Model and Its Application to Asian Countries
Dong-Sung Cho and Hwy-Chang Moon, 1998

Summary and Key Points

In Chapter 1, we discussed absolute advantage and comparative advantage. In today's global economy, the strategic implication concerning absolute advantage is to beat other countries, while that concerning comparative advantage is to complement other countries. Countries with similar characteristics in a certain stage (e.g., Korea and Taiwan) compete with each other, based on absolute advantages; but countries in different stages (e.g., Korea and the United States; Korea and Vietnam) complement each other, based on comparative advantages. Therefore, defining stages of economic development is important to derive strategic implications for a nation's competitiveness.

A nation's competitiveness strategy is an art of balancing and enhancing a country's absolute advantages and comparative advantages. In each stage of development, the country has to decide which factors to utilize; in which industries to invest; and where to innovate. Porter's (1990) classifications of factor-driven, investment-driven, innovation-driven and wealth-driven stages are important in development. However, factors can be further classified into physical factors and human factors, which can again be subcategorized. For this purpose, Cho (1994) presented a life cycle model and applied it to the Korean economy. Cho and Moon (1998) extended this model by adding the government variable, and studied several Asian economies.

By using two dimensions (i.e., quantity and quality) of development, Cho and Moon classify four different stages of development. In each stage they explain different sources of international competitiveness in terms of

175

physical factors, human factors, and government. This new model fits well for explaining the development patterns and strategies of Asian countries.

Source:
Cho, Dong-Sung and H. Chang Moon. 1998. A nation's international competitiveness in different stages of economic development. *Advances in Competitiveness Research*, 6(1): 5-19.

INTRODUCTION

Adam Smith told us to leave the economy alone. The invisible hand would take care of it. People would sort things out, do what they can do best, and augment the wealth of nations. However, many countries still have low income and an absence of economic growth. These countries are called "underdeveloped," "less developed," "developing," or just "poor" countries. Modern development economics studies how the development of these countries can be achieved. While their policy recommendations vary, development economists in general agree that something should be done for economic growth and development. In other words, economic growth and development cannot be achieved just by the invisible hand.

There are two important points here. One is to distinguish economic growth and economic development. Economic growth simply means quantitative growth in per capita GNP, whereas economic development means quantitative growth plus qualitative change. This qualitative change may include the rising share of industry and increasing percentage of urbanization [Gillis et al 1992]; increased self-esteem [Kasliwal 1995]; and the protection of life opportunities [United Nations Development Programme 1994]. However, one problem of these views is that they are not direct measures for economic development. More direct economic variables such as improved techniques of production are needed to measure economic development.

The other important point is to distinguish different stages and patterns of economic development. The use of terms such as "third world," "poor countries," or "developing countries" tends to obscure the diversity of these countries. They need to be further categorized into different levels of development. It should also be noted that countries follow different patterns of economic development. For example, some countries emphasize quantitative growth, while other countries (e.g., communist countries) try to achieve qualitative development rather than just GNP growth. However, most of the existing stage theories [e.g., Smith 1937; Marx 1962; Rostow 1971; Porter 1990] are not satisfactory in explaining the different paths of economic development because they focus primarily on unidirectional views of development. A new model should employ more than one explanatory variable to explain the variety of development paths.

This paper is divided into three sections. The first section discusses two dimensions of economic development and develops a new framework for measuring economic development. Based on this framework, a new model for development stages is also introduced. The subsequent section then explains the sources of a nation's international competitiveness in each stage of economic development. The final section provides a summary and conclusions.

PATTERNS OF ECONOMIC DEVELOPMENT

Two Dimensions of Economic Development

Because GNP alone is not a good measure for economic development, some alternative methods have been developed. Two of the most popular methods are Purchasing Power Parities (PPP) and Physical Quality of Life Index (PQLI). The PPP attempts to adjust international comparisons for the real purchasing power parities of national currencies. The PQLI is a composite index of infant mortality, life expectancy, and basic literacy. Based on these two methods, the first Human Development Report [United Nations Development Programme 1990] introduced a new way of measuring development—the human development index (HDI). The HDI is a composite of three basic components of human development: longevity, knowledge, and standard of living. *Longevity* is measured by life expectancy. *Knowledge* is measured by a combination of adult literacy (two-thirds weight) and mean years of schooling (one-third weight).[49] *Standard of living* is measured by purchasing power, based on real GDP per capita adjusted for the local cost of living (PPP).

The report [United Nations Development Programme 1994, p. 91] maintains that the HDI offers an alternative to GNP for measuring economic development. However, there are two problems with the HDI method. First,

---

[49] This variable is used as a proxy for development quality in this study. It is calculated as follows. For example, Japan's literacy rate is 99% and its mean years of schooling is 10.8 years. The maximum value for schooling is 15 years. The schooling index is then 0.72 (10.8 divided by 15). Therefore, Japan's education index is: 0.99 x 2 (two-thirds weight) + 0.72 x 1 (one-third weight) = 2.70. See the Human Development Report's [United Nations Development Program 1994, p. 108] technical notes for more information.

longevity is not a direct measure for economic development. Longevity may be affected by the development of medicine which is a result of economic development, but also affected by climate, geographic location, and resources such as water supply which have little to do with an economic effort. Furthermore, longevity may be negatively affected by the pollution produced in the process of economic growth in some developing countries. Second, the HDI uses the GNP per capita based on PPP to reflect not just income but also what that income can buy. The report [United Nations Development Programme 1994, p. 92] says, for example, housing and food are cheaper in Bangladesh than in Switzerland, so a dollar is worth more in Bangladesh than in Switzerland. However, a dollar is a dollar and worth the same in the global market. If you buy a Boeing 747, for instance, both Bangladesh and Switzerland have to pay the same amount of dollars, although a dollar is worth more in Bangladesh than in Switzerland. Therefore, traditional GNP serves better than PPP-based GNP to compare international purchasing power, but not domestic purchasing power.

With these two problems, the HDI may not be an alternative to traditional GNP. However, the other variable, *knowledge,* of the HDI may serve a good measure for the quality of economic development. The development quality can be defined as a capability for further growth with improved techniques of production and management. The most important variable for measuring this quality is human capital. Workers use the wide variety of skills embodied in the human mind and human capital represents the skills acquired by education. There are two types—extensity and intensity—of education. Extensity means the range of the minimum education achieved among the people in a country. Extensity of education is important because countries with people who have at least some relevant education are better positioned for development. Literacy rate is a good proxy for extensity of education. On the other hand, intensity means the depth of education which can measure the level of the workforce skills. Average years in school can serve a proxy for this variable.

Educational attainment, one of the HDI, is measured by a combination of adult literacy (two-thirds weight) and mean years of schooling (one-third weight). This index can thus serve to measure the quality of development. The Human Development Report introduced the HDI as a new method. However, this is not a good alternative to GNP, but one of the three variables of HDI can be a supplement to GNP in measuring economic development. In this paper both per capita GNP and the education index are used to measure the quantity and the quality of economic development, respectively. The data for these two dimensions of economic development for some Asian countries are shown in Table 8-1.[50]

Figure 8-1 illustrates the development patterns of these countries, measured by development quality on the horizontal axis and development quantity on the vertical axis.[51] The sample can be divided into six groups and demonstrates some interesting patterns. First, the general development pattern is to balance quantity and quality of economic development as shown in Group 1 through Group 4. The most developed country, Japan (Group 4), is followed by Asian Newly Industrialized Countries (NICs) —Singapore, Hong Kong, and South Korea (Group 3), then by the Southeast Asian countries—Malaysia and Thailand (Group 2), and finally by the less developed countries—India, Bangladesh, and Nepal (Group 1). Second, the resource-based countries such as Kuwait and Saudi Arabia (Group 5) show high levels of development quantity but low levels of development quality. Finally, communist countries such as China and Viet Nam (Group 6) show low levels of development quantity but fairly high levels of development quality. One important implication of this finding is that existing stage models of economic development, mostly focusing on unidirectional movement, need to be reconsidered in order to understand various types of development patterns.

---

[50] Data for Taiwan are not available. Philippines and Indonesia can be classified between less developed countries and developing countries. To simplify the model, however, these two countries are left out. Most of the other countries are classified as less developed countries.

[51] Vertical axis is not proportionally scaled.

Table 8-1. Data for Quantity and Quality of Economic Development

COUNTRIES	P.C.GNP US$ (1993)	LITERACY INDEX (1992)	SCHOOLING INDEX (1992)	EDUCATION INDEX (1992)
Japan	31,490	0.99	0.72	2.70
Singapore	19,850	0.92	0.27	2.11
Kuwait	19,360	0.74	0.37	1.85
Hong Kong	18,060	0.90	0.48	2.28
South Korea	7,660	0.97	0.62	2.55
Saudi Arabia	7,510	0.64	0.26	1.54
Malaysia	3,140	0.80	0.37	1.97
Thailand	2,110	0.94	0.26	2.14
Philippines	850	0.90	0.51	2.31
Indonesia	740	0.84	0.27	1.96
China	490	0.80	0.33	1.93
India	300	0.50	0.16	1.16
Bangladesh	220	0.37	0.13	0.87
Cambodia	200	0.38	0.13	0.89
Nepal	190	0.27	0.14	0.68
Viet Nam	170	0.89	0.33	2.10

Source: *World Development Report (1995)* and *Human Development Report (1994)*

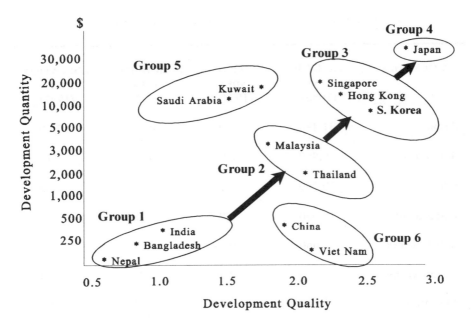

Figure 8-1. Patterns of Economic Development

A Stage Model for Economic Development

Several writers have introduced development models in terms of different stages. Smith [1937] referred to the sequence of hunting, pastoral, agricultural, commercial, and manufacturing stages. Marx [1962] proposed stages of feudalism, capitalism, and socialism. Rostow [1971] presented the famous five-stages: the traditional society, the preconditions for take-off, the take-off, the drive to maturity, and the age of high mass-consumption. Most recently, Porter [1990] suggested four distinct stages of national competitive development: factor-driven, investment-driven, innovation-driven, and wealth-driven. However, there are three problems with these traditional models. First, all of these models have adopted one type of development path. In other words, they argue that every economy always follows the same course of development with a common past and the same future. However, there are different patterns of economic development when we consider two dimensions—quantity and quality—of development as shown in Figure 8-1. Second, all of these models show some societal and industrial characteristics of development stages, but not the different levels of economic development. Smith explains just the predominant industries; Marx, the social systems; Rostow, the investment and societal characteristics; and Porter, the sources of competitiveness. These scholars overschematized the complex features of economic development. Third, the traditional models are difficult to operationalize because they do not have consistent measures across different stages.

In order to solve these problems we introduce a new framework of economic development based on our observation of the development patterns of some selected countries. The stages of economic development are illustrated in Figure 8-2. This new framework is different from the existing models as follows:

Firstly, the development pattern in this model is multidirectional starting from the less developed country. In contrast, it is unidirectional in the other existing frameworks. As the arrows in Figure 8-2 indicate, the typical development pattern is to go through less developed country, developing country, semi-developed country, and developed country in which both quantity and quality are emphasized almost on an equal weight. In contrast, two groups show different patterns of development. Resource-based developing countries such as Kuwait and Saudi Arabia have achieved a significant quantity development, but not a quality development. This is the reason why these economies are not classified as developed countries although they have high per capita GNP. Therefore, one important policy implication for these countries is to enhance their development quality. Communist countries such as China and Viet Nam are the opposite. They have made more judicious use of their income to improve the capabilities of their people, i.e., the quality of development. However, the relatively low level of per capita income and the rigid economic system have not given economic incentives to their people. A policy advice to these countries is to increase economic growth by providing more incentives to economic performance. Some countries have adopted different patterns of economic development because of the abundance of natural resources or because of different political systems. In the long run, however, they have to follow the normal pattern of development in which quantity and quality of development are balanced.

Secondly, this new model uses comprehensive terms in identifying different stages of development—less developed country, developing country, semi-developed country, and developed country. These development stages are then explained by two dimensions of quantity and quality. In contrast, other scholars use very specific terms thereby policy implications are very limited. Porter [1990], for example, used terms for development stages, i.e., factor-driven, investment-driven, etc. However, factors are important not just in the initial stage but in every stage of economic development. The question is: "which factor is important in which stage of development?" From this perspective, Cho [1994] explained development stages with two types of factors—physical and human factors. In this study we employ one more variable, *government*, which is also very important in every stage of economic development. These three are the main sources of international competitiveness for enhancing the levels of the two dimensions—quantity and quality—of development. This will be discussed in the next section.

Finally, this model is useful in operationalizing the development concepts, i.e., in comparing and contrasting various types or stages of development by using two consistent criteria—quantity and quality—of development. In contrast, the traditional models have different criteria in each development stage, thereby having difficulty in operationalization. For example, Porter [1990] distinguishes investment-driven and innovation-driven stages. What if a country has both more investment and innovation than the other country? For operationalization a development model should have consistent criteria to compare different levels of development.

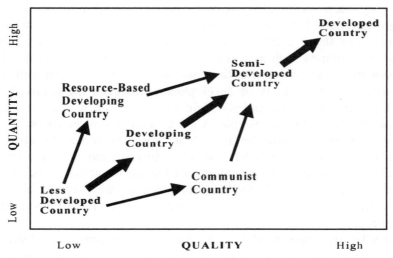

Figure 8-2. Stages of Economic Development

In this new framework the initial stage is less developed country which is the poorest country and the potential for growth is also the lowest. The next stage is developing country which is dynamic, industrializing, and moving forward in terms of both quantity and quality of development. The terms less developed country and developing country have been interchangeably used in the literature of development economics and international business. However, there is a clear distinction between these two types. A less developed country is stagnated and has not moved forward yet, while a developing country, as its name implies, is moving ahead and one stage further developed than a less developed country. A further advanced stage is Semi-Developed Country which is no longer poor and has a great potential for quality in further development. Asian Newly Industrialized Countries (NICs) fall in this category. These countries have usually been called high-income less developed countries or developing countries. However, it is appropriate to call them Semi-Developed Countries because they are not poor and they are different from developing countries. The final stage is developed country which has high achievements in both quantity and quality of development.

SOURCES OF INTERNATIONAL COMPETITIVENESS

Competitiveness and the relevant strategies should be understood and designed at various levels of product, firm, industry, and nation [Moon & Peery 1995]. The most popular definition of competitiveness at the national level can be found in the Report of the President's Commission on Competitiveness, written for the Reagan administration in 1984 as follows:

A nation's competitiveness is the degree to which it can, under free and fair market conditions, produce goods and services that meet the test of international markets while simultaneously expanding the real incomes of its citizens. Competitiveness at the national level is based on superior productivity performance.

Some scholars have a similar view to this. For example, Porter [1990, p. 6] says that the only meaningful concept of competitiveness at the national level is national productivity. One problem with this definition is that competitiveness is confused with productivity. Competitiveness and productivity are different. A nation can sometimes enhance its competitiveness by changing strategies (e.g., protectionism, currency devaluation), without any increase in productivity. Productivity refers to the internal capability of an organization, while competitiveness refers to the relative position of an organization against its competitors. These two important concepts are often confused and are used interchangeably. The relative competitive position in the international market, not just the absolute amount of productivity, is the critical element for a nation's competitiveness.

There is another important point in defining a nation's competitiveness. It is meaningful only among the nations endowed with similar comparative advantages competing in similar industries. For example, it may not be very meaningful to say that Korea is in general less competitive than the United States because these two countries have different comparative advantages. In contrast, it is very meaningful to say that Korea is less (or more) competitive than Taiwan because these two countries are very similar in terms of comparative advantages and the areas of competition in the international market. Therefore, the relative competitive position among similar countries in a certain stage of economic development, but not among all the countries in the world, is another important element for a nation's competitiveness.

Combining these two important elements, a nation's competitiveness can now be defined as a nation's relative competitive position in the international market among the nations of a similar economic development. It is thus very important to have a good model of development stages for an analysis of a nation's competitiveness. In this section we will discuss the sources of international competitiveness of a nation based on the stage model of economic development developed in the previous section. The sources of international competitiveness will be discussed from three perspectives— physical factors, human factors, and government. The relationship between the stages of economic development and the sources of international competitiveness is summarized in Table 8-2.

Less Developed Stage

Countries in this stage are characterized by low quantity and low quality of development. Their per capital GNP is less than US$ 1,000 in 1993.[52] Their

---

[52] The World Development Report [World Bank 1995] has a different classification for groups. They are: low-income, $695 or less; lower-middle-income, $696~$2,785; upper-middle-income, $2,786~$8,625; and high-income, $8,626 or

education index is lower than 1.5. India, Bangladesh, and Nepal fall in this category. The sources of international competitiveness in this stage are natural resources (physical factors) and/or non-trained workers (human factors). However, because their incomes are low and their production capabilities are quite limited, these resources are not efficiently utilized. The government role here is critical. The government must pursue an open-door policy and encourage inbound foreign direct investment (FDI). These countries need capital for investment and technology for production. They can solve these two problems simultaneously by attracting multinational firms through FDI. Therefore, the most important source of international competitiveness in this less developed stage is the pro-Western or pro-capitalist policy of the government. Many less developed countries do not have this kind of policy and leave their economies stagnated.

Table 8-2.Development Stages and the Sources of International Competitiveness

	LESS DEVELOPED STAGE	DEVELOPING STAGE	SEMI-DEVELOPED STAGE	DEVELOPED STAGE
PHYSICAL FACTOR	Natural Resources	Basic Infrastructure	Clustering	Advanced Infrastructure
HUMAN FACTOR	Non-trained Workers	Trained Workers	Entrepreneurs	Professionals
GOVERNMENT	Inbound FDI Open-door	Exporting Learning	Outbound FDI ST Industry	World-class Fair Resource Distribution
EXAMPLES	India Bangladesh Nepal	Malaysia Thailand	Singapore Hong Kong Korea	Japan

more. According to this classification, however, Malaysia ($3,140) and Thailand ($2,110) should be in different groups. Korea ($7,660) and other NICs should also be in different groups. In order to put similar countries in the same group we use the classification, for the quantitative dimension of development, as follows: less developed stage, $1,000 or less; developing stage, $1,000—$5,000; semi-developed stage, $5,000—$20,000; and developed stage, $20,000 or more.

Scholars advocating dependency theory share the view that economic problems in poor nations arise from unequal relations of power between rich and poor nations. They also provide a common solution that progress for a poor nation is possible only if its ties to the international capitalist system are severed. However, the weakest point in this analysis is that it views the international capitalist system as a zero-sum game. In other words, it views that the rich nation or the multinational firm always exploits the poor nation, but not that there is a possibility of mutual benefits. Multinational firms in general increase the productivity of the host country's factors of production and contribute to its economic development [Moon & Roehl 1993]. In reality many countries with close ties to the international capitalist system have achieved rapid economic growth and, in some cases, even a reduction in income inequality. Asian NICs are good examples. There are few countries which have achieved economic development without increasing their involvement in the international economic system. The government of a country in this less developed stage must increase the productivity of natural resources and workers by integrating them into the capital and technology of multinational firms. Opening the door to international business is the first step for a less developed country to move forward.

Developing Stage

The countries in this stage overcome the inertia of the less developed stage and begin to move forward. Their per capita GNP is growing fast and their workers are now being trained. Their per capital GNP is between US$ 1,000 and 5,000 in 1993. Their education index is around 2.0. Malaysia and Thailand are included in this group. The sources of international competitiveness in this stage are basic infrastructure (e.g., roads, ports, financial markets, and other socio-economic environments) and trained workers. The government must make a significant effort to enhance the quality of these physical and human factors to ensure continuous growth.

International involvement is also important in this stage. Countries in this stage usually produce labor-intensive products in mature industries with technologies learned from multinational firms. Therefore, the government must pursue policies to promote technology transfers from multinational firms. These countries must also depend on foreign markets for the sale of their products because their own domestic markets are not well developed. To promote exports, the government may have to pursue various policies such as export subsidies and currency devaluation. Despite the increase in exports, these countries may have current account deficits because of increased imports of raw materials and other intermediary goods. The government may have to impose trade barriers to reduce imports and to protect some infant industries. Macroeconomic policies such as technology transfer, export subsidies, currency devaluation, and protectionism are thus very important and popular policies in this stage of economic development.

In the development process, the government has two alternative strategies. One is "balanced growth"—the simultaneous investment in a wide range of industries [Nurkse 1953]. The other is "unbalanced growth" —investment in a few of the most productive industries that take advantage of forward and backward linkages in the production process. The government usually allocates scarce resources to a few industries and even to a few companies in each industry at a time. Major industries in this stage of development are thus monopolized by a single or a few firms. One side-effect of this unbalanced growth strategy is an inequality in income distribution.

However, income inequality is not always bad for economic development. Some scholars [e.g., Lewis 1954] argue that inequality is not just a necessary effect of economic growth; it is also a cause of growth. The rationale is that a distribution of income that favors high-income groups contributes to growth because high-income profit-earners save to obtain funds for expanding their enterprises. The more income they receive, the more they invest. In many high-performing economies, inequality first increases, but later diminishes as development takes place. A World Bank Policy Research Report [1993] studied 40 economies in terms of the ratio of the income share of the richest fifth of the population to the income share of the poorest fifth and per capita real GDP growth during 1965—1989. The report found that rapid growth and declining inequality have been shared virtues for the high-performing Asian economies including Japan, the four tigers (Korea, Taiwan, Hong Kong, and Singapore), and some Southeast Asian countries (Malaysia, Thailand, and Indonesia). Fair distribution of income may be one of the economic objectives that countries have to achieve in the long run, but a certain degree of inequality may be unavoidable in the process of rapid growth.

Semi-Developed Stage

Countries in this stage have graduated from the developing stage. They are no longer poor. Their per capital GNP is between US$ 5,000 and 20,000 in

1993. Their education index is around 2.5. Korea, Hong Kong, and Singapore fall in this stage. They are not in the developing, but partially developed stage. Their international strategies are now quite different. They cannot compete with other developing countries in the labor-intensive products. Their labor costs are now much higher than those of other developing countries. They now must compete with other developed countries. Their area of competition is no longer mature industries, but new and growing industries. Therefore, the most important strategic recommendation for these countries is to develop some world-class industries such as semi-conductors which have great effects on the backward and forward linkages.

Since they are late comers vis-à-vis other developed countries, these countries must be more efficient than their competitors in developing world-class industries. Two important strategies may be suggested. One strategy is to create a clustering such as a science park where several related industries are located close together. This will maximize synergies among the related sectors and will minimize transportation and transaction costs. This can be done at the corporate level as well as the industry level. Samsung Electronics Co., for instance, has enhanced synergies among the related businesses of electronics and become a world-class producer of semi-conductors. One important implication is that the Korean government should not try just to dismantle the conglomerates or *chaebols*, but to encourage synergies among the related businesses.

The other strategy is to encourage entrepreneurship. Entrepreneurs are innovative, proactive, and risk-taking. They are critically important in undertaking the most productive, but risky enterprises. Entrepreneurship, unlike other human skills, cannot be cultivated by spending money on education. To encourage entrepreneurship, the government should provide venture capital, a rewarding system (e.g., awards, patents), and so on. In this stage of development, the role of government is very important in creating and promoting new physical and human factors as the sources of international competitiveness.

Developed Stage

Countries in the developed stage are advanced in terms of both quantity and quality of development. In our sample only one country—Japan—is categorized in this stage. Japan's per capita GNP is greater than US$ 30,000 and its education index is 2.7. Countries in this stage also need quite different sources of competitiveness from those of the countries in other stages.

Countries in this stage must develop an advanced infrastructure which is the world-best. Advanced infrastructure means more than just basic infrastructure such as roads and ports. It means a quality education system, well-developed research & development facilities, socio-political stability, and other environments in which businesses can be performed most efficiently. The role of entrepreneurs (i.e., the human factor) becomes less important in this stage as the economy becomes more stable and predictable. Instead, professional managers, engineers, and educators become important to sustain the advanced status of development.

In the developed stage, the government should be very careful in directing the flow of resources because the economy is so comprehensive. The main role of government in this stage is to help maintain a fair distribution of resources and let the professionals do their work. This does not mean that government should not do anything. On the contrary, the role of government is critical. The government should constantly monitor and respond to the changing international environment to maintain the world-class business location where the resources are most efficiently allocated.

SUMMARY AND CONCLUSIONS

The quantitative measure of per capita GNP is not enough to measure the level of economic development; development should also include the qualitative dimension. This paper developed a model which employed the educational index as a qualitative measure, together with the quantitative measure of per capita GNP. This two-dimensional model is useful in explaining different patterns of economic development. For example, the model explains why Kuwait and Saudi Arabia are not classified as developed countries, although their per capita GNP is high. The model also explains the development pattern of communist countries. The model is useful in suggesting some important policy recommendations for countries in a certain group of economic development. In the semi-developed stage, for instance, Hong Kong and Singapore have higher levels of development quantity, but lower levels of development quality than Korea. These economies thus have to focus more on enhancing the development quality for further and more balanced development.

Countries used to be broadly classified as poor and rich countries. The poor countries have been interchangeably referred to less developed countries, developing countries, or newly industrialized (semi-developed) countries. This paper distinguishes these countries and develops a stage model for economic development. There are three important differences between this new model and the traditional stage models. First, the new model shows a possibility of multi-directional development paths, while the existing models are mostly uni-directional. Second, the new model uses more general, comprehensive terms for describing the development stages, while the existing models use very specific terms which describe some characteristics of stages but not their general status of development. Third, the new model is useful in operationalizing the development concepts by comparing two consistent variables across different stages, while the existing models are weak in operationalization because they use different criteria in different stages.

Finally, this paper explains different sources of international competitiveness in each stage of economic development. The role of government is particularly important in improving both physical and human factors in each stage. If the government is unable to play an active, positive role, the government itself can be a barrier to development. This does not mean that the government should be involved in every aspect of the economy. The areas of government intervention change as development stages evolve. Protectionism, for instance, may be a useful policy in the developing stage, but certainly not in the developed stage. An active, positive role of government should be conducted in the right areas in the right stage of economic development.

This paper can be further extended. First, the data used in this study are for Asian countries. It would be interesting to compare these countries with those of other regions such as Europe and Latin America. Second, this paper explains sources of international competitiveness from three perspectives—physical factors, human factors, and the government. If updated data for these variables are available for a group of countries in a certain level of development, the NICs, for instance, some interesting policy implications can be derived.

REFERENCES

Cho, Dong-Sung. 1994. A dynamic approach to international competitiveness: The case of Korea. *Journal of Far Eastern Business.* 1(1): 17-36.

Gillis, Malcolm, Dwight H. Perkins, Michael Roemer & Donald R. Snodgrass. 1992. *Economics of development.* New York: Norton & Company.

Hirschman, Albert O. 1958. The strategy of economic development. New Haven, Conn.: Yale University Press.

Kasliwal, Pari. 1995. *Development economics.* Cincinnati: South-Western Publishing Co.

Kravis, Irving B. 1986. The three faces of the international comparison project. *World Bank Research Observer*, January.

Lewis, Arthur W. 1954. Economic development with unlimited supplies of labor. *The Manchester School* 22 (May): 139-191.

Marx, Karl. 1962 (1894). *Capital: A critique of political economy.* In Vol, 3, F. Engels, editor. Moscow: Foreign Languages Publishing.

Moon, H. Chang & Newman Peery. 1995. Competitiveness of product, firm, industry, and nation in a global business. *Competitiveness Review.* 5(1): 37-43.

Moon, H. Chang & Thomas W. Roehl. 1993. An imbalance theory of foreign direct investment. *Multinational Business Review.* Spring: 56-65.

Nurkse, Ragnar. 1953. Problems of capital formation in underdeveloped countries. New York: Oxford University Press.

Porter, Michael E. 1990. *The competitive advantage of nations.* New York: The Free Press.

President's Commission on Industrial Competitiveness. 1985. *Global competition: The new reality.* Washington, D.C.: U.S. Government Printing Office.

Rostow, Walt W. 1971 (1960) *Stages of economic growth.* 2nd ed. New York: Cambridge University Press.

Smith, Adam. 1937 (1776). *An inquiry into the nature and causes of the wealth of nations.* New York: The Modern Library.

United Nations Development Programme. 1990. *Human development report 1990.* New York: Oxford University Press

United Nations Development Programme. 1994. *Human development report 1994.* New York: Oxford University Press

World Bank. 1995. *World development report: Workers in an integrating world.* Oxford: Oxford University Press.

World Bank Policy Research Report. 1993. The East Asian miracle: Economic growth and public policy. Oxford: Oxford University Press.

9.   HOW TO MEASURE COMPETITIVENESS

National Competitiveness Report:
Critical Comparison of Their Theoretical and Methodological Soundness

Hwy-Chang Moon and Dong-Sung Cho

Summary and Key Points

The two most popular institutes publishing competitiveness reports are the International Institute for Management Development (IMD) and the World Economic Forum (WEF). From 1989 to 1995 these two institutes had published the report in cooperation, but since 1996 they have been publishing two separate reports. Although they are separate, both institutes use almost the same variables to measure competitiveness. However, there are significant discrepancies in the rankings of countries between the two reports, mainly because they use different methodologies, including different weights on each variable. We will critically evaluate the theoretical and the methodological approaches of these reports.

The main problem of existing reports is due to their lack of strong theoretical background. Without a rigorous theoretical explanation, it is not clear why some factors are important while others are not. In order to solve the problems of existing competitiveness reports, we introduce a new competitiveness report, based on the nine-factor model, an extension of Porter's diamond model. We have chosen the nine-factor model because it is particularly useful in understanding the role of different types of people for a nation's competitiveness.

In this new report, a nation's competitiveness is defined as a nation's relative competitive position in the international market among the nations of a similar economic development. In this regard, the report contains rankings among similar nations, as well as the overall rankings. Among the factors of competitiveness, the current report focuses on resources, which are classified into human, natural, and capital resources. Other factors will be studied in the future issues of this report. Although the current report does not include all the variables, the results of this report support some of the interesting arguments of the new competitiveness models we have discussed in previous chapters and provide important implications to understand the real world.

INTRODUCTION

Competitiveness is now a buzzword, despite the fact that there is no consensus of what competitiveness really is. Factors affecting competitiveness are quite controversial. In recent years of rapid globalization, competitiveness is often compared across countries by rankings. However, rankings may be misleading if they are not based on a rigorous model and an appropriate methodology.

There are already several existing competitiveness reports, but these reports are not satisfactory. Policy makers are often so sensitive to the results of these reports that they may be misled to pursue undesirable policies. We have introduced a new competitiveness report in which we have corrected some theoretical and methodological problems of the existing reports. We hope that both scholars and practitioners will find useful implications from this report. This new competitiveness report has collected and analyzed the data for competitiveness variables, based on the nine-factor model that is an extension of the diamond model. In this report, three types of resources are highlighted. Other competitiveness variables will be treated in the future issues of this report.

All the relevant data have been collected from statistical sources published by international and government organizations. The Korean Trade-Investment Promotion Agency (KOTRA) offices abroad have greatly helped us obtain the data. Raw data are transformed to standardized indices in order to control different scales of data values. An overall index for each of the three main factors is then calculated by taking a simple average of the standardized indices for all sub-factors within each main factor. Finally, rankings are given based on the overall indices.

Competitiveness can be defined as a nation's relative competitive position in the international market among the nations with similar economic development. This implies that competitiveness scores and rankings may be more meaningful among similar nations. The new report contains rankings among similar nations, as well as the overall rankings.

WHY DO WE NEED A NEW COMPETITIVENSS REPORT?

The two most popular institutes publishing competitiveness reports are the International Institute for Management Development (IMD) and the World Economic Forum (WEF). From 1989 to 1995 these two institutes published the report in cooperation. Since 1996 they have published separate reports. When these reports are published they send shock waves through some nations that make headlines in the newspapers for several days. However, readers are confused because there are significant discrepancies in the rankings between these two reports.

For example, the IMD 1997 report ranks Korea 30th among 46 countries. This is a three-step fall from 27th place in 1996. According to this report, Korea is evaluated below China and Argentina. In the WEF 1997 report, Korea is ranked 21st among 53 countries. This is an one-step fall from 20th place in 1996. In this report, however, Korea is evaluated above China and Argentina. Rankings of other countries such as Japan and Malaysia are also confusing. Japan is far above Malaysia in the IMD 1997 report, but far below in the WEF 1997 report. For the most recent 1999 rankings, Korea, for example, is ranked in the lower group (38th among 47 countries) in the IMD report, but ranked in the higher group (22nd among 59 countries) in the WEF report. With these big differences the validity of these reports is very doubtful.

PROBLEMS OF EXISTING COMPETITIVENESS REPORTS

A careful examination of these two reports reveals some significant problems that can be summarized as follows:

Theoretical Background

The two reports have different views on the definition of competitiveness. The IMD defines competitiveness as "the ability of a country to create added value and thus increase national wealth ... (IMD, 1996, p. 42)." This definition may imply that GDP and productivity can be proxies for competitiveness, but the IMD argues that competitiveness cannot be reduced to the mere notions of GDP and productivity (IMD, 1996, p. 42). In contrast, the WEF accepts GDP and/or productivity as proxies for competitiveness by defining competitiveness as "the ability of a national economy to achieve sustained high rates of economic growth, as measured by the annual change in gross domestic product per person (WEF, 1996, p. 19).

While their definitions of competitiveness are different, both institutes have chosen almost the same factors of competitiveness. The IMD has first chosen two factors—domestic economy and internationalization—and then added six other factors—government, management, finance, infrastructure, science and technology, and people. However, there are conceptual redundancies between the first two factors and the additional six factors because the latter six factors can be classified as either domestic or international variables. In the WEF report, the first two factors are slightly changed: from domestic economy to civil institutions and internationalization to openness, while the other six factors are the same. The factors of competitiveness in these two reports are contrasted in Table 9-1.

Table 9-1. Comparing the Existing two Reports

IMD Report	WEF Report
Domestic Economy	(Civil) Institutions
Internationalization	Openness
Government	Government
Management	Management
Finance	Finance
Infrastructure	Infrastructure
Science and Technology	Technology
People	Labor

Different Weights

The IMD report contains both hard data that are statistical indicators published by organizations, and soft data which are survey data compiled from executives. Because soft data may be volatile, the IMD applies a one-third/two-thirds balance between hard and soft data. On the other hand, the WEF applies quite different weights. According to this report, the four factors—openness, government, finance, and labor—are given a weight of three; the two other factors—infrastructure and technology—are given a weight of two; the remaining two factors—management and civil institutions are given a weight of one. Hence, the weighting of factors is somewhat arbitrary.

The WEF argues that weights have been chosen both using evidence in academic literature, as well as its own preliminary evidence using the most recent data. However, weights should vary across different environments and stages of economic development. For example, technology may be more important for developed countries, but natural resources may be more important for less developed countries. The role of government may also be different as a nation develops from one stage to another. It is not appropriate to apply pre-determined, arbitrary weights to all nations in different stages of economic development.

Subjective Opinions

A great portion of data in the two reports is based on executive opinion survey. They are very subjective and thus may not be very reliable. In addition, the low response rate makes this problem more serious. For example, the IMD (1996, p. 44) sent questionnaires to about 21,000 executives, but only 15% of them have been returned. Although the sample size is big, there is a significant non-response bias. The survey method is useful when we need data that are not published, but important for our research purpose. However, extreme dependence on the survey data, together with their arbitrary weights, will produce volatile and unreliable results.

THE NEW COMPETITIVENESS REPORT

In order to solve the problems of existing competitiveness reports, this new competitiveness report is designed as follows:

An Extended Diamond Model

The main problem of existing reports is due to their lack of strong theoretical background. Without a rigorous theoretical explanation, it is not clear why some factors are important and others not. Our new competitiveness report is based on the nine-factor model, an extension of Michael Porter's (1990) diamond model.

To investigate why nations gain competitive advantage in particular industries and the implications for company strategy and national economies, Porter conducted a four-year study of ten nations. Porter concluded that nations succeed in particular industries because their home environment is the most forward-looking, dynamic, and challenging. Specifically, the determinants are factor conditions; demand conditions; related and supporting industries; and firm strategy, structure, and rivalry, as shown in Figure 9-1. In addition, there are two outside variables: government and chance.

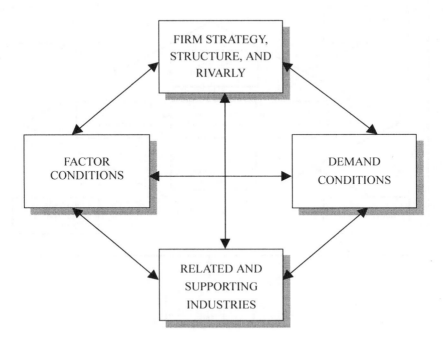

Figure 9-1. The Diamond Model

Porter's diamond model has been extended by several scholars. Moon, Rugman, and Verbeke (1995, 1998) extended it to a generalized double diamond model that appropriately incorporates multinational activity and government. Cho (1994) also argued that Porter's original model has a limited application to developing countries. He emphasized different groups of human factors and different types of physical factors in explaining a nation's competitiveness. Human factors include workers, politicians and bureaucrats, entrepreneurs, and professionals. Physical factors include endowed resources, domestic demand, related and supporting industries, and other business environment. An external factor, chance, is added to these eight internal factors to make a new paradigm, the nine-factor model, as shown in Figure 9-2. As a basis for this report, we have chosen the nine-factor model because it is particularly useful in understanding the role of different types of people for a nation's competitiveness.

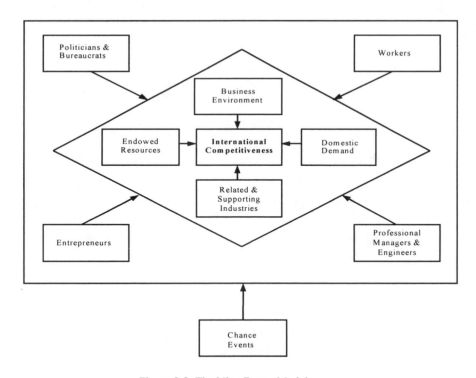

Figure 9-2. The Nine Factor Model

Equal Weights

Arbitrary weights overstate or understate the effects of variables. Thus, results of the study may be misleading. Both IMD and WEF reports have eight factors that are almost the same, but produce quite different results. This is mainly due to the fact that they apply different weights to the variables. In our report, equal weights are applied. However, as stated before, the relative importance of factors varies across national environments and stages of economic development. Policy makers can thus modify the data of this report by applying different weights to fit the unique situations of their economies.

Quantitative Data Only

Our report uses quantitative data only, not survey data. As mentioned, survey data are subjective and thus unreliable. All of our data were obtained from publications by international and government organizations. This would have been impossible without the cooperation of KOTRA. Many of the data needed were either missing or out-dated in the available publications. KOTRA offices abroad helped us obtain the necessary data from the most recent publications of the local governments.

SCOPE OF THIS REPORT

Competitiveness and the relevant strategies should be understood and designed at various levels of product, firm, industry, and nation. The most popular definition of competitiveness at the national level can be found in the Report of the President's Commission on Competitiveness, written for the Reagan administration in 1984 as follows:

> *A nation's competitiveness is the degree to which it can, under free and fair market conditions, produce goods and services that meet the test of international markets while simultaneously expanding the real incomes of its citizens. Competitiveness at the national level is based on superior productivity performance.*

Some scholars have a similar view to this. For example, Porter (1990, p. 6) says that the only meaningful concept of competitiveness at the national level is national productivity. Krugman (1994, p.32) also says that competitiveness would turn out to be a funny way of saying productivity and would have nothing to do with international competition. However, competitiveness and productivity are conceptually different. A nation can sometimes enhance its competitiveness by changing strategies (e.g., protectionism, currency devaluation), without any increase in productivity. Productivity refers to the internal capability of an organization, while competitiveness refers to the relative position of an organization against its competitors. These two important concepts are often confused and used interchangeably. The relative competitive position in the international market, not just the absolute amount of productivity, is a critical element for a nation's competitiveness.

Another important point in defining a nation's competitiveness is that it may be more meaningful among the nations endowed with similar comparative advantages competing in similar industries (Cho and Moon, 1998). For example, it may not be very meaningful to say that Korea is in general less competitive than the United States because these two countries have different comparative advantages. In contrast, it is very meaningful to say that Korea is less (or more) competitive than Taiwan because these two countries are very similar in terms of comparative advantages and the areas of competition in the international market. Therefore, the relative competitive position among similar countries in a certain stage of economic development, but not among all the countries in the world, is another important element for a nation's competitiveness.

If we combine these two important elements, a nation's competitiveness can now be defined as a nation's relative competitive position in the international market among the nations of a similar economic development. In this regard, our report contains rankings among the similar nations, as well as the overall rankings.

Among the factors of competitiveness, the current report focuses on resources. Other factors will be studied in the future issues of this report. Resources are classified into three categories—human, natural, and capital resources. The three main factors and their sub-factors that are used to determine the competitiveness of the main factors are shown in Table 9-2. Major differences between this report and other reports are illustrated in Table 9-3.

Table 9-2. Competitiveness Variables in the New Report

Main Factors	Sub-Factors
Human Resources	Total Employment Employment Rate Output-Input Index Education Index Attitude Index Working Hours
Natural Resources	Oil Balance Energy Balance Tourism Receipts Land Area per capita
Capital Resources	Capital Liquidity Capital Value Exchange Rate Stability

Table 9-3. Comparing the Three Competitiveness Reports

	IMD	WEF	IPS
Name of the report	The World Competitiveness Yearbook	The Global Competitiveness Report	The National Competitiveness Report
Sponsoring Institution	International Institute for Management Development	World Economic Forum	The Institute of Industrial Policy Studies
Location	Lausanne, Switzerland	Geneva, Switzerland	Seoul, Korea
Year started	1989	1996	1998
Theoretical base	No particular theory	No particular theory	Extended diamond model (9-factor model)

Table 9-3. (Continued)

Name of the report	IMD The World Competitiveness Yearbook	WEF The Global Competitiveness Report	IPS The National Competitiveness Report
Key factors	A collection of 8 factors - Domestic economy - Internationalization - Government - Management - Finance - Infrastructure - Science & Technology - People	A collection of 8 factors - Civil institutions (C) - Openness (O) - Government (G) - Management (M) - Finance (F) - Infrastructure (I) - Technology (T) - Labor (L)	A collection of 9 factors **4 human factors** - Workers - Politicians & bureaucrats - Entrepreneurs - Professionals **4 Non-human factors** - Resources - Demand - Related industries - Business environment **Chance event**
Source of data	- Published data - Questionnaire survey	- Published data - Questionnaire survey	- Published data - 114 KOTRA offices
Weights	**Hard vs. Soft data** - All hard data: 2/3 of total - All soft data: 1/3 of total - Not individual, but total **Number of criteria** Domestic economy (28) Internationalization (40) Government (43) Finance (20) Infrastructure (30) Management (34) Science & Tech. (20) People (44)	**Hard vs. Soft data** - 75% hard 25% soft: O, G, F, L - 25% hard 75% soft: I, T - 100% soft: M, C **Factor Weights** (Civil) Institutions (1/18) Openness (1/6) Government (1/6) Management (1/18) Finance (1/6) Infrastructure (1/9) Technology (1/9) Labor (1/6)	**Equal weights** In the final report of the year 2000, different weights of the variables will be applied for countries at different stages of development (e.g., more weight on technology and less weight on natural resources for developed countries; and vice versa for less developed countries).
Number of countries in the study	Overall ranking: 46 countries	Overall ranking: 53 countries	Overall ranking: 51 countries Intra-group ranking:* - 29 OECD countries - 4 first NICs - 4 second NICs - 15 LDCs

Table 9-3. (Continued)

Name of the report	IMD	WEF	IPS
	The World Competitiveness Yearbook	The Global Competitiveness Report	The National Competitiveness Report
Strengths	– The first, largest survey on Competitiveness – Direct information from executives	Similar to IMD, but better than IMD in elaborating the variables	– Strong theoretical basis with minimum multicollinearity – Consistent survey through KOTRA offices – Useful information of intra-group rankings
Weaknesses	– Weak theoretical basis – Redundancies between the first two variables (domestic economy, internationalization) and other six variables. – Low response rate and subjective methodology – Inappropriateness of executives' opinions for national competitiveness	In general, similar to IMD, but more emphasis on soft data. Specifically, – Weak theoretical basis and redundancies between variables – Unconvincing methodology and weights – Inappropriateness of executives' opinions for national competitiveness	– No soft data – Incomplete (the whole report will be completed in 2000)

* Generally speaking, OECD members are developed countries; the first Newly Industrialized Countries (NICs) are semi-developed countries; the second NICs are developing countries; LDCs are less developed countries. For this new classification of countries, see Cho and Moon (1998). Specifically, the first NICs are Singapore, Hong Kong, Taiwan, and Korea; the second NICs are Malaysia, Indonesia, Thailand, and the Philippines. Since Korea is also a member of OECD, it is double counted in both the first NICs and OECD.

METHODOLOGY

Because the data have different scales, the first step is to standardize all the values of sub-factors as follows:

Index = (actual X_i - minimum X_i) / (maximum X_i - minimum X_i) x 100

The second step is to take a simple average of these standardized (STD) indices for all sub-factors within a main factor in order to get an overall index for the factor. The final step is to give rankings based on these overall indices. Calculating steps can be summarized as follows:

Raw Data $\Rightarrow$ STD Index $\Rightarrow$ Overall Index $\Rightarrow$ Ranking

The data are calculated and analyzed based on the principles as shown in Table 9-4. Major data sources for the variables are shown in Table 9-5.

Table 9-4. Principles of Calculation and Analysis

Human Resources	
Total Employment	Annual average for 3 years
Employment Rate	Annual average for 3 years
= 1 - Unemployment Rate	
Output-Input Index	Annual change for 3 years
= GDP/ Wages	
Education Index	Most recent data
= Literacy Rate + Enrollment Ratio	
Attitude Index	Annual average for 3 years
= 1 - Labor Disputes	
= 1 - X_i/Maximum X	
Where X_i is the number of workers involved in strikes and lockouts in each country	Annual average for 3 years
	Working Hours
Natural Resources	
Oil Balance (Export - Import)	Annual average for 3 years
Energy Balance (Export - Import)	Annual average for 3 years
Tourism Receipts	Annual average for 3 years
Land Area per capita	Most recent data
Capital Resources	
Capital Liquidity	Annual average for 3 years
= 1- Lending Interest Rate	
Capital Value	Annual average for 3 years
= 1- Inflation Rate	
Exchange Rate Stability	Annual change for 3 years
= 1 - Exchange Rate Fluctuations	

Table 9-5. Variables and Major Sources

Human Resources

Total Employment	IFS: 67e, HDR: Table 16 & 32, ISY, SYT
Unemployment Rate	IFS: 67r, YLS: Ch. 3, ISY, SYT
GDP	IFS: 66..c, SYT
Wages	IFS: 65ey, YLS: Ch.5 & 6, ISY, SYT
Education Index	HDR: p.146 (1997 edition)
Labor Dispute	YLS: Ch. 9, ISY, SYT
Working Hours	YLS: Ch. 4, HDR: Table 32, ISY, SYT

Natural Resources

Oil Balance	ISY, SYT
Energy Balance	ISY, HDR: Table 23 & 43, SYT, ESY
Tourism Receipts	ISY, UNS, SYT
Area per capita	HDR: Table 22 & 42, ISY, SYT

Capital Resources

Lending Interest Rate	IFS: 60p
Inflation Rate	IFS: 64
Exchange Rate Fluctuations	IFS: aa

ESY:	Energy Statistics Yearbook 1995 Ministry of Trade, Industry and Energy, Republic of Korea
HDR:	Human Development Report 1996, 1997 United nations Development Program, New York.
IFS:	International Financial Statistics Yearbook 1996, April 1997 International Monetary Fund, Washington
ISY:	International Statistics Yearbook 1996 National Statistical Office, Republic of Korea
SYT:	Statistical Yearbook of Taiwan 1995 Taiwan
UNS:	Statistical Yearbook 1995 United Nations, New York
YLS:	Yearbook of Labor Statistics 1996 International Labour Office, Geneva

*Additional data have been collected by the KOTRA overseas offices.

IMPLICATIONS AND DISCUSSIONS

Several important implications can be derived from the findings of this report.

Firstly, Japan is on the top in the overall rankings of human resources (Table 9-6), but at the bottom in the overall rankings of natural resources (Table 9-7). In contrast, Russia is on the top in natural resources, but only in the 21st place in human resources. This finding supports Michael Porter's competitiveness theory that national prosperity is not inherited, but created. It also supports the nine-factor model in which the role of human resources is emphasized for economic development.

Secondly, in the intra-group rankings of human resources (Table 9-7), it is interesting to note that Korea is 3rd in each of the three groups—OECD, NICs, and the 2nd NICs. This also means that the top countries in these three groups have similar overall scores and thus similar competitiveness of human resources. Also, interestingly, all of these nations have relatively poor natural resources, as shown in Table 9-8. Even the United States is only in 8th place, which may look low for its abundant natural resources. However, the United States is not a resource-rich country in the relative sense because it consumes and thus imports large amounts of resources from abroad.

Finally, in the overall rankings of capital resources (Table 9-10), France is on the top, followed by Japan and Luxembourg. Except Singapore, non-OECD countries are not ranked high. Korea is 14th among the OECD countries, 4th among NICs, and 2nd if it is ranked among the 2nd NICs (Table 9-11). This means that, unlike in the case of human resources, the top countries in these three groups are different in the competitiveness of capital resources. For further economic development, NICs, including Korea, and the 2nd NICs can thus derive some important implications from this area of capital resources.

This new competitiveness report is useful in explaining the recent economic problems of Korea and some Southeast Asian countries. These countries have been bailed out by the International Monetary Fund (IMF). As suggested by the IMF, the economic crisis in these countries primarily came from the inefficient allocation of capital resources.

The relative inefficiency of the capital sector in these countries is well reflected in the rankings of this report. It measures the competitiveness of capital resources with a composite index of capital liquidity, capital value and exchange rate stability. As shown in Table 9-11, Korea (94.9) has a lower score than other Asian NICs: Singapore (96.3), Hong Kong (95.4), and

Taiwan (95.2). Compared with other Southeast Asian countires, Korea is lower than Malaysia (95.3), but higher than Thailand (92.3), the Philippines (89.3) and Indonesia (87.6). Hence, this result also explains IMF bailouts for Thailand and Indonesia. The Philippines may be economically very unstable because this country has a very low score. Singapore has the highest score among the countries in the region, but may not be perfectly safe because Singapore is economically much related to the neighboring countries in the region. It should be noted that scores of this report measure the relative ranks, but have little meaning in the absolute sense. (Refer to the methodology of calculating the scores.)

Interestingly, most of these countries have relatively high scores in human resources (Table 9-6), but have relatively low scores in natural resources (Table 9-8). This explains that human resources have been an engine for the economic success of these countries. Hence, one important implication is that economic progress cannot be sustained only with human resources. Capital sector should be well developed to expedite an efficient use of human and other resources. Capital sector is not the only factor, but definitely one of the important factors for economic development.

CONCLUSION

The most serious problem of the existing reports on international competitiveness is that they are lacking in a rigorous theoretical basis. This paper introduced a new competitiveness report that is based on a new competitiveness theory. The results support some of the interesting arguments of Porter's diamond model and its extended nine-factor model. For example, the results show that not the natural resources, but human and capital resources may be more important as an economy progresses to a more advanced stage.

This new competitiveness report is limited because it does not include all the independent variables. It would be also interesting to further study the relative importance of the independent variables for competitiveness at different stages of economic development. Notwithstanding, this report has shown that some important implications can be found. In our future research, a more comprehensive study will be reported.

Table 9-6. Human Resources: Overall Rankings

Main Factor Rankings					
Country	Score	Rank	Country	Score	Rank
Japan	73.2	1	Ireland	61.4	27
United States	73.0	2	Jordan	61.2	28
Indonesia	72.1	3	Belgium	60.0	29
Thailand	70.9	4	United Kingdom	59.7	30
Singapore	70.7	5	Czech Republic	59.4	31
Taiwan	69.0	6	Switzerland	58.8	32
Korea	67.9	7	Peru	58.4	33
Hong Kong	67.7	8	Hungary	58.2	34
Malaysia	66.5	9	Brazil	57.8	35
Austria	65.7	10	Finland	57.0	36
Mexico	65.7	11	Greece	56.5	37
Iceland	65.6	12	Denmark	56.1	38
New Zealand	65.6	13	Portugal	56.1	39
Sri Lanka	65.1	14	Kenya	55.6	40
Colombia	65.0	15	Germany	53.8	41
Netherlands	64.9	16	Romania	52.5	42
France	64.5	17	Pakistan	52.2	43
Philippines	64.1	18	Bangladesh	49.4	44
Luxembourg	64.0	19	India	46.2	45
Norway	63.8	20	Australia	45.9	46
Russia	63.7	21	Italy	45.8	47
Egypt	63.0	22	South Africa	42.9	48
Turkey	63.0	23	Poland	42.9	49
Panama	62.8	24	Spain	40.2	50
Sweden	61.9	25	Guatemala	30.3	51
Canada	61.7	26			

Table 9-7. Human Resources: Intra-Group Rankings

Main Factor Rankings					
Country	Score	Rank	Country	Score	Rank
OECD (Organization for Economic Cooperation and Development)			Italy	45.8	27
			Poland	42.9	28
Japan	73.2	1	Spain	40.2	29
United States	73.0	2	1st NICs (Newly Industrialized Countries)		
Korea	67.9	3	Singapore	70.7	1
Austria	65.7	4	Taiwan	69.0	2
Mexico	65.7	5	Hong Kong	67.7	3
Iceland	65.6	6	2nd NICs		
New Zealand	65.6	7	Indonesia	72.1	1
Netherlands	64.9	8	Thailand	70.9	2
France	64.5	9	Malaysia	66.5	3
Luxembourg	64.0	10	Philippines	64.1	4
Norway	63.8	11	LDCs (Less Developed Countries)		
Turkey	63.0	12	Sri Lanka	65.1	1
Sweden	61.9	13	Colombia	65.0	2
Canada	61.7	14	Russia	63.7	3
Ireland	61.4	15	Egypt	63.0	4
Belgium	60.0	16	Panama	62.8	5
United Kingdom	59.7	17	Jordan	61.2	6
Czech Republic	59.4	18	Peru	58.4	7
Switzerland	58.8	19	Brazil	57.8	8
Hungary	58.2	20	Kenya	55.6	9
Finland	57.0	21	Romania	52.5	10
Greece	56.5	22	Pakistan	52.2	11
Denmark	56.1	23	Bangladesh	49.4	12
Portugal	56.1	24	India	46.2	13
Germany	53.8	25	South Africa	42.9	14
Australia	45.9	26	Guatemala	30.3	15

Table 9-8. Natural Resources: Overall Rankings

Main Factor Rankings					
Country	Score	Rank	Country	Score	Rank
Russia	74.1	1	Czech Republic	44.0	27
Australia	69.1	2	Luxembourg	44.0	28
Canada	62.8	3	Thailand	43.2	29
Iceland	60.3	4	Brazil	42.9	30
Austria	53.7	5	Hong Kong	42.7	31
Norway	53.1	6	Portugal	42.1	32
France	48.6	7	Germany	41.8	33
United States	48.5	8	Netherlands	41.0	34
Spain	47.5	9	Sri Lanka	40.5	35
Italy	47.5	10	Singapore	40.0	36
United Kingdom	47.2	11	Poland	39.4	37
Mexico	46.5	12	Hungary	39.4	38
New Zealand	46.3	13	Philippines	39.1	39
Switzerland	46.0	14	Greece	39.0	40
Indonesia	45.7	15	Taiwan	38.6	41
Malaysia	45.3	16	Turkey	38.3	42
Egypt	44.9	17	Pakistan	37.7	43
Colombia	44.8	18	Guatemala	37.7	44
Kenya	44.8	19	Bangladesh	37.1	45
South Africa	44.7	20	Korea	36.7	46
Sweden	44.6	21	Jordan	35.4	47
Peru	44.5	22	Romania	35.2	48
Finland	44.5	23	India	33.8	49
Denmark	44.3	24	Panama	32.2	50
Ireland	44.2	25	Japan	30.3	51
Belgium	44.1	26			

Table 9-9. Natural Resources: Intra-Group Rankings

Main Factor Rankings					
Country	Score	Rank	Country	Score	Rank
OECD (Organization for Economic Cooperation and Development)			Turkey	38.3	27
			Korea	36.7	28
Australia	69.1	1	Japan	30.3	29
Canada	62.8	2	1st NICs (Newly Industrialized Countries)		
Iceland	60.3	3	Hong Kong	42.7	1
Austria	53.7	4	Singapore	40.0	2
Norway	53.1	5	Taiwan	38.6	3
France	48.6	6	2nd NICs		
United States	48.5	7	Indonesia	45.7	1
Spain	47.5	8	Malaysia	45.3	2
Italy	47.5	9	Thailand	43.2	3
United Kingdom	47.2	10	Philippines	39.1	4
Mexico	46.5	11	LDCs (Less Developed Countries)		
New Zealand	46.3	12	Russia	74.1	1
Switzerland	46.0	13	Egypt	44.9	2
Sweden	44.6	14	Colombia	44.8	3
Finland	44.5	15	Kenya	44.8	4
Denmark	44.3	16	South Africa	44.7	5
Ireland	44.2	17	Peru	44.5	6
Belgium	44.1	18	Brazil	42.9	7
Czech Republic	44.0	19	Sri Lanka	40.5	8
Luxembourg	44.0	20	Pakistan	37.7	9
Portugal	42.1	21	Guatemala	37.7	10
Germany	41.8	22	Bangladesh	37.1	11
Netherlands	41.0	23	Jordan	35.4	12
Poland	39.4	24	Romania	35.2	13
Hungary	39.4	25	India	33.8	14
Greece	39.0	26	Panama	32.2	15

Table 9-10. Capital Resources: Overall Rankings

Main Factor Rankings					
Country	Score	Rank	Country	Score	Rank
France	97.3	1	Iceland	93.4	27
Japan	96.9	2	Bangladesh	92.4	28
Luxembourg	96.4	3	Thailand	92.3	29
Singapore	96.3	4	Italy	92.2	30
United Kingdom	96.2	5	Portugal	90.8	31
Norway	96.0	6	Philippines	89.3	32
Denmark	95.8	7	Sri Lanka	88.0	33
Netherlands	95.6	8	Egypt	87.8	34
United States	95.6	9	Indonesia	87.6	35
Hong Kong	95.4	10	Pakistan	87.4	36
Belgium	95.3	11	South Africa	87.2	37
Australia	95.3	12	India	85.0	38
Malaysia	95.3	13	Czech Republic	84.1	39
Switzerland	95.2	14	Greece	82.8	40
Taiwan	95.2	15	Guatemala	74.4	41
Panama	95.2	16	Colombia	70.6	42
Finland	95.2	17	Hungary	70.0	43
Canada	95.0	18	Mexico	66.7	44
Korea	94.9	19	Kenya	66.0	45
Austria	94.9	20	Poland	50.3	46
Sweden	94.4	21	Peru	39.9	47
Germany	94.4	22	Romania	15.3	48
Spain	94.2	23	Turkey	7.9	49
Ireland	94.1	24	Brazil	0.0	50
Jordan	94.1	25	Russia	0.0	50
New Zealand	93.9	26			

Table 9-11. Capital Resources: Intra-Group Rankings

Main Factor Rankings					
Country	Score	Rank	Country	Score	Rank
OECD (Organization for Economic Cooperation and Development)			Mexico	66.7	27
			Poland	50.3	28
France	97.3	1	Turkey	7.9	29
Japan	96.9	2	1st NICs (Newly Industrialized Countries)		
Luxembourg	96.4	3	Singapore	96.3	1
United Kingdom	96.2	4	Hong Kong	95.4	2
Norway	96.0	5	Taiwan	95.2	3
Denmark	95.8	6	2nd NICs		
Netherlands	95.6	7	Malaysia	95.3	1
United States	95.6	8	Thailand	92.3	2
Belgium	95.3	9	Philippines	89.3	3
Australia	95.3	10	Indonesia	87.6	4
Switzerland	95.2	11	LDCs (Less Developed Countries)		
Finland	95.2	12	Panama	95.2	1
Canada	95.0	13	Jordan	94.1	2
Korea	94.9	14	Bangladesh	92.4	3
Austria	94.9	15	Sri Lanka	88.0	4
Sweden	94.4	16	Egypt	87.8	5
Germany	94.4	17	Pakistan	87.4	6
Spain	94.2	18	South Africa	87.2	7
Ireland	94.1	19	India	85.0	8
New Zealand	93.9	20	Guatemala	74.4	9
Iceland	93.4	21	Colombia	70.6	10
Italy	92.2	22	Kenya	66.0	11
Portugal	90.8	23	Peru	39.9	12
Czech Republic	84.1	24	Romania	15.3	13
Greece	82.8	25	Brazil	0.0	14
Hungary	70.0	26	Russia	0.0	14

REFERENCES

Cho, Dong-Sung. 1994. A dynamic approach to international competitiveness: The case of Korea. *Journal of Far Eastern Business*, 1(1): 17-36.
Cho, Dong-Sung & H. Chang Moon. 1998. A nation's international competitiveness in different stages of economic development. *Advances in Competitiveness Research*, 6(1): 5-19.
International Institute for Management Development. 1996, 1997, 1998, 1999. *The world competitiveness yearbook*. Lausanne, Switzerland.
Krugman, Paul. 1994. Competitiveness: A dangerous obsession. *Foreign Affairs*, 73(2): 28-44.
Moon, H. Chang, Alan M. Rugman & Alain Verbeke. 1995. The generalized double diamond approach to international competitiveness. In Alan M. Rugman, editor, *Research in Global Strategic Management: A Research Annual*, 5: 97-114.
Moon, H. Chang, Alan M. Rugman & Alain Verbeke. 1998. A generalized double diamond approach to the global competitiveness of Korea and Singapore. *International Business Review*, 7: 135-150.
Porter, Michael E. 1990. *The competitive advantage of nations*. New York: Free Press.
World Economic Forum. 1996, 1997, 1998, 1999. *The global competitiveness report*. Geneva, Switzerland.

BIBLIOGRAPHY

Baker, M.J. and S. J. Hart, *Marketing and Competitive Success,* Philip Allan,1989: 5-8.

Brown, C. & T. D. Sheriff, De-industrialization: A Background Paper, in F. Blackaby (ed.), *De-industrialization,* London: Heinemann, 1978.

Buckley, P. J. and M. C. Casson, *The Future of the Multinational Enterprise,* MacMillan, 1976:.33-65.

Buckley, P. J. and M. C. Casson, Ch.2, *Multinational Enterprises in Less Developed Countries: Cultural and Economic Interactions*, P.J. Buckley and J. Clegg (eds.), Multinational Enterprises in Less Developed Countries. London: MacMillan, 1991: 27-55.

Cartwright, Wayne R. 1993. Multiple linked diamonds: New Zealand's experience. *Management International Review*, 33 (2): 55-70.

Cho, Dong-Sung. 1994. A dynamic approach to international competitiveness: The case of Korea. *Journal of Far Eastern Business.* 1(1): 17-36.

Cho, Dong-Sung & H. Chang Moon. 1998. A nation's international competitiveness in different stages of economic development. *Advances in Competitiveness Research,* 6(1): 5-19.

Cho, Dong-Sung, Jinah Choi & Youjae Yi. 1994. International advertising strategies by NIC multinationals: The case of a Korean firm. *International Journal of Advertising*, 13: 77-92.

Chungang Daily Newspaper. 1995. Wages of Korea and other major countries. February 25.

Crane, David, "High Level of Foreign Ownership Hampers Our Ability to Compete," *The Toronto Star,* 19th October 1991.

Crocombe, F.T., M.J. Enright & M. E. Porter. 1991. *Upgrading New Zealand's competitive advantage.* Auckland: Oxford University Press.

Dialogue. 1992. Canada at the crossroads. *Business Quarterly* (Winter, Spring, and Summer).

Dunning, J. H. 1992. "The Competitive Advantage of Countries and the Activities of Transnational Corporations." *Transnational Corporations* l(l):135-168.

Dunning, J.H. 1993. Internationalizing Porter's diamond. *Management International Review,* 33 (2): 7-15.

The Economist Intelligence Unit. 1992. South Korea 1992-93: Annual survey of political and economic background. *EIU Country Profile.*

Economist. 1994. Professor Porter Ph.D., October 8: 75.

Europa Publications Limited. 1995. *The Europa world year book 1995*. London, England.

Francis, A. and P. K. M. Tharakan, (eds.), *The Competitiveness of European Industry*, London and NY: Routledge,1989: 5-20.

Gillis, Malcolm, Dwight H. Perkins, Michael Roemer & Donald R. Snodgrass. 1992. *Economics of development*. New York: Norton & Company.

Goldsmith, W. and D. Clutterbuck, *The Winning Streak: Britain's Top Companies Reveal Their Formulas for Success*, Weidenfeld&Nicolson,1984.

Grant, R. M. 1991. "Porter's Competitive Advantage of Nations: An Assessment." *Strategic Management Journal* 12(7):535-548.

Grossman, M. Gene, editor. 1992. *Imperfect competition and international trade*. Cambridge: MIT Press.

Gwynne, Peter. 1993. Directing technology in Asia's dragons. *Research Technology Management*, March/April 32(2): 12-15.

Heckscher, Eli F. 1949 (1919). The effect of foreign trade on the distribution of income. In Howard. S. Ellis & Lloyd A. Metzler, editors, *Readings in the theory of international trade*. Homewood: Irwin.

Hirschman, A. O. 1958. *The Strategy of Economic Development*. New Haven, CT: Yale University Press.

HMSO, Report from the Select Committee of the House of Lords on Overseas Trade, The Aldington Report, 1985.

Hymer, Stephen H. 1976 (1960). *The international operations of national firms: A study of direct foreign investment*. Cambridge: MIT Press.

IMD. 1992. *The world competitiveness report*. Lausanne, Switzerland.

International Institute for Management Development. 1996, 1997, 1998, 1999. *The world competitiveness yearbook*. Lausanne, Switzerland.

International Monetary Fund. 1996. *International financial statistics*, February.

Kasliwal, Pari. 1995. *Development economics*. Cincinnati: South-Western Publishing Co.

KIET, Future Picture of Automobile Industries, *Series of Future Industries*,1987.

Kindleberger, C. P., *American Business Abroad,* New Haven: Yale University Press, 1969, p.13.

Kogut, B., *Designing Global Strategies: Comparative and Competitive Value-Added Chains*, Sloan Management Review (Summer 1985): 15-28

Korea Electronic Industries Promotion Institute, *Prospect for Long-term Development of Electronic Industries*, 1989. 9.

Kravis, Irving B. 1986. The three faces of the international comparison project. *World Bank Research Observer*, January.

Krugman, Paul R. 1979. Increasing returns, monopolistic competition and international trade. *Journal of International Economics*, 9: 469-479.

Krugman, Paul R. 1994. Competitiveness: A dangerous obsession. *Foreign Affairs*, 73(2): 28-44.

Kreinin, Mordechai. 1965. Comparative labor effectiveness and the Leontief scarce factor paradox. *American Economic Review*, 64 (April): 143-155.

Lancaster, Kelvin J. 1979. *Variety, equity and efficiency.* New York: Columbia University Press.

Leontief, Wassily. 1953. Domestic production and foreign trade: The American capital position re-examined. *Proceedings of the American Philosophical Society,* 97: 331-349. Reprinted in Richard Caves and Harry Johnson, editors, *Readings in International Economics* (Homewood, Illinois: Richard D. Irwin, Inc., 1968).

Leontief, W. 'Factor Proportions and Structure of American Trade: Further Theoretical and Empirical Analysis', *Review of Economics and Statistics,* Vol.38.

Lewis, Arthur W. 1954. Economic development with unlimited supplies of labor. *The Manchester School* 22 (May): 139-191.

Linder, S. 1961. *An Essay on Trade and Transformation.* New York: John Wiley.

Management Today. 1989. Guru on the riverbank (August): 52-56.

Marx, Karl. 1962 (1894). *Capital: A critique of political economy.* In Vol, 3, F. Engels, editor. Moscow: Foreign Languages Publishing.

Moon, H. Chang. 1992. New challenges for Korean conglomerates. In Thomas Chen, Young B. Choi and Sung Lee, eds. *Economic and political reforms in Asia.* New York: St. John's University Press.

Moon, H. Chang. 1994. A revised framework of global strategy: Extending the coordination-configuration framework. *The International Executive,* 36(5): 557-574.

Moon, H. C. & K. C. Lee. 1995. Testing the diamond model: Competitiveness of U.S. software firms. *Journal of International Management,* 1 (4): 373-387.

Moon, H. Chang & Newman Peery. 1995. Competitiveness of product, firm, industry, and nation in a global business. *Competitiveness Review.* 5(1): 37-43.

Moon, H. Chang & Thomas W. Roehl. 1993. An imbalance theory of foreign direct investment. *Multinational Business Review,* Spring: 56-65.

Moon, H. Chang, A. M. Rugman & A. Verbeke. 1995. The generalized double diamond approach to international competitiveness. In Alan M. Rugman, editor, *Research in Global Strategic Management: A Research Annual,* 5: 97-114.

Moon, H.C., A. M. Rugman, and A. Verbeke. 1997. The new global competitiveness of Korea and the generalized double diamond approach. *The Korean Economic and Business Review* (Fall): 48-57.

Moon, H. Chang, A. M. Rugman & A. Verbeke. 1998. A generalized double diamond approach to the global competitiveness of Korea and Singapore. *International Business Review,* 7: 135-150.

New York Times. 1992. Economic analyst says U.S. needs long-term investments (September 7).

Nurkse, Ragnar. 1953. Problems of capital formation in underdeveloped countries. New York: Oxford University Press.

Porter, M. E. 1980. *Competitive strategy: Techniques for analyzing industries and companies.* New York: Free Press.

222   *From Adam Smith to Michael Porter*

Porter, M. E. 1986. Competition in global industries: A conceptual framework. In Michael E. Porter, ed. *Competition in global industries*. Boston: Harvard Business School Press.

Porter, M. E. 1990. *The competitive advantage of nations*. New York: Free Press.

Porter, M. E. 1994. Competitiveness of the Korean economy. *Mae-il-kyung-jai* [Daily Economic Review], January 4, 5, 6.

Porter, M. E. & J. Armstrong. 1992. Canada at the crossroads: Dialogue. *Business Quarterly*, Spring: 6-10.

Porter, M. E. & the Monitor Company. 1991. *Canada at the crossroads: The reality of a new competitive environment*. Ottawa: Business Council on National Issues and Minister of Supply and Services of the Government of Canada.

President's Commission on Industrial Competitiveness. 1985. *Global competition: The new reality*. Washington, D.C.: U.S. Government Printing Office.

Ricardo, David. 1971 (1817). *The principles of political economy and taxation*. Baltimore: Penguin.

Rostow, Walt W. 1971 (1960) *Stages of economic growth*. 2nd ed. New York: Cambridge University Press.

Rostow, Walt W., Theories of Economic Growth from David Hume to the Next Century, Oxford University Press, 1990.

Rugman, Alan M., 1981. *Inside the multinationals*. New York: Columbia University Press, 1981.

Rugman, A. M. 1990. *Multinationals and Canada-United States Free Trade*. Columbia: University of South Carolina Press.

Rugman, A. M. 1991. "Diamond in the Rough." *Business Quarterl* 55(3):61-64.

Rugman, A. M. 1992. "Porter Takes the Wrong Turn." *Business Quarterly 56(3):59-64.*

Rugman, A. M. and John McIlveen, *Megafirms: Strategies for Canada's Multinationals*, Toronto, Methuen/Nelson, 1985.

Rugman, A. M. and J. R. D'Cruz, *New Visions for Canadian Business: Strategies for Competing in the Global Economy*, Toronto: Kodak Canada, 1990.

Rugman, A. M. and J. R. D'Cruz. 1991. *Fast Forward: Improving Canada's International Competitiveness.* Toronto: Kodak Canada Inc.

Rugman, A. M. and J. R. D'Cruz. 1993. The double diamond model of international competitiveness: Canada's experience. *Management International Review*, 33 (2): 17-39.

Rugman, A. M. and A. Verbeke. 1990. *Global Corporate Strategy and Trade Policy*. London/New   York: Croom Helm/ Routledge.

Ryan, Richard. 1990. A Grand Disunity. *National Review*, July 9, 42(13): 46-47.

Safarian, A.E., FIRA and FIRB: *Canadian and Australian Policies on Foreign Direct Investment*, Toronto: Ontario Economic Council, 1985

Samuelson, Paul. 1948. International trade and the equalization of factor prices. *Economic Journal* 58: 165-184.

Shin, Uh Sun, *Resource Economics*, Park-Young Sa, 1988: 9-11.

Smallwood, J.E., The Product Life Cycle: A Key to Strategic Marketing Planning, in B.A. Weitz and R. Wensley (ed.), *Strategic Marketing: Planning Implementation and Control*, Boston, MA: Kent Publishing Company, 1984: 184-92

Smith, Adam. 1937(1776). An inquiry into the nature and causes of the wealth of nations. In Charles W. Eliot, editor, The Harvard Classics. New York: P. F. Collier & Son Corporation.

Spring, D. 1992. "An International Marketer's View of Porter's New Zealand Study." *Business Quarterly* 56(3): 65-69.

Stolper, Wolfgang and Paul Samuelson. 1941. Protection and real wages, Review of Economic Studies 9: 58-73.

Thain, Donald H., "The War Without Bullets," *Business Quarterly*, Summer 1990, Volume 55, Number 1, pp. 13-19.

Toffler, Alvin, 1980, *The Third Wave*, New York : Morrow.

United Nations Development Programme. 1990. *Human development report 1990*. New York: Oxford University Press

United Nations Development Programme. 1994. *Human development report 1994*. New York: Oxford University Press

United States Department of Commerce. 1995. *Statistical abstract of the United States 1995.*

Vanek, Jaroslav. 1963. The natural resource content of United States foreign trade, 1870-1955, Cambridge: MIT Press.

Vernon, Raymond. 1966. International investments and international trade in the product cycle. Quarterly Journal of Economics, May: 190-207.

Vernon, Raymond. 1979. The product cycle hypothesis in a new international environment. OBES, 41 (4): 255-267. Reprinted in Heidi Wortzel and Lawrence Wortzel, editors, Strategic Management of Multinational Corporations: The Essentials, New York: John Wiley & Sons, 1985.

World Bank. 1995. *World development report: Workers in an integrating world.* Oxford: Oxford University Press.

World Bank Policy Research Report. 1993. The East Asian miracle: Economic growth and public policy. Oxford: Oxford University Press.

World Economic Forum. 1996, 1997, 1998, 1999. *The global competitiveness report.* Geneva, Switzerland.

Wu, F. 1991. "The ASEAN Economies in the 1990s and Singapore's Regional Role." *California Management Review* 34(1):103-114.

Yamazawa, I. 1970. *Intensity Analysis of World Trade Flow*, Hitotsubashi Journal of Economics: 61-90.

DATE DUE

MAY 1 4 2007